Approaches and Methods in Event Studies

The recent proliferation of events as a subject of study in its own right has signalled the emergence of a new field – event studies. However, while the management-inspired notion of planned events, which strives for conceptual slenderness, may indeed be useful for event managers, the moment we attempt to advance knowledge about events as social, cultural and political phenomena, we realise the extent to which the field is theoretically impoverished. Event studies, it is argued, must transcend overt business-like perspectives in order to grasp events in their complexities.

This book challenges the reader to reach beyond the established modes of thinking about events by placing them against a backdrop of much wider, critical discourse. *Approaches and Methods in Event Studies* emerges as a conceptual and methodological tour de force – comprising the works of scholars of diverse backgrounds coming together to address a range of philosophical, theoretical and methods-related problems. The areas covered include the concepts of eventification and eventual approaches to events, a mobilities paradigm, rhizomatic events, critical discourse analysis, visual methods, reflexive and ethnographic research into events and indigenous acumen.

Researchers and students engaged in the study of events will draw much inspiration from the contributions and from the volume as a whole.

Tomas Pernecky is with the Faculty of Culture and Society at the Auckland University of Technology, New Zealand. An advocate of post-disciplinary approaches to knowledge, his wide-ranging interests extend to examining a variety of philosophical, conceptual, theoretical and methodological issues. Examples include ontological inquiry into the constitution of social worlds through the phenomenon of events (e.g. *Ideological, Social and Cultural Aspects of Events* by CABI), sustainability-related concerns (e.g. *Events, Society and Sustainability: Critical and Contemporary Approaches* by Routledge) and the application of constructionist philosophy and hermeneutic phenomenology in tourism research. Tomas recently co-chaired the second Tourism Postdisciplinary Conference (Copenhagen, 22–24 June 2015) and co-edited a special issue on tourism post-disciplinarity for the journal *Tourism Analysis*.

Routledge advances in event research series
Edited by Warwick Frost and Jennifer Laing
Department of Marketing, Tourism and Hospitality, La Trobe University, Australia

For full list of titles in this series please visit www.routledge.com.

Events, Society and Sustainability
Critical and contemporary approaches
Edited by Tomas Pernecky and Michael Lück

Exploring the Social Impacts of Events
Edited by Greg Richards, Maria deBrito and Linda Wilks

Commemorative Events
Memory, identities, conflict
Warwick Frost and Jennifer Laing

Power, Politics and International Events
Socio-cultural analyses of festivals and spectacles
Edited by Udo Merkel

Event Audiences and Expectations
Jo Mackellar

Event Portfolio Planning and Management
A holistic approach
Vassilios Ziakas

Conferences and Conventions
A research perspective
Judith Mair

Fashion, Design and Events
Edited by Kim M. Williams, Jennifer Laing and Warwick Frost

Food and Wine Events in Europe
A stakeholder approach
Edited by Alessio Cavicchi and Cristina Santini

Event Volunteering
International perspectives on the event volunteering experience
Edited by Karen Smith, Leonie Lockstone-Binney, Kirsten Holmes and Tom Baum

The Arts and Events
Hilary du Cros and Lee Jolliffe

Sports Events, Society and Culture
Edited by Katherine Dashper, Thomas Fletcher and Nicola McCullough

The Future of Events and Festivals
Edited by Ian Yeoman, Martin Robertson, Una McMahon-Beattie, Elisa Backer and Karen A. Smith

Exploring Community Events and Festivals
Edited by Allan Jepson and Alan Clarke

Event Design
Social perspectives and practices
Edited by Greg Richards, Lénia Marques and Karen Mein

Rituals and Traditional Events in the Modern World
Edited by Warwick Frost and Jennifer Laing

Battlefield Events
Landscape, commemoration and heritage
Edited by Keir Reeves, Geoffrey Bird, Laura James, Birger Stichelbaut and Jean Bourgeois

Events in the City
Using public spaces as event venues
Andrew Smith

Event Mobilities
Politics, place and performance
Edited by Kevin Hannam, Mary Mostafanezhad and Jillian Rickly-Boyd

Approaches and Methods in Event Studies
Edited by Tomas Pernecky

Visitor Attractions and Events
Locations and linkages
Adi Weidenfeld, Richard Butler and Allan Williams

Approaches and Methods in Event Studies

Edited by Tomas Pernecky

LONDON AND NEW YORK

First published 2016
by Routledge
2 Park Square, Milton Park, Abingdon, Oxon OX14 4RN

and by Routledge
605 Third Avenue, New York, NY 10017

First issued in paperback 2021

Routledge is an imprint of the Taylor & Francis Group, an informa business

Publisher's Note
The publisher has gone to great lengths to ensure the quality of this reprint but points out that some imperfections in the original copies may be apparent.

British Library Cataloguing in Publication Data
A catalogue record for this book is available from the British Library

Library of Congress Cataloging in Publication Data
A catalog record for this book has been requested

ISBN 13: 978-1-03-224248-4 (pbk)
ISBN 13: 978-1-138-78052-1 (hbk)

DOI: 10.4324/9781315770642

Typeset in Times New Roman
by Cenveo Publisher Services

Contents

Illustrations

Figures

Tables

Contributors

Alison Booth is a specialist in ethnography, festivalisation, social sustainability, the cultural representation of diasporic communities, event management theory and event production practices. Her research focuses on event production practices, diasporic cultures and the role producers play in representing minority cultures. Her PhD, 'Performance Networks: Indian Cultural Production in Aotearoa', explores the processes and relationships that support the production of cultural events, with specific reference to events that are of interest to and/or produced by New Zealand's Indian communities. Alison holds a Master's in Creative and Performing Arts with honours from the University of Auckland specialising in Arts Management with a primary world music production focus. She is a performer as well as an event producer. She has been involved in numerous event collaborations across the event industry including conferences, concerts and national tours.

William G. Feighery is an independent scholar whose research interests embrace qualitative research methodologies, visual research methods and critical discourse studies. Currently based in Switzerland, he has previously lived and worked in the United Kingdom, Oman and China. He is Editor-in-Chief of the journal *Visual Methodologies*.

Kevin Hannam is Professor of Tourism at Edinburgh Napier University, UK and a research affiliate at the University of Johannesburg, South Africa. Previously he was at Leeds Beckett University and the University of Sunderland, UK. He is the founding co-editor of the journals *Mobilities* and *Applied Mobilities* (Routledge), co-author of the books *Understanding Tourism* (Sage) and *Tourism and India* (Routledge) and co-editor of the *Routledge Handbook of Mobilities Research* and *Moral Encounters in Tourism* (Ashgate). He has extensive research experience in South and South-East Asia. He has a PhD in geography from the University of Portsmouth, UK and is a Fellow of the Royal Geographical Society (FRGS), a Member of the Royal Anthropological Institute (RAI) and Vice-Chair of the Association for Tourism and Leisure Education and Research (ATLAS).

Temple Hauptfleisch is a drama teacher, playwright and theatre researcher. Currently Emeritus Professor at the University of Stellenbosch, he was the head of the Centre for SA Theatre Research (CESAT – 1979–87), chair of the University of Stellenbosch Drama Department (1995–2005), director of the Centre for Theatre and Performance Studies at Stellenbosch (1994–2009) and co-founder/editor of the *South African Theatre Journal* (1987–2011). He has published widely on the history of South African theatre, research methodology and the sociology of theatre. His current project is an open-access, online Encylopaedia for South African Theatre, Film, Media and Performance (ESAT).

Keith Hollinshead is a Romano-British historian who nowadays investigates the agency and authority of tourism to inscribe the history/culture of populations and places. Having worked in Wales, Australia (predominantly) and the USA, he inspects (from the University of Bedfordshire, England) the representational systems through which received inheritances are regularised for psychic cum political advantage. Long interested in Indigenous cosmologies, he critiques how both Indigenous and non-Indigenous visions of the world imbricate each other today. A Distinguished Professor of the International Tourism Studies Association (nested at Peking University, China) and thrice Vice President (International Tourism) of the International Sociological Association, Keith functions as a long-standing Masthead Editor for both *Tourism Analysis* and *Tourism, Culture and Communication*.

Welby Ings is a Professor in Design at AUT University. He holds a PhD in Applied Narratology and is an elected Fellow of the British Royal Society of Arts. He has been a consultant to many international organisations on issues of creativity and learning and has published and spoken widely on issues related to the nature of the socially marginalised voice, post-hierarchical structures, pedagogy and individual agency. Related publications include: 'Trade talk: the historical metamorphosis of the language of the New Zealand male prostitute between 1900–1981', *Women's History Review* (2012); 'Queer as a two-bob watch: the implications of cultural framing and self-declaration', in A. C. Engels-Schwarzpaul and M. Peters (eds), *Of Other Thoughts: Nontraditional Ways to the Doctorate* (2013); and *The Rage of Silence: Type and Marginalisation*, at the International Symposium on Typographic Landscaping, Göteborg, Sweden, 17–18 June 2013.

Welby is also a designer, film-maker and playwright whose films have been shortlisted for the Oscars and won numerous international awards.

Iain MacKenzie is a Senior Lecturer in Politics and Co-Director of the Centre for Critical Thought at the University of Kent, UK. Publications include: *The Edinburgh Companion of Poststructuralism* (Edinburgh University Press, 2013) co-edited with Benoît Dillet and Robert Porter; *Dramatizing the Political: Deleuze and Guattari* (Palgrave, 2011) co-authored with Robert Porter; *Politics: Key Concepts in Philosophy* (Continuum, 2009); *The Idea of Pure Critique* (Continuum, 2004).

Jared Mackley-Crump currently teaches on the Event Management Programme at AUT University in Auckland, New Zealand. He holds a PhD in Ethnomusicology from the University of Otago and his research to date has primarily focused on the festivalisation of diasporic Pacific cultures in New Zealand. He recently published a book on this topic, *Negotiating Place and Identity in a New Homeland: The Pacific Festivals of Aotearoa New Zealand*, with the University of Hawai'i Press. His other research and teaching interests include the festivalisation of food, commercial popular music festivals in New Zealand, popular music and gender, Pacific/indigenous epistemologies and methodologies.

Tomas Pernecky is with the Faculty of Culture and Society at the Auckland University of Technology, New Zealand. An advocate of post-disciplinary approaches to knowledge, his wide-ranging interests extend to examining a variety of philosophical, conceptual, theoretical and methodological issues. Examples include ontological inquiry into the constitution of social worlds through the phenomenon of events (e.g. *Ideological, Social and Cultural Aspects of Events* by CABI), sustainability-related concerns (e.g. *Events, Society and Sustainability: Critical and Contemporary Approaches* by Routledge), and the application of constructionist philosophy and hermeneutic phenomenology in tourism research. Tomas recently co-chaired the 2nd Tourism Postdisciplinary Conference (Copenhagen, 22–24 June 2015) and co-edited a special issue on tourism post-disciplinarity for the journal *Tourism Analysis*.

Robert Porter teaches Cultural and Political Theory at the University of Ulster, UK. His publications include: *The Edinburgh Companion of Poststructuralism* (Edinburgh University Press, 2013) co-edited with Benoît Dillet and Iain MacKenzie; *Dramatizing the Political: Deleuze and Guattari* (Palgrave, 2011) co-authored with Iain MacKenzie; *Deleuze and Guattari: Aesthetics and Politics* (University of Wales Press, 2009); *Ideology: Contemporary Social, Political and Cultural Theory* (University of Wales Press, 2006)

Rukeya Suleman is a Cultural Geographer schooled at the University of Cambridge who now works as a Lecturer in Tourism Studies/Related Subjects at the University of Bedfordshire in England. Currently completing a doctorate on the Muslim diaspora in and from the UK, she is deeply interested in matters of Islamic modernity. Rukeya's other research interests concern geopolitical issues as they relate to the traditional/transitional use of space and place today and she has published articles and chapters in the realm of public culture and Indigeneity. She is an innovative thinker on the application of emergent critico-interpretive/soft science approaches in the humanities (in general) and on spirituality (in particular).

Dennis Zuev graduated from Krasnoyarsk State University, Russia. He is a co-founder and vice-president (research) of ISA Working Group 03 Visual Sociology. He is currently working as a researcher at Lancaster University, UK.

Preface

What and when is an 'event'? A short prelude to event studies

Tomas Pernecky

The word 'event' can be used as a generic term to capture the kind of social phenomena which have been described in the events, social science and humanities literature as festivals, carnivals, civic anniversaries, celebrations, rituals, protests, conferences, congresses, exhibitions, indigenous ceremonies, performances and many others. In the domain of event management, these have been classified as *planned events* – those events that are 'created to achieve specific outcomes, including those related to the economy, culture, society and environment' (Getz, 2007: 21) – and *unplanned events* – those which are often 'clearly set in motion by people (maybe agitators, publicity agents or social activists) and … have a purpose' (p. 27) but which are more difficult to tidily define. The term 'event' thus has the capacity to encompass a broad spectrum of human manifestations – extending to such diverse phenomena as spontaneous gatherings, creative outbursts, rhizomatic events (see Ings, Chapter 4, this volume), online conferences and web-based music festivals.

If we were to think of the event in a very broad sense, we can approach it as the 'coming together' of people for various purposes, desires, needs and goals, and as a phenomenon that signifies 'an aspect of human activity that pertains to modes of socio-cultural being' (Pernecky, 2013: 16). So understood, the study of events – or event studies – calls for multiple strategies of sense-making and must be open to a wide methodological repertoire and to theoretical innovation. If we were to stretch our minds even further and go beyond the rhetoric of business literature, the event can be grasped as a 'novelty-bearing' phenomenon – a notion advanced by MacKenzie and Porter in Chapter 2.

To underscore the necessity of thinking more expansively about events, we need only consider that social life is not neatly organised into homogenous schemas. The management-inspired notion of planned events, which strives for conceptual slenderness, may indeed be useful for event managers, but the moment we attempt to advance knowledge about events as social, cultural, political and worldmaking phenomena, we realise the extent to which the field is theoretically impoverished. Event studies, it is argued, must transcend overt business-like perspectives in order to grasp events in their complexities. The conceptual and methodological stretching solicited in this book may be more familiar to scholars situated in other disciplines, but increasingly it is reverberating in inter- and multi-disciplinary works (e.g. Herold and Marolt, 2011).

The chief tenet of this book is that we should not think of events only in terms of given conceptual stereotypes carved out by disciplinary thinking. Events, understood more profoundly as speaking to the human condition, demand a wide-ranging theoretical treatment and epistemic sophistication. It is necessary, therefore, to think more deeply and critically about the ways in which events manifest in societies, what functions they serve and for whom. It is equally important to contemplate the transformative role of events in the making, remaking and de-making of societies (e.g. Hollinshead, 2009; Pernecky, 2014) and scrutinise them in light of different types of mobilities (see Hannam, Chapter 5, this volume). Moreover, when we ask *When is an event?*, we open the door to intentional acts of framing, representation and interpretation – topics that occupy several authors in this volume.

Rigid conceptualisations and simplistic definitions fall short of meaningfully accessing our ways of being, becoming, belonging and relating. What and when is an 'event', then, cannot be a matter of a crude definition. Answering such questions demands that we approach the study of events critically, creatively and with the help of philosophical, theoretical and methodological tools – enabling us to sculpt new understandings. This book hopes to take a step in this direction.

References

Getz, D. (2007) *Event Studies: Theory, Research and Policy for Planned Events*. Oxford: Butterworth-Heinmann.

Herold, D. K. and Marolt, P. (eds) (2011) *Online Society in China: Creating, Celebrating, and Instrumentalising the Online Carnival*. Abingdon: Routledge.

Hollinshead, K. (2009) 'The "worldmaking" prodigy of tourism: the reach and power of tourism in the dynamics of change and transformation', *Tourism Analysis*, 14 (1): 139–52.

Pernecky, T. (2013) 'Events, society, and sustainability: five propositions', in T. Pernecky and M. Lück (eds), *Events, Society and Sustainability: Critical and Contemporary Approaches*. London: Routledge, pp. 15–29.

Pernecky, T. (2014) 'The making of societies through events: on ideology, power and consent', in O. Moufakkir and T. Pernecky (eds), *Ideological, Social and Cultural Aspects of Events*. Wallingford: CAB International, pp. 28–46.

Acknowledgements

There are several people who ought to be acknowledged. First and foremost, this book would have been impossible without the commitment and dedication of the contributing authors. I am grateful to Iain MacKenzie, Robert Porter, Temple Hauptfleisch, Welby Ings, Kevin Hannam, William G. Feighery, Dennis Zuev, Alison Booth, Keith Hollinshead, Rukeya Suleman and Jared Mackley-Crump for their professionalism and care preparing the manuscripts. I would also like to thank Trish Brothers, who has helped with the proofing and copy-editing of the text, and the Routledge team for their help throughout the editorial process.

Tomas Pernecky
Mākoha Cottage, New Zealand
31 October 2015

Part I

Introduction

1 The epistemic foundations of event studies

Tomas Pernecky

The problem with the study of events: the need to articulate a much broader vision of event studies

The recent proliferation of events as a subject of study in its own right has signalled the emergence of a new field. The notion of event studies, first articulated by Donald Getz (2007), arose from business and management perspectives, which sought to establish a body of knowledge in response to the needs of a growing events industry. The 'event' thus became firmly rooted within the rhetoric of managerial practices – a business-like entity, capable of not only generating revenues but delivering a host of other acclaimed benefits, including job creation, destination development and event tourism. Regardless of the typology employed, knowledge about events has been advanced mainly under the rubric of event management, whereby students are taught about topics such as event production, design and marketing – all of which contribute to an event manager's practical know-how.

While it is appropriate for specialised forms of knowledge to develop according to disciplinary, field-specific or vocational needs, the danger which this book seeks to address lies in limiting event studies to the standpoint of event management. To make this point clear, the claim put forward here is that event studies ought to resist domination by a business paradigm, and instead serve as a platform for a multitude of scholarly investigations. As such, it ought to comprise a body of knowledge nourished by methodological diversity and conceptual and philosophical acumen. Such inquiries into events must navigate a much broader landscape than the notion of the event as something to be planned, bid for, marketed, designed, managed and executed.

Despite the fact that some event scholars have started to pay attention to the social, cultural and political aspects of events (for example, Merkel, 2013; Moufakkir and Pernecky, 2014; Richards *et al.*, 2013; Rojek, 2013), these are on the fringe of the mainstream event curriculum. Critiques of the lack of theoretical sophistication and critical insight have come mainly from disciplinary thinkers like Rojek (sociology), who remarks that

> [...] overwhelmingly, the professional event literature provides a *technocratic* view of events. It focuses on the nuts and bolts in the machine and when and

> where to oil the parts. The crucial issues of who owns the machine, who controls it and what is its purpose are confined to the backwaters.
>
> (2013: xii)

The prevalent conception of event studies is, for the most part, a well-articulated extension of the event management curriculum. For example, Getz (2007) states that it is dependent 'on the already well-established event design/production and management professions' (p. 3; see also Figure 1.2 on p. 4). This suggests that there is a fundamental bond between event management and event studies, and that the former holds an a priori status upon which the latter depends. Such an assumption, however, speaks of disciplinary predisposition, and is explicitly contested in this volume by MacKenzie and Porter (Chapter 2). There is nothing more or less fundamental about social phenomena other than when an inquiry is framed by a disciplinary or interdisciplinary eye, knowledge is skewed towards what is deemed important by the discipline(s) in question. In other words, what is accepted as noteworthy and legitimate has to conform to the vision of discrete communities of practice.

It would seem that event studies needs to swap its straitjacket for a looser, more comfortable cloak. If its ambitions go far beyond producing knowledge on the type of event described in the event management literature, and if disciplinary, cross-disciplinary, and interdisciplinary visions are all too narrow and restricting, then we must develop a more flexible reading of the field: *event studies is whatever researchers invested in the study of events do.*[1] Such a definition speaks of possibilities and inclusiveness: it says that there is no privileged reading of events, and that events inquiry is open to a range of ontological, epistemological and methodological views. In this light, event studies becomes neutral territory, erected upon the ideals of epistemological freedom and academic creativity. It extends, but is not limited, to disciplinary, multi-disciplinary, cross-disciplinary, inter-disciplinary, trans-disciplinary and post-disciplinary modes of inquiry, whose delineation will occupy us for the remainder of this chapter.

Disciplines vs professions

The challenges faced by event studies in its nascence are typical in the growth and development of new and emerging fields. In addressing the question of whether or not human movement studies[2] is a discipline, Abernethy *et al.* (2013) differentiate between disciplines and professions. In their reading, disciplines are viewed as coherent bodies of knowledge that describe, explain and predict 'key phenomena from the domain of interest (or subject matter)', whereas professions draw on knowledge from a variety of disciplines in order to 'improve the conditions of society' (p. 5). Accordingly, the profession of engineering, for example, is argued to require the disciplinary know-how of mathematics, physics and computer science for solving engineering problems. Similarly, various medical professions apply knowledge from physiology, anatomy, pharmacology, psychology and biochemistry when attending to medical problems. Hence, the distinction at hand sees disciplines as theory- and research-building, and professions in terms of applied learning. Nevertheless, such a distinction – as indeed recognised by Abernethy *et al.* (2013) – is limiting for it does not help us to differentiate between disciplines, fields of studies and vocational training/profession-based curricula. Before we examine this point further, it is useful to note some of the shared characteristics that professions have in common:

- an identified set of jobs or service tasks over which they have jurisdiction or monopoly;
- organisation under the framework of a publicly recognised association;
- identified educational competencies and formalised training and education criteria (this generally includes the mastery of complex skills and the presence of a theory and evidence base for their practice);
- political recognition, usually through acts of government legislation (including, in some cases, establishment of licensing or registration boards); and
- a code of ethics defining minimal standards of acceptable practice.

(Abernethy *et al.*, 2013: 5)

All of the above traits can be applied to the applied field of event management. In light of the points above, there are specific jobs, professional bodies, associations and training programmes for event professionals. The importance of planned events has been recognised not only by the industry, but also in many countries by governments via legislation (e.g. the Major Events Management Act 2007, which provides protection for major events in New Zealand), regulation (e.g. local by-laws dealing with noise restrictions, health and safety, traffic management, waste management, etc.), strategic planning (e.g. events featuring in a variety of strategic documents), and funding to support the development of new events as well as the bidding for international events. In addition, with the growth of planned events come new industry standards, codes of ethics and the emergence of associations that strive to improve industry practices and support event stakeholders. In the UK alone, several associations have emerged over the past few years: the Association of Event Organisers (AEO), the Event Supplier and Services Association (ESSA), the Association of Event Venues (AEV), the Association for Events Management Education (AEME), the National Outdoor Events Association (NOEA), the Association of British Professional Conference Organisers (ABPCO), the Event Marketing Association (EMA) and the Meetings Industry Association (MIA).

From this vantage point, we can understand event management – as opposed to event studies – as a phenomenon that arose to cater to the needs of industry and event professionals. In the words of Getz (2012), it is 'an applied, professional field devoted to understanding and improving the management of planned events' (p. 5). The event industry and the applied field of event management have developed symbiotically, as reflected in the exponential growth in the number of events organised internationally, the increase in university programmes offering courses in event management and the number of students choosing to study event management over other subject areas.

It has been argued that event management and event studies are not disciplines because both derive their theoretical perspectives from, and are therefore dependent on, other disciplines and fields. Among the figures supporting this view is Getz (2012), who has provided a list of what he calls the foundation disciplines and closely related fields – showing that psychology, for instance, contributes to the understanding of the event experience and people's personal needs, motives and preferences – which have direct value for event planning, production, marketing and design. Such disciplinary importing has been depicted as playing a fundamental role in the still emerging field of event studies. Also worthy of mention is Tribe's (1997) critical analysis of tourism studies, which similarly rejected the conception of tourism knowledge as conforming to a discipline. He proposed that tourism studies is jointly made up of a business field and a non-business field. In his subsequent work, these have been labelled Tourism Field 1 (TF1) and Tourism Field 2 (TF2) (Tribe, 2004). Whereas TF1 includes marketing, management and corporate-focused inquiry, TF2 covers social, environmental and other non-business areas of inquiry.

Event studies may be seen as following a similar path: event management, with its focus on planned events representing the business arm and social, cultural, political, environmental and critical research into events representing the non-business arm. This dichotomy must be resisted. Event studies comprises a broad body of academic knowledge, of which event management is one of many sub-strands; event management should not be seen as a necessary or a priori prototype of the field of event studies. Put another way, event studies is a loose, umbrella-like, broad-ranging area that includes all types of modes of knowledge production: disciplinary, cross-disciplinary, multi-discipinary, inter-disciplinary, trans-disciplinary and post-disciplinary. To better understand this view, it is necessary to engage with each of these terms.

Disciplinary and inter-, multi-, cross-, trans- and post-disciplinary approaches

The task of delineating inter-, multi-, cross-, trans- and post-disciplinarity is a challenging one. Not only are these terms defined inconsistently in the literature, they can be applied to different domains: from research, teaching and curriculum development to conferences, academic publications and researchers' situatedness. Therefore, attempts to draw precise boundaries can be immensely problematic. This is perhaps most true of new and recent generations of scholars who are the 'product' of inter-disciplinary, multi-disciplinary and trans-disciplinary educational trends and influences and do not feel a strong allegiance to any single discipline. This problematic has been addressed, for instance, by Munar (see Munar's account in Pernecky *et al.*, 2016b). The difficulty of locating oneself epistemically may also resonate with the so-called 'first-generation scholars' (Pritchard and Morgan, 2007) who started out as geographers, economists, anthropologists and sociologists, but who have since migrated to other fields, embraced new interdisciplinary research interests and are working in inter-, multi-, and trans-disciplinary programmes. Despite these pitfalls, it is useful to have an understanding of the different modes of knowledge production and outline the fundamental differences, as they all have something to offer to event studies. A summary of each is available in Table 1.1.

Disciplinarity

The division of knowledge into distinct scholarly domains has to do with the systems of organisation throughout the ages. Historically, we can observe as many as six different ways in which knowledge has been produced with the help of various institutions: libraries, monasteries, universities, the 'republic of letters', disciplines and the laboratory (McNeely and Wolverton, 2008). Disciplinarity started to materialise in Europe during the Age of Enlightenment (circa eighteenth century) and the rise of empiricism – heralded by the Scientific Revolution and the establishment of the modern sciences, such as mathematics, physics, biology and astronomy. Disciplines 'have established their own vocabularies, even code words, and procedures, which function as union cards for

Table 1.1 Modes of knowledge production

Mode of inquiry	*Symbol*	*Description*
Disciplinarity		Disciplinary knowledge is specific to distinct branches of learning – it has its own procedures, methods, concepts and ways of framing research problems.
Cross-disciplinarity		Cross-disciplinary knowledge is the 'viewing of one discipline from the perspective of another' (Stember, 1991: 4) or the 'importing' of knowledge from other disciplines.
Multi-disciplinarity		Multi-disciplinarity occurs when 'researchers work in parallel or sequentially from [a] disciplinary-specific base to address [a] common problem' (Rosenfield, 1992: 1351).
Inter-disciplinarity		Inter-disciplinarity occurs when 'researchers work jointly but still from [a] disciplinary-specific basis to address [a] common problem' (Rosenfield, 1992: 1351).
Trans-disciplinarity		Trans-disciplinarity is the most collaborative approach to research: 'researchers work jointly using [a] shared conceptual framework drawing together disciplinary-specific theories, concepts, and approaches to address [a] common problem' (Rosenfield, 1992: 1351).
Post-disciplinarity		Post-disciplinarity weaves a unique inquiry thread. It is an 'escape' from disciplines – marked by flexibility, creative problem-solving and intellectual disobedience.

admission to the guild' (Rousseau, 1991: xii). They stem from unique ways of thinking about and framing research problems – a disciplined mode of thinking (Costa, 2008) – and are demarcated by their specialised body of knowledge, distinctive set of concepts, logical structure of propositions, processes of validation and methodological rigour (Cutrofello, 1994; Donald, 1995).

It should come as no surprise that the earliest studies of events are disciplinary in character. They are disciplinary because social sciences and humanities were initially made up of specific forms of knowledge and methodologies. This means that inquiry into events was – and to some extent continues to be – bounded by distinct methodological, theoretical and philosophical walls. It also means that any knowledge generated within these walls tends to remain there, although disciplinary fortifications have been crumbling since the arrival of inter-, cross-, multi- and trans-disciplinarity. Thus events – be they carnivals, rituals, protests or festivals – became the research foci for advancing knowledge of a given discipline. Historians, for example, have studied events by drawing on methods accepted by their peers (e.g. historical methodology) and have disseminated research within established networks, academic conferences, symposia and edited books (for example, see Spalinger and Armstrong, 2013). This applies to other disciplines – including psychology, sociology, anthropology and economics – and subdisciplines, such as social psychology which is a subdiscipline of psychology. When disciplinary knowledge is imported into other fields, we are speaking of cross-disciplinarity.

Cross-disciplinarity

Cross-disciplinarity is among the most inconsistently defined terms. For instance, Østreng (2010) states that all forms of cross-disciplinarity are 'different integrative expressions of academic interdisciplinarity' (p. 113), and proposes that it can lead to the absolute synthesis of disciplines, which he calls 'all-encompassing crossdisciplinarity'. However, there is also the notion of cross-disciplinarity as 'a viewing of one discipline from the perspective of another', say 'a physics professor describing the physics of music or the art department offering a course in art history' (Stember, 1991: 4). We will follow the latter conception of cross-disciplinarity by Stember and employ the term to denote the 'importing' or application of knowledge from other disciplines. In regard to the event management curriculum, all textbooks have a cross-disciplinary undertone as they draw on concepts and theories developed outside of the field. Consider Bladen *et al.*'s (2012) *Events Management: An Introduction*. The text uses Maslow's (1943) hierarchy of needs to explain the social evolution of humans and the need for events, Clawson's (1963) multi-phased nature of experience and Pine and Gilmore's (2011) work *The Experience Economy* to understand the experience of event attendees, Boyle and Simms' (2009) approach to economics as part of contemplating the future of the events industry and so forth. None of these works were produced by event scholars; rather, they have been 'imported' into the event management curriculum to advance knowledge on events.

Multi-disciplinarity

When a research problem is not distinctively disciplinary and its solution can benefit from the insights and knowledge of other disciplines, there is scope, and increasingly also a greater need, for collaboration. In contrast to disciplinary and cross-disciplinary research strategies, multi-, inter- and trans-disciplinarity speak to joint efforts that vary in intensity and implementation. Multi-disciplinarity means that more than one discipline (or field of study) is involved in tackling a problem at hand – each providing a different perspective (Stember, 1991). Coles *et al.* (2009) describe multi-disciplinary approaches as those that recognise and incorporate 'information derived in other disciplinary arenas without scholars stepping beyond their own boundaries' (p. 83). In the words of Rosenfield (1992), researchers 'work in parallel or sequentially from [a] disciplinary-specific base to address [a] common problem' (p. 1351). This book, for example, can be described as a multi-disciplinary endeavour because it gathers the work of academics from different fields. Another example given by Stember (1991) is faculty members from sociology, literature and history teaching in a women's studies programme. Overall, multi-disciplinarity can be understood as requiring very little or no collaboration in problem-solving; instead, each discipline approaches the problem in its own right.

Inter-disciplinarity

Inter-disciplinary research is also firmly grounded in disciplinary thinking, but is marked by increased cooperation among researchers. Inter-disciplinarity occurs when academics of different disciplinary backgrounds work together on a research problem while maintaining a sense of disciplinarity (Rosenfield, 1992). In the view of Østreng (2010), inter-disciplinary scholarship breaks down the walls that separate communities of knowledge and fosters a more holistic understanding of a given topic. He further asserts that 'the craft of this type of interdisciplinarity is to create wholeness out of pieces, to see how the individual contributions of disciplines affect, connect, relate, integrate and interact in composite reality' (Østreng, 2010: 26). Tourism scholars have described it as '(temporary) forays outside "home" disciplinary boundaries in order to advance knowledge production' (Coles *et al.*, 2009: 83). To use an example in the context of events, consider a research team made up of experts from environmental psychology, urban design, event management and sports studies to jointly investigate the problem of event crowding. Whereas cross-disciplinary approaches merely import disciplinary knowledge and multi-disciplinary approaches address the same problem (but remaining within their disciplinary silos), inter-disciplinarity is a team effort – striving for a team-based solution. It is important to note, however, that the research results – although the outcome of collaborative work – are often reported in a 'partial, discipline-by-discipline sequence' (Rosenfield, 1992: 1351). In other words, the disciplinary walls come down temporarily while the team members each make their contribution, but we are not

speaking of a complete merging of concepts and methodologies – such intensive integration comes with trans-disciplinarity.

Trans-disciplinarity

Trans-disciplinarity has the highest level of collaboration, often leading to transformative and wider-ranging outcomes. As with the previous approaches, disciplinary knowledge is recognised as playing a necessary role, especially in the early stages of the research project. However, it is also acknowledged as a limiting factor. In the view of Rosenfield (1992), team members share and strive to become familiar with each other's concepts and approaches, but disciplinary authorisation eventually fades away: individual disciplinary perspectives are transcended and give way to a 'new process of collaboration' and 'qualitatively different results' (p. 1344). Articulated similarly by Stember (1991), trans-disciplinarity is 'concerned with the unity of intellectual frameworks beyond the disciplinary perspectives' (p. 4).

We can draw on the example used earlier to explain inter-disciplinary research – i.e. a team of experts from environmental psychology, urban design, event management and sports studies jointly investigating the problem of event crowding – to see what it would take for it to become trans-disciplinary. For such research to progress to a trans-disciplinary stage, the researchers would have to eventually consolidate their theoretical, conceptual and methodological perspectives and generate a more comprehensive model or framework or strategy to solve the problem, which would be informed by, but no longer belong to, any single field or a discipline. Although trans-disciplinary strategies are not yet very common in the field of event studies, they are slowly being implemented across university programmes, as shown in Table 1.2.

Table 1.2 is part of a summary of McGregor and Volckmann's (2011) research on institutions that have transitioned to a trans-disciplinary mode of operation. It is worth noting that according to the authors' reading of trans-disciplinarity there is a strong emphasis on the inclusion of other stakeholders, such as the local community, who are considered an integral part of the project. McGregor and Volckmann echo other commentators on trans-disciplinarity in stating that disciplines must not be abolished because they offer important perspectives. However, they are quick to add that if universities wish to move toward trans-disciplinary modes of research, teaching and curriculum development, disciplines must not be treated as 'protected silos of specialised knowledge' (p. 7); rather, 'disciplines need to be taught and research conducted in the *context of their dynamic relationships with each other* and with societal problems' (p. 7).

Post-disciplinarity

Post-disciplinarity stands out as the most contentious but also the least understood approach. As with multi-, inter-, cross- and trans-disciplinary stances, post-disciplinarity is grounded in the critique, but not abolishment, of solely disciplinary knowledge. Menand (2001: 52) explains the 'escape from disciplines' in the

Table 1.2 Examples of trans-disciplinary approaches at universities

Country/region	*Institution*	*Approach*
United States	Arizona State University prototype for a 'new American university'	Redesigned the entire university using eight design aspirations: created multiple research centres, institutions, merged departments, created new academic units; view the research centres and institutes as the interface between the academy, industry and civil society; the trans-disciplinary work happens at the interface (in the research centres and institutes) – called *working at the seams* (permeable boundaries); faculty are cross-appointed between one or more departments and one or more research centres.
Austria	BOKU University Institute of Landscape Development, Recreation and Conservation Planning	Using trans-disciplinary projects (notably the Luben 2014 Life Project), the university collaborates with local citizens (to gain diverse perspectives) using a dialogic process, striving especially to find a common language to help cross boundaries. Developed advanced degrees (MA and PhD) in trans-disciplinarity.
Australia	University of Technology, Sydney, the Institute for Sustainable Futures	Using behaviour change theory, the institute, funded mainly by non-university grants and contracts (80%), contracts its services for trans-disciplinary research projects. The university institute does not teach traditional university courses or have undergraduate or even postgraduate teaching degrees; it does have PhD and Master's level degrees. The students help the academics conduct the research.

Source: adapted from McGregor and Volckmann (2011: see Table 1).

context of the changing demographics in American higher education, and attributes the first *anti-disciplinary* attitudes to the influx of women and non-white students at universities in the 1970s and 1980s. In his words, 'the new populations inevitably created a demand for new subject matter, a demand to which university departments, among the most sluggish and conservative institutions in America, were slow to respond' (p. 53). It was in this milieu, Menand asserts, that new areas of study emerged, such as women's studies, which was a reaction to hesitation within the traditional disciplinary programmes of history, sociology and English to sanction the creation of gender-based courses. Many of the centres that sprouted within universities (focusing on, for example, postcolonial studies, gay and lesbian studies and African American studies) can thus be understood as 'anti-disciplinary in temper' but 'inter-disciplinary by definition' because they comprise professors from various disciplines (Menand, 2001: 54). But post-disciplinarity is more than just an anti-disciplinary attitude.

In tourism studies, Coles *et al.* (2009) have called for 'flexibility and freedom from the constraints of established and orthodox disciplinary boundaries and

dogmas' (p. 80) – freedom to follow ideas to their 'logical conclusions', as opposed to 'some contrived or preordained end point determined by artificial disciplinary strictures' (p. 87). In their view, post-disciplinarity necessitates more flexible and creative approaches to investigating and defining objects, and so 'post-disciplinary studies emerge when scholars forget about disciplines and identify with learning rather than with disciplines' (Coles *et al.*, 2005: 32). Moreover, post-disciplinarity 'encourages new hybrid, more flexible forms of knowledge production' (Coles *et al.*, 2009: 89). Similar notions had been articulated earlier but had gone mostly unnoticed by other tourism academics, such as Hollinshead. He anticipated a vision of tourism researchers as *bricoleurs*[3] 'much less reliant on the spin-offs from other disciplinary endeavours in their work' (Hollinshead, 1996: 72). Despite the contributions of Hollinshead (see also Hollinshead, 2010, 2012) and Coles *et al.*, post-disciplinarity has remained largely a misnomer, and it is only recently that tourism academics have begun to come together to debate and articulate its prospects and challenges.[4]

There is no unified outlook or clearly shared programme by proponents of post-disciplinary approaches, only the different concerns held by various thinkers. These have been recently gathered in a special issue of *Tourism Analysis* on tourism post-disciplinarity (see Munar *et al.*, 2016). Among the most prominent points listed were: (1) the critique of traditional universities failing to prepare students to become critical and literary global citizens; (2) the acknowledgement of post-disciplinarity as a deeper, critical concern about knowledge production and dissemination; (3) the widespread misconception and misreading of post-disciplinarity as replacing disciplinary approaches; and (4) the endorsement of epistemological, semantic and methodological flexibility, which can manifest through pluralist and constructionist approaches, but also via reflexive methodologies, visual methods and relational, emic and subjective accounts of tourism (for a summary see Pernecky *et al.*, 2016a). In addition to these views, there is also a post-disciplinarity flavour that manifests as disobedience, rebellion and scholarly creativity.

Post-disciplinarity as disobedience, rebellion and scholarly creativity

Mourad (1997) asserts that any attempt to spell out in detail what post-disciplinary work entails is inconsistent with the postmodern critique of modern approaches to research 'because it would impose another preexisting reality on inquiry before it has been undertaken' (p. 100). When framed by a discipline, or across a number of disciplines, research is shaped by cultural practices which are always 'at work', so to speak, arranging objects, people and problems in distinct ways. Put in different terms, disciplinarity (but also inter-disciplinarity, cross-disciplinarity, multi-disciplinarity and to some extent trans-disciplinarity) creates what Scheff (1997) calls 'disciplinary habitus'. The discipline of economics, for instance, is governed by quantitative methods, mathematical models and the assumption that the free market is the solution to all economic problems. Even when disciplines intermingle or are applied simultaneously, the inquiry is still shaped by disciplinary

conventions. In this respect, post-disciplinary inquiry begins with a blank slate: there are no methodological and epistemological prerequisites to investigating the world. As Mourad elaborates:

> Outside the disciplines, words and objects that have been arranged to produce knowledge within the disciplines would be rearranged to produce intellectually compelling inquiries that are not about explaining preexisting reality. Rather, they would be about what reality could become. Inquiry, thus conceived, would bring together ideas that, from particular standpoints within the disciplines, do not belong together as consistent parts of a disciplinary language or of a cross-disciplinary language. From the standpoint of modern inquiry, these alternative constellations may appear to be disparate, paradoxical or even a-logical and a-rational arrangements. However, disparity or paradox ends inquiry only if one insists on limiting inquiry to the pursuit of preexistent reality. Similarly, what is a-logical or a-rational intellectual activity is not predetermined for any particular inquiry.
>
> (Mourad, 1997: 100)

What Mourad alludes to is that, while post-disciplinarity may draw upon already established ideas, unlike the traditional, disciplinary progressive view of knowledge, these are not to provide secure foundations upon which new knowledge is to be built. Instead, disparate ideas can be 'arranged, rather than extended, improved upon, or refuted' (p. 102). So understood, social reality – including events phenomena – 'becomes something that is produced in the course of inquiry rather than an object that is essentially separate from the inquiry and that inquiry seeks to discover, accurately represent, and explain' (p. 102). This reading of post-disciplinarity resonates with some varieties of constructionist philosophy, for knowledge is inseparable from the investigator's intellectual activity, and any hope of epistemic objectivity is lost. Underpinned by these ideals, a post-disciplinary approach does not seek to describe beyond doubt the world and its phenomena as they truly are: researchers play 'active parts rather than being observers of stable, preexisting disciplinary realities' (Mourad, 1997: 107).

Post-disciplinarity shares some common ground with Ings' (2013) notion of creativity as disobedient thought.[5] It is when we leave our preconceived ideas behind – when we become intellectually disobedient – that novel solutions may come to the fore. The act of questioning and contemplating other ways in which to see the world is an act in creativity. To Ings, 'questioning is the very source of creative thought' (2013). Those who find inspiration in the views of Mourad and Ings may also concur with St Pierre, who states that 'inquiry should be provocative, risky, stunning, astounding. It should take our breath away with its daring. It should challenge our foundational assumptions and transform the world' (St Pierre, 2011: 623). Conceived jointly as disobedience, rebellion and scholarly creativity, this variety of post-disciplinarity is the most outspoken of the aforementioned means of approaching knowledge. Despite this, it must be cherished, not feared, as it cultivates the creative and imaginative capacity to conceive of events in ways that may prove useful, meaningful, important – even inspirational and empowering.

The structure and possible uses of this text

This volume was conceived to include a variety of voices, topics and theoretical outlooks – a vision that was fulfilled due to the commitment and dedication of the contributors to this project. Every author in this book was approached directly for their expertise, innovative ideas, criticality and inspirational research. The backdrop against which the following chapters unfold thus covers a range of scholarly domains, including event studies, ethnomusicology, cultural studies, tourism, sociology, theatre and performance studies, culture and political theory, design, qualitative research methodologies and critical discourse studies. The content is organised into four thematic parts: aside from this introduction (Part I) and conclusion (Part IV), the remaining works are nested in Part II, 'Articulating a broader philosophical, conceptual and theoretical vision for event studies', and Part III, 'Towards critical capacity and methodological vigilance for the study of events'. A brief outline of each chapter is provided below, followed by suggestions on using the book to inform different research trajectories.

Part I Introduction

Chapter 1

The central argument of this introductory chapter is that event studies is a body of knowledge nourished by a variety of methods, conceptual and philosophical insights, and methodological diversity. Inquiry into events must therefore take on a far broader scope than the notion of events as mere business entities to be planned, bid for, marketed, designed, managed and executed. Events, understood more profoundly as speaking to the human condition, demand wide-ranging theoretical treatment and epistemic sophistication. The chapter has distinguished between event studies and the applied field of event management, and has outlined disciplinary and multi-, cross-, inter-, trans- and post-disciplinary approaches to events research. Post-disciplinarity has been presented as the most contentious, creative and disobedient of the aforementioned epistemic stances.

Part II Articulating a broader philosophical, conceptual and theoretical vision for event studies

Chapter 2

Events are recognised as social phenomena, but their ontological status – how they ought to be considered in terms of analytical metaphysics – is rarely examined in event scholarship. 'Evental approaches to the study of events' is the second chapter, by Iain MacKenzie and Robert Porter. The authors argue that the field would be impoverished if we were to think of events solely as occurrences or happenings – as is often purported and reiterated in the management and business literature. Instead, events are fundamentally 'novelty-bearing' – bringing novelty into the world. To understand events, we are urged to study the difference they make. However, if social science methods and methods influenced by attitudes in the natural sciences are inadequate for this task, as claimed by the duo, what are we to do? The answer to the question 'Is it possible to study events in a manner that reveals their significance without neutralising it?' is worked out with care by enlisting the philosophies of Slavoj Žižek, Michel Foucault, and Gilles Deleuze.

Chapter 3

Temple Hauptfleisch develops his latest thoughts on the power of events to impact a person, the community and societies at large. Revisiting his earlier work on the concept of *eventification*, the notion of the *theatrical event* is presented as a 'complex, subjective process of framing, enacting and performance, which takes place in a specific venue and in a particular context'. The theatrical event is offered as a framing device and we are invited to think about events not as innocent and unbiased messages, but as mediated accounts of reality. Eventification, Hauptfleisch argues, is a fundamental process embedded in socio-cultural contexts driven by cultural and social systems.

Chapter 4

Welby Ings shows the extent to which events are rhizome-like in nature – generated by communities and collectives, and lacking the hierarchical models of facilitation that can be observed with planned events. In this chapter, we learn that rhizomatic events 'build cultures of practice, facilitation, and dissemination by interfacing online and maker-oriented physical communities'. Furthermore, events organised by maker-oriented movements not only promote the groups' artefacts but also carry ideological, political and personal messages. In the words of Ings, such events 'reconceive spaces as local within the global, while simultaneously empowering practice, distribution, and a sense of belonging'.

Chapter 5

Kevin Hannam's contribution completes the second part of the book. It adds another layer of conceptual richness by situating events within a mobilities paradigm. Not only do events enable and promote a range of mobilities, such as the movement of people, material objects, thoughts and fantasies, some events, such as weddings, 'involve complex orderings of mobility and proximity in the social, familiar, and religious obligations to travel to the event'. Hannam's chapter advances the key conceptual dimensions needed to engage with mobilities and introduces the reader to what he sees as interconnected dimensions of *interruptions*, *transitions*, *framings* and *materialities*.

Part III Towards critical capacity and methodological vigilance for the study of events

Chapter 6

William G. Feighery's opening statement positions events as 'an outcome of the human desire to construct and articulate shared understandings and to mark identities within broader socio-cultural contexts'. Events communicate a variety of messages and are imbued with a host of trepidations: social, cultural, political, economic and environmental. Critical discourse analysis (CDA) is presented as a useful tool for investigating what Feighery terms 'the language of events' – defined as the ways in which events are constructed and represented through language, and where the language of events is understood to produce desired effects.

Chapter 7

Denis Zuev offers a comprehensive account of how to approach events from a visual sociology perspective, pointing out that standard social science methods are not necessarily sufficient for the study of events – phenomena which comprise multiple sensory, emotional and kinaesthetic elements. Visual methods, when combined with other methods, can reveal the otherwise invisible patterns of human behaviour. The application of visual sociology can also be highly valuable in critical scholarship, whereby researchers can employ visual data (e.g. photographs, videos, three-dimensional material objects) as a way of questioning the dominant readings of events.

Chapter 8

Keith Hollinshead and Rukeya Suleman scrutinise the agency of the tourism and events industry in the encoding and decoding of 'Aboriginality'. The authors draw on *Lonely Planet* to accentuate the world-making authority of texts, organisations and people that organise and interpret different worlds for tourism and events consumption. In their words, the chapter inspects 'not only the power of representations of peoples, places, pasts, and presents but also the consequentiality of misrepresentations and derepresentations (either consciously or not consciously engaged in!) of these cultural and cosmological storylines'.

Chapter 9

Alison Booth's 'Ethnography in the diaspora: Indian cultural production and transnational networks' is a personal, reflexive account of ethnographic research that seeks to understand Indian cultural identity as a global phenomenon. Events and festivities are portrayed as important community-building vehicles – providing opportunities for preserving traditional cultures of diasporic communities, and also for building local and transnational community.

Chapter 10

Jared Mackley-Crump describes an unconventional method that he implemented during his doctoral research on Pacific festivals in New Zealand. In order to collapse the social distance between the researcher – describing himself as a young, male *Pākehā*[6] *– and the participants – who were mostly Pacific Islanders – he baked. The act of baking, when placed in an Indigenous context, amplifies his alertness and sensitivity to the research process. It also resonates with the message in this book: that researchers should not be afraid to challenge the established norms and conventions and dare to be creative inquirers. His account demonstrates how traditional Western methods can fall short of forging trust, rapport, mutual respect and ongoing connections with co-researchers.*

Part IV Conclusion

Chapter 11

The second contribution by Keith Hollinshead and Rukeya Suleman, 'Events and the framing of people and places: acts of declaration/acts of devilry', was chosen as the concluding chapter for its comprehensive thirty-term glossary, which is bound to leave the reader with much to think about. Whereas some of the earlier works in this volume point to the problem of social science methods as 'neutralising' the significance of events in philosophical terms (i.e. MacKenzie and Porter's Chapter 2), Hollinshead and Suleman further present *normalisation* and *naturalisation* under the premise of what they call the 'historical correlation of events' and as one of many research topics they carefully delineate for the reader. Hence, the book concludes with an abundance of inquiry possibilities that can be applied in future event scholarship.

How to use this book and possible trajectories

Although organised into four thematic parts, the chapters can be read, combined and re-ordered in different ways. Indeed, it is by disturbing the prescribed flow that novel sensitivities may emerge. For example, students interested in the study of indigenous events may wish to ease into the topic by starting with Mackley-Crump's (Chapter 10) innovative solution to overcoming the barrier between a Western researcher and non-Western participants, then move onto Chapter 3 by Hauptfleisch on eventification and, finally, supplement it with the critical reading on world-making and the encoding and decoding of 'Aboriginality' by Hollinshead and Suleman (Chapter 7). In this way, the reader will have to confront a number of methodological and theoretical issues and begin to shape a critical outlook (see 'Critical Indigenous Inquiry', in Figure 1.1). Another possible trajectory may consist of chapters that are more philosophically and conceptually inclined (see 'Philosophical Inquiry', in Figure 1.1). Here, the chapters by MacKenzie and Porter (Chapter 2),

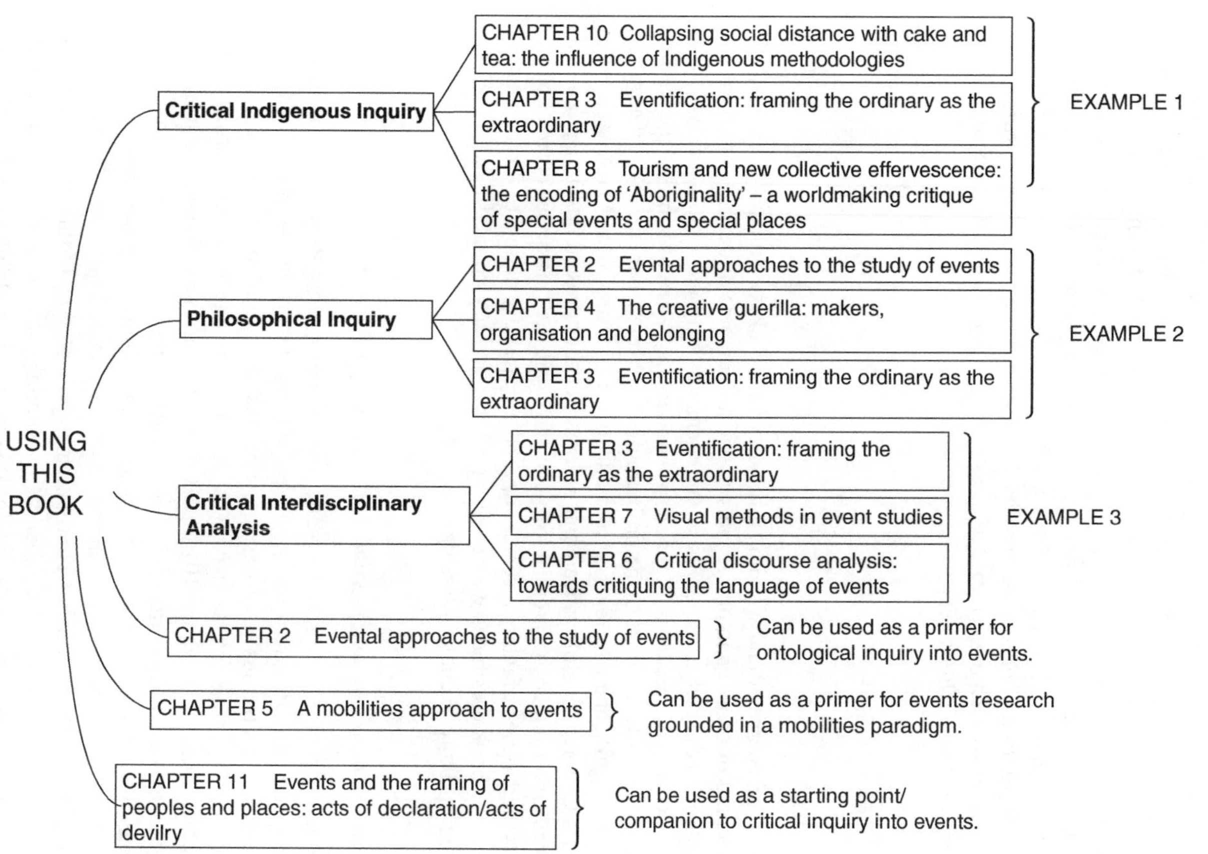

Figure 1.1 Different ways of interacting with this text

Ings (Chapter 4), and Hauptfleisch (Chapter 3) can offer much food for thought about the nature of events. In addition, some scholars may be interested in critical theory and the use of multi-disciplinary and inter-disciplinary approaches to events, in which case the work by Hauptfleisch (Chapter 3) can be combined with Chapter 7 by Zuev and Chapter 6 by Feighery. The implementation of discourse analysis, visual methods and the concept of eventification would indeed result in a powerful contribution to knowledge about events. Importantly, many of the chapters stand on their own. For instance, one can draw inspiration from the work of Hannam (Chapter 5) and examine events in the context of mobilities. Alternatively, one can focus on the ontology of events, in which case Chapter 2 may be a useful starting point – leading the researcher, perhaps, to further exploration and implementation of the ideas of philosophers such as Deleuze, Rorty, Foucault, Gadamer, Nietzsche, and many others. Finally, the concluding chapter by Hollinshead and Suleman will prove to be a great resource for any critical scholar. These latter examples are shown as stand-alone chapters in Figure 1.1.

The following pages together contribute to four main discourses:

- *ontological* – what can be said about events ontologically, metaphysically and also in regard to social reality;
- *epistemological* – what can be known about events and what are the issues, challenges and prospects that are tied in with obtaining such knowledge;
- *methodological/methods-related* – what strategies and tools ought to be adopted to study events and to address the complexity with which researchers have to grapple; and
- *critical theoretical* – what is at stake for different groups vis-à-vis events.

By engaging with the content and reading the text as a whole, the mind can witness trans-disciplinary, perhaps even post-disciplinary horizons.

Notes

1. Inspired by Menand's pragmatic definition of the discipline of anthropology (see Menand, 2001).
2. Human movement studies is described by the authors as 'academic inquiry concerned with systematically understanding *how* and *why* people move and the factors that limit and enhance our capacity to move' (Abernethy *et al.*, 2013: 4).
3. Hollinshead borrowed this term from qualitative research (see, for example, Denzin and Lincoln, 2000; Kincheloe, 2001).
4. There have been two conferences dedicated to post-disciplinarity: 'Welcoming Encounters: Tourism Research in a Postdisciplinary Era' (Neuchâtel, 19–22 June 2013) and 'The 2nd Tourism Postdisciplinary Conference: Freedom. Art. Power' (Copenhagen, 22–24 June 2015).
5. See https://www.youtube.com/watch?v=aumxbgOdkRU and also Pernecky *et al.* (2016b).
6. *This is a Māori-language term used to describe New Zealanders of European descent.*

References

Abernethy, B., Kippers, V., Hanrahan, S. J., Pandy, M. G., McManus, A. M. and Mackinnon, L. (2013) *Biophysical Foundations of Human Movement*, 3rd edn. Champaign, IL: Human Kinetics.

Bladen, C., Kennell, J., Abson, E. and Wilde, N. (2012) *Events Management: An Introduction*. Abingdon: Routledge.

Boyle, D. and Simms, A. (2009) *The New Economics: A Bigger Picture*. London: Earthscan.

Clawson, M. (1963) *Land and Water for Recreation: Opportunities, Problems and Policies*. Chicago: Rand McNally.

Coles, T., Hall, C. and Duval, D. T. (2005) 'Mobilizing tourism: a post-disciplinary critique', *Tourism Recreation Research*, 30 (2): 31–41.

Coles, T., Hall, C. M. and Duval, D. T. (2009) 'Post-disciplinary tourism', in J. Tribe (ed.), *Philosophical Issues in Tourism*. Bristol: Channel View Publications, pp. 80–100.

Costa, A. L. (2008) *The School as a Home for the Mind: Creating Mindful Curriculum, Instruction, and Dialogue*. Thousand Oaks, CA: Sage.

Cutrofello, A. (1994) *Discipline and Ccritique: Kant, Poststructuralism, and the Problem of Resistance*. Albany, NY: State University of New York Press.

Denzin, N. K. and Lincoln, Y. S. (eds) (2000) *Handbook of Qualitative Research*, 2nd edn. Thousand Oaks, CA: Sage.

Donald, J. G. (1995) 'Disciplinary differences in knowledge validation', *New Directions for Teaching and Learning*, 1995 (64): 6–17.

Getz, D. (2007) *Event Studies: Theory, Research and Policy for Planned Events*. Oxford: Butterworth-Heinemann.

Getz, D. (2012) *Event Studies: Theory, Research and Policy for Planned Events*, 2nd edn. Abingdon: Routledge.

Hollinshead, K. (1996) 'The tourism researcher as bricoleur: the new wealth and diversity in qualitative inquiry', *Tourism Analysis*, 1 (1): 67–74.

Hollinshead, K. (2010) 'Tourism studies and confined understanding: the call for a "new sense" postdisciplinary imaginary', *Tourism Analysis*, 15 (4): 499–512.

Hollinshead, K. (2012) 'The under-conceptualisations of tourism studies: the case for postdisciplinary knowing,' in I. Ateljevic, N. Morgan and A. Pritchard (eds), *The Critical Turn in Tourism Studies: Creating an Academy of Hope*. Abingdon: Taylor & Francis, pp. 55–72.

Ings, W. (2013) *Disobedient Thinking: Welby Ings at TEDxAuckland* [TEDxTalks]. Retrieved 29 October 2015 from: https://www.youtube.com/watch?v=aumxbgOdkRU.

Kincheloe, J. L. (2001) 'Describing the bricolage: conceptualizing a new rigor in qualitative research', *Qualitative Inquiry*, 7: 679–92.

McGregor, S. L. T. and Volckmann, R. (2011) 'Transdisciplinarity in higher education, Part 7: Conclusion', *Integral Leadership Review*, June. Retrieved from: http://integralleadershipreview.com/2630-transdisciplinarity-in-higher-education-part-7/.

McNeely, I. F. and Wolverton, L. (2008) *Reinventing Knowledge: From Alexandria to the Internet*. New York: W. W. Norton.

Maslow, A. H. (1943) 'A theory of human motivation', *Psychological Review*, 50: 370–96.

Menand, L. (2001) 'Undisciplined', *Wilson Quarterly*, Autumm, pp. 51–9.

Merkel, U. (ed.) (2013) *Power, Politics and International Events: Socio-cultural Analyses of Festivals and Spectacles*. Abingdon: Routledge.

Moufakkir, O. and Pernecky, T. (eds) (2014) *Ideological, Social and Cultural Aspects of Events*. Wallingford, England: CABI.

Mourad Jr, R. P. (1997) *Postmodern Philosophical Critique and the Pursuit of Knowledge in Higher Education*. Westport, CT: Bergin & Garvey.

Munar, A. M., Pernecky, T. and Feighery, W. (2016) 'An introduction to tourism postdisciplinarity', Special issue of *Tourism Analysis*, 21 (1) (forthcoming).

Østreng, W. (2010) *Science Without Boundaries: Interdisciplinarity in Research, Society, and Politics*. Lanham, MD: University Press of America.

Pernecky, T., Munar, A. M. and Feighery, W. (2016a) 'Tourism in a postdisciplinary milieu: final demarcation points', *Tourism Analysis*, 21 (1) (forthcoming).

Pernecky, T., Munar, A. M. and Wheeller, B. (2016b) 'Existential postdisciplinarity: personal journeys into tourism, art and freedom', *Tourism Analysis*, 21 (1) (forthcoming).

Pine, J. B. and Gilmore, J. H. (2011) *The Experience Economy*, rev. edn. Boston: Harvard Business Review Press.

Pritchard, A. and Morgan, N. (2007) 'De-centring tourism's intellectual universe, or traversing the dialogue between change and tradition', in I. Ateljevic, A. Pritchard and N. Morgan (eds), *The Critical Turn in Tourism Studies: Innovative Research Methodologies*. Amsterdam: Elsevier, pp. 11–28.

Richards, G., de Brito, M. and Wilks, L. (eds) (2013) *Exploring the Social Impacts of Events*. Abingdon: Routledge.

Rojek, C. (2013) *Event Power: How Global Events Manage and Manipulate*. London: Sage.

Rosenfield, P. L. (1992) 'The potential of transdisciplinary research for sustaining and extending linkages between the health and social sciences', *Social Science and Medicine*, 35: 1343–57.

Rousseau, G. S. (1991) *Enlightenment Crossings: Pre- and Post-modern Discourses, Anthropological*. Manchester: Manchester University Press.

St Pierre, E. A. (2011) 'Introduction: the discipline and practice of qualitative research', in N. K. Denzin and Y. S. Lincoln (eds), *The Sage Handbook of Qualitative Research*. Thousand Oaks, CA: Sage, pp. 611–25.

Scheff, T. J. (1997) *Emotions, the Social Bond, and Human Reality: Part/Whole Analysis*. Cambridge: Cambridge University Press.

Spalinger, A. and Armstrong, J. (eds) (2013) *Rituals of Triumph in the Mediterranean World*, Vol. 63. Leiden: Koninklijke Brill NV.

Stember, M. (1991) 'Advancing the social sciences through the interdisciplinary enterprise', *Social Science Journal*, 27 (1): 1–14.

Tribe, J. (1997) 'The indiscipline of tourism', *Annals of Tourism Research*, 24: 638–57.

Tribe, J. (2004) 'Knowing about tourism: epistemological issues', in J. Phillimore and L. Goodson (eds), *Qualitative Research in Tourism: Ontologies, Epistemologies and Methodologies*. London: Routledge, pp. 46–62.

Part II

Articulating a broader philosophical, conceptual and theoretical vision for event studies

2 Evental approaches to the study of events

Iain MacKenzie and Robert Porter

Introduction

If it is assumed that events are *at least* as ontologically basic as, and therefore non-reducible to, 'things' then it is by no means obvious that the ways in which we study 'things' will be transferable to the study of events. It is worth clarifying aspects of this assumption at the very beginning, as it will guide this foray into the methodological issues surrounding the way we approach the study of events in general and political events in particular. While it is an assumption that reaches back into the traditions of Western and non-Western philosophical reflection, it came to contemporary prominence in the analytical philosophy of Donald Davidson. According to Davidson (1980), our ordinary language use gives us ample reason to claim that the world is not simply composed of things. The language we use, indeed, suggests that we cannot make sense of the world without appeal to the equally basic category of 'happenings' or events. Furthermore, Davidson argues that the category of events implied in ordinary language use is not reducible to changes attributable to the mutations of things. In this sense, events and things have *at least* an equal ontological status. In many respects, and despite the now canonical series of debates in analytical metaphysics that this claim inaugurated (see, for example, Lowe, 2002), the methodological ramifications of this position are still underdeveloped. This is especially true in the social sciences where it seems necessary to delve into what it is that we are talking about when we talk about events, and not just how the category is mobilised in our everyday language. The sense of necessity emerges from one of the key features of events as understood in the social domain, namely that events are not simply 'happenings' or 'occurrences' but phenomena that contain within them, so to speak, a novelty-bearing quality. If we treat events as simple occurrences then we run the risk of leaving them trapped in ordinary language (a category of everyday speech but nothing more) or, as is the case in some recent management and marketing work on the category of events (Getz, 2012), turn them back into things in the service of competitive advantage. Whatever we understand by events, it is necessary to find a way to conceive of the novelty-bearing quality they express if we are to understand the impact they can have on our personal, social, cultural, economic and political lives. Whatever else events may be, it is important that we retain the notion that they are not just occurrences but occurrences that make a difference, a difference marked by their capacity to bring novelty into the world. In studying events, therefore, we should aim to study the difference they make.

There is no doubt that this raises the stakes in terms of philosophical complexity and, to this extent, may appear to take us further from the aim of finding ways to study these phenomena. The differences that we are used to studying in the social sciences tend to be differences in things or, more precisely, phenomena that we treat as things. We may consider the difference that voting systems make on party composition, the difference between old and new social movements, the difference that class background makes on educational achievement, and so on. But to the extent that we treat these differences as quantifiable dimensions of existing things, even if we think of them as 'social things', we *obscure* any evental component they may have by shrouding it in analyses of cause and effect and/or we *neutralise* this same component by deeming it secondary to the phenomenon itself – something that requires subsequent debate and discussion based on the 'facts'. If we are to avoid these tendencies toward concealment and domestication then the task must be to develop a method appropriate to the study of *events qua events*: a method that is able to express their intrinsic novelty-bearing qualities. At the core of this endeavour is the claim that events can be differentiated from mere occurrences to the extent that they are intrinsically *significant*. The method that we need to study events, therefore, must be a method appropriate to the study of significance.

The first clarification of our opening assumption, therefore, is that events cannot be studied like things (or as mutations of things, occurrences) because events must be understood as intrinsically significant. However, this brings us on to a new set of problems. If it is assumed that events can be differentiated from mere occurrences then a central task of studying events is the identification of the novelty-bearing qualities that constitute their significance. Is it possible to identify such qualities? What methods would seem appropriate to this task? An obvious place to turn is to the idea that the significance that constitutes events *as* events is significance *for us*. Philosophically, this is the route taken by hermeneutics. Paul Ricœur (1992), for example, develops Davidson's insight in this manner when he locates the significance of events within narratives of personal identity. Methodologically, this sits neatly within the domain of qualitative approaches that seek to identify the meaning attributed to events by agents. Such identification, however, would seem to be hampered by the ineluctably subjective nature of this treatment of significance, even to the point that, to put it colloquially, 'one person's event may be another person's mere occurrence' (MacKenzie, 2008: 4–6). For all the gains in understanding the subjective complexity of events that such approaches engender, the loss is that in moving from the thing to the subject the event qua event remains obscured and neutralised. It is *obscured* to the extent that it becomes a matter of detailing the subject's, perhaps changing, perceptions of the event rather than the significant qualities of the event itself. It is *neutralised* to the extent that qualitative approaches tend toward diminishing the non-subjective differences that can be constituted by and through events. No matter how complicated the hermeneutic circle, or spiral as Ricœur (1981) prefers, the emphasis upon the subjective basis of significance puts the event qua event forever at a distance. While it is not possible to develop in depth why this remains the case, we can say in sum that it is because the subject itself is deemed to have a thing-like quality of persistence.

Given this we can clarify further the opening assumption: that we should not presume to be able to apply the methods we use to study things to study events. Whether it is the methods of the natural sciences imported to the social sciences as the study of social things *or* the interpretive methods focused on the attribution of the subject's (thing-like) perception of events, in both cases the significance of the event qua event seems obscured and neutralised. This helps us frame the guiding question of the following discussion. Is it possible to study events in a manner that reveals their significance without neutralising it?

Evental approaches: eventalisation

In his recent book on the category of the event, Slavoj Žižek approaches the same problem and gives an interesting and characteristically elegant answer. For Žižek (2014), the category of events is caught between the transcendental and empirical dimensions of thought, dimensions that map on to the subjective and objective focus of the methods highlighted above. Considering how best to proceed in order to avoid the traps of both of these tendencies, he says: 'The only appropriate solution is … to approach events in an evental way' (p. 6). This is a motif that we will carry forward in this discussion, albeit in a manner slightly different from Žižek's own version. Žižek uses it as a motif for a series of insightful reflections on different ideas of the event itself, presenting it as 'a subway trip with stops and connections' (p. 6). While this metaphor of the journey with many stops does capture an important element of how we should approach events, namely that an evental approach to events must take seriously the serial nature of events, it is fundamentally a textual device for the presentation of ideas about the event rather than a methodological device for revealing the significance of events in the world without neutralising them. If we are to carry this motif further then we must consider what an evental approach to events means from the perspective of method. We can do this by turning to the work of Michel Foucault, though there will be much to be gained by returning to Žižek's presentations of the different ways in which the event has been conceptualised as we follow the methodological reading of his useful motif.

In one of the most important moments of methodological reflection that marked Foucault's genealogical work of the 1970s, 'Questions of Method', he was asked to consider the relationship of his analyses of the penal system to more traditional historical accounts. During this conversation he says: 'I am trying to work in the direction of what one might call "eventalization"' (Foucault, 2002: 226). The brief account he gives of this 'procedure of analysis' is instructive for us in highlighting what is at stake in evental approaches to the study of events, at least initially. He outlines two ways of thinking about what is meant by eventalisation. The first is referred to as 'a breach of self-evidence'. He goes on: 'It means making visible a *singularity* at places where there is a temptation to invoke a historical constant ... to show that things "weren't as necessary as all that"' (p. 226). In the terms set out above, this means paying attention to the significance events have as novelty-bearing ruptures within the domain of mere occurrences. This significance is given by the quality events have to displace our common assumptions about the apparently inexorable journey of social practices toward the alleged obviousness of the present configuration of forces and domains. Therefore, as Foucault points out, the significance of events is first given by paying attention to the challenge they express to our knowledge of the present order. That events are singular, however, does not mean that they are simply 'a fact to be registered' (p. 227), a mere anomalous instance, as this would imply a notion of continuity that would undermine the novelty-bearing quality they express. It would, in other words, obscure their significance. Rather – and this brings us to the second of Foucault's claims about eventalisation – if we are to 'rediscover' the evental quality of events then it means 'rediscovering the connections, encounters, supports, blockages, plays of forces, strategies and so on that at a given moment establish what subsequently counts as being self-evident' (pp. 226–7). In this sense, paying attention to the singular and disruptive nature of events requires an investigation into the deeply plural nature of their 'causes'. We should, however, note the complicated temporality within Foucault's claim. The multiple causes of events are not just those that happened 'before the event' but also those that we can only recognise by virtue of the subsequent process of sedimentation that makes the present order appear self-evident. In this sense, one of the cornerstones of any method for the study of events qua events is ineluctably forged in the present, while also considering the complex flows of forces that shape the event in the past, so to speak. Between these two opening claims – that we should stress the singular nature of events as novelty-bearing ruptures and the multiple nature of their causes across time – Foucault adroitly spells out what he calls the 'theoretico-political function' of eventalisation (p. 226). But why is this deemed a political as well as a theoretical function?

Foucault (2002) insists that eventalisation as method works by constructing a '"polyhedron" of intelligibility' around the event 'the number of whose faces is not given in advance and can never properly be taken as finite' (p. 227). This polyhedron of intelligibility is composed of the different elements brought into relation by the event, the different forms of relation that these elements express and the different domains to which the event refers. Considering the 'movement by which imprisonment as a form of punishment and technique of correction becomes a central component of the penal order' (p. 227), he gives examples of what each of these faces of the polyhedron mean. The elements include pedagogical practices, British empirical philosophy and a new division of labour; the relations include the trajectory of technical models such as surveillance, and the domains include new regimes of power linked to the development of capitalist economies (p. 228). This multifaceted exploration of the nature of the event of carceralisation leads to a 'saturation' of the significance of the event that makes it impossible to see it simply as part of a self-evident process of modernisation, liberalisation or any other grand narrative. It is impossible, in other words, to conduct such an analysis without impacting on the political order of the present time and, therefore, one should acknowledge that eventalisation has an ineluctable political function as much as a theoretical one. While he recognises that the political nature of the method of eventalisation will be 'too much and too little' from the perspective of traditional history – too many things to consider and too few necessary connections between them – he says that 'this is precisely the point at issue; both in historical analysis and political critique. We aren't, nor do we have to put ourselves, under the sign of a unitary necessity' (pp. 228–9).

What have we achieved through this foray into Foucault's account of eventalisation? Recalling Žižek's (2014) motif that the appropriate way to study events is to approach events in an evental way, we can now say that this can be detailed in the two key features of eventalisation highlighted by Foucault. First, maintaining the singular disruption of the order from which they emerge is crucial to revealing the evental nature of events. This means approaching events as phenomena that are significant in terms of the challenge they pose to the order of the past, the time of the present in the past, so to speak. Secondly, recognising that this past order is always defined by a sense of the 'unitary necessity' of the present is essential if we are to approach events in a manner that does not neutralise their significance, now. Taken together, the upshot is that the study of events from the methodological perspective of eventalisation is inescapably a form of 'political critique' because it has as its *raison d'être* the practice of calling into question the sense of necessity that shapes the present orders of power and control, whatever these are deemed to be.

That said, there are risks associated with an all too ready adoption of Foucault's account of eventalisation, especially for those of us working in the social sciences. These risks fall under three broad categories. First, it would be wise to acknowledge that Foucault's main targets are forms of traditional history that emphasise continuity and progress. Is it the case that the method of eventalisation can travel outside of this context to the study of contemporary events? Within the social sciences we are often dealing with events in the present rather than the past, or, more precisely, moments in which the event and its evental analysis appear to occupy 'the same time'. We must reflect further on such contemporaneity if we are to avoid transporting a method from one domain of inquiry to another in a manner that may not be appropriate. Secondly, Foucault's notes on eventalisation give us a strong sense of attunement to certain key features of events qua events – their singularity and multiple causes – but are we any closer to identifying what this means we should do in our analyses of events, especially those of a more contemporary nature? While it true that every method can be said to begin with such attunement, it is also the case that methodological innovation requires a set of tools that can be placed ready-to-hand beside the investigator. In order to approach events in an evental way, what do we actually have to do? Thirdly, we must grasp the ontological nettle if we are to appreciate the full resonance of a method of eventalisation. What, exactly, is the ontological status of events in evental analyses? Only if we answer this question can we then understand fully why the study of events will inevitably involve 'political critique' or, more simply, critique.

Each of these concerns raises fundamental matters of philosophical importance – 'what is the temporality of an event?', 'what is the relationship between theory and practice?', 'what is the nature of critique?' – that cannot be explored in the depth they deserve in the remainder of this chapter. However, we can clarify certain key features of an evental approach to the study of events by considering an example drawn from the contemporary political domain and by developing this example with arguably the twentieth century's most developed philosophy of the event: that found in the work of Gilles Deleuze (especially 1990, 1994; for insight into the debates surrounding Deleuze's philosophy of the event see Bowden, 2011; Williams, 2008; Zourabichvili, 2012). If the prima facie case can be established for evental approaches to the study of events then further work will be required to chart the full philosophical implications of such methods.

Evental approaches: dramatisation

One of the most interesting political developments of recent years has been the Occupy Movement. Usually thought to have begun with the Occupy Wall Street protests of September 2011, it became a movement as similar protests spread around the world within a month (Lang and Lang/Levitsky, 2012). If we assume, for the moment, that the Occupy Movement constitutes an event in contemporary political life how should we study it? Leaving to one side the voluminous pro- and anti-Occupy polemics in the blogosphere, the literature seems divided into two broad-based approaches. First, there are a number of works that seek to analyse Occupy as a form of social movement (indicatively Conover *et al.*, 2013; Langman, 2013; Pickerill and Krinsky, 2012). These vary in style from those that see it as an outcrop of existing movements to those that try to account for its particularity in some way or another. Both approaches, however, tend to rely on the theoretical frameworks developed over decades to study social movements in general, such as framing, mobilisation and opportunity perspectives. Whatever differentiates Occupy, therefore, is discussed within established frames of reference and, in this sense, its evental character is obscured by virtue of being domesticated within the self-evident knowledge formations of the present epoch. Secondly, there are a number of first-hand accounts that detail the intricacies of various occupations from the perspective of the occupiers (notably Lang and Lang/Levitsky, 2012). These may vary from the sympathetic to the critical but they tend to prioritise the subjective perspective and thereby neutralise any deeper sense of significance that may be expressed through the Movement itself.

We can certainly get closer to the evental nature of Occupy by adopting Foucault's call to approach it in terms of both its singularity and its plural causes. The 'polyhedron of intelligibilities' that results would certainly be an improvement on the standard literature: it would bring an appreciation of the diverse elements of the movement, the new constellations of activists it brought together but also the new use of space and artistic practice (among many things); the new relations forged in the process, not simply between people but those that spoke to the identification of a class of the super-rich that seemed only to profit from the financial crisis of 2008 (for example); and, lastly, new domains of reference that brought together the politics of the square (linking to events in Tahrir Square and elsewhere) and dispossession (linking to the Indignados movement in Spain) with the politics of mainstream America (again, just to mention some possible lines of inquiry). If this gives even a hint of the evental character of the Occupy Movement, it is because it enables us to reflect on the singular nature of what happened in ways that could not be constrained by either the existing academic discipline of social movement studies or the populist first-hand accounts of the occupiers.

It also allows us to address the problem of the temporality of the event. In the case of the Occupy Movement – one that is relatively recent and still continuing to this day – is it possible to distil the singularity of the event and the plurality of its causes while we are still embedded within it, so to speak? The answer is 'no' if we make one of two assumptions about our temporal embeddedness in the time of Occupy. First, if we assume that the present time is simply the culmination of a linear progression from one moment to the next, the linear time of modernity, then we will treat 'continuity as a self-sufficient reality that carries its own raison d'etre within itself' (Foucault, 2002: 227). Secondly, if we treat the present moment as the culmination of some deep world-historical process, the dialectical time of modernity, then we may fall into the trap of presuming that the event we focus on is *the real event*, that which is truly significant. In both cases, the present time will be de-eventalised; either movements such as Occupy are mere occurrences like any other or they are mere reflections of deeper processes working themselves out more or less inexorably. However, the answer is 'yes' if we have a more subtle appreciation of the temporality of events in relation to the present.

Two of Deleuze's claims about temporality can be usefully imported at this stage to give us a more complicated understanding of the contemporary nature of events and their evental analyses. The first is metaphysical. According to Deleuze (1990), the present is not the culminating point of the past shut off from the future; rather it is the moment at which we are both becoming-past and becoming-future. In other words, the present moment is always *split*: 'instead of a present which absorbs past and future, a future and past divide the present at every instant and subdivide it ad infinitum into past and future, in both directions at once' (Deleuze, 1990: 164). This means that the temporality of the event is always already a split temporality; on the one hand it appears to be the case that evental significance has an eternal dimension – something that has always existed – while, on the other hand, it is necessary to think of the significance of the event as something that is happening now and that must pass as we move into the future. The tension in these two claims is central to Deleuze's understanding of the time of events. As Williams (2008) puts it: 'the eternal event is always past and yet to come but never present, whereas the present event is always passing away and opening to the future but never past or future' (p. 144). This tension is not disabling because for Deleuze it signals that the time of events is always a dual time, each necessary for the understanding of the other but non-reducible to each other. Early in *The Logic of Sense*, he puts it like this: 'Only the present exists in time and draws together, absorbs the past and future; but the past and future alone subsist in time, and infinitely divide each present. Not three successive dimensions, but two simultaneous readings of time' (Deleuze, 1990: 5). As one might expect, this complex dual temporality of the event raises significant metaphysical issues to which Deleuze returns many times in his *oeuvre*. In the context of thinking about how to conduct an evental analysis of events, the main contribution can be summed up in the idea that the time of events is always already split, not between past and present as in Foucault's account of eventalisation, but between the becoming-past and becoming-future of the eternal event and the passing of the present event.

The second important claim we can develop with Deleuze is structural. Once the novelty-bearing quality of events has been attributed this temporal significance, or, better yet, once the temporal complexity of events is understood as a condition of their significance, then we can understand how the novel event leads to further processes. The emergence of an event is a radical cut in our knowledge of the self-evident workings of the present order, as we noted with Foucault. We can understand this with the Occupy Movement in terms of the difficulty of capturing its significance from within the established frames of reference deployed in the literature that surrounds it. Following on from the complicated temporality of the event we can also add that the Occupy Movement has significance both as something that was always there – the power of the people, for example – and as something that is so radically new that it is already passing into a different future – whatever the Occupy Movement will become. But, in fact, Deleuze's account of the temporality of events leads to a rather more radical conclusion. According to Deleuze, every event changes everything. We can understand why this is such an important claim by recalling the earlier hint about the importance of seriality, Žižek's 'stops on the train journey'. Deleuze's version of structuralism is based on the idea that the structures that condition our experience of the world are formed by linked series that result from events; it is his version of the poststructuralist claim that structures are always contingent and therefore open to radical change. This means that each new event retroactively changes the 'past' elements of the series *and* the possible future elements at the same time. This is not such a strange idea; indeed, it is a commonplace in psychoanalysis, as Žižek (2014) acknowledges. The present revelation of the past traumatic event changes the nature of that event and of every other event connected to it, including those that stretch into the future. Deleuze's claim is simply that this is true of an ontological as well as a psychoanalytical account of events. Žižek (2014) sums it up well (referring to Bergson, one of Deleuze's major influences): 'when something radically New emerges, this new retroactively creates its own possibility, its own causes/conditions' (p. 111).

While it may appear that the metaphysical baggage heaped upon an evental analysis of events is rather weighty at this stage, it is nonetheless necessary to have both a dual sense of the temporality of events and a serial account of their relationship if we are to transport Foucault's method of eventalisation from the domain of history/genealogy to that of contemporary evental studies. Without these weighty metaphysical components, the novelty-bearing quality of events that marks their significance will remain forever obscured and neutralised. Moreover, it enables the taking of perspectives in the present that speaks directly to the ways in which the 'polyhedron of intelligibilities' may be constructed when the time of the event and the time of the evental analysis are the same, so to speak, in essence because the time of the event is always already *split*. But, doesn't a danger remain: that the time of the evental analysis will reabsorb the split time of the event? By what means can an evental analysis proceed if one cannot simply appeal to the self-evident practices of contemporary knowledge formation for fear that they may suture the split of the present? The answer is deceptively simple: to express the novelty-bearing quality of the event *within and through* novelty-bearing analyses. This is the core gesture at the heart of Deleuze's (2004: 94–116) method of dramatisation.

To say that dramatisation expresses the novelty of events within and through novelty-bearing analyses is to highlight the twofold nature of evental approaches as processes of discovery and creation (we discuss the ontological claims implied in this relationship more fully elsewhere: MacKenzie and Porter, 2011a, 2011b). This becomes clear if we take the motif of dramatisation seriously. To dramatise a text, for example, is to activate the forces at work in the text in a manner that 'brings them to life'. In this sense, the novelty contained in the work of art is expressed *within* the dramatised version. This can be described as a process of discovery. The potential dynamics of the text are intensified in order to reveal certain qualities of the original. Shakespearean monologues may be powerful on the page but when performed they can have a life and intensity that reveals the hidden forces at work. In the same way, the dramatisation of an event is the practice of intensifying the complex arrangement of forces animating the rupture with the present social order; Foucault's method of eventalisation captures this aspect of the analysis well. Of course, not all performances have this revelatory quality vis-à-vis the text, and not all conceptualisations of the event can reveal its evental quality. To understand what it is that makes the difference between those that do and those that do not, we need to consider the second dimension of dramatisation. For the forces animating a text to be discovered, its dramatisation must be as much a creative process as a process of discovery. In this sense, the novelty contained within the script is created *through* the performance of the dramatised version. Staging Macbeth's monologues as those of an urban gang leader on a housing estate creates a new series of resonances for the forces at work in the text, hardly envisaged by Shakespeare, that nonetheless express an integral quality of the script, namely its timeless potential for novel recreation. Considering events, we can also say that it is through the *creation of concepts* to express the novelty-bearing quality of the event that one is able to discover that quality within it (Deleuze and Guattari, 1994). It is this twofold dynamic of discovery and creation that marks the method of dramatisation as an evental approach to the study of events. The singular and disruptive nature of the event can be expressed by dramatising the forces *within* the event, while this dramatisation, if it is to be successful, must involve the creation of new ways of expressing this dynamism *through* an equally singular and disruptive analytical process. To dramatise events is not 'to restage what happened'. Rather, dramatisation is the expression of the potential contained *within* the event *through* the construction of a new event. This can be summarised in the following manner: an evental approach to the study of events must itself be an event. It is this creative side of the eventalisation process that Deleuze brings out so well in the idea of dramatisation as method.

Conclusion

Are we any closer to how we should study events in an evental way? It is worth making a brief methodological recap of the claims so far before closing with a gesture back to the opening assumption about the ontological status of events. If the category of event means anything, it must refer to the novelty-bearing quality of certain ruptures with the given rather than to the domain of mere occurrences which sustain and replicate the given. In order to approach the study of events, however, we must give up on the standard methods – naturalist and interpretivist – that operate within the social sciences as both tend toward obscuring and neutralising the significance that characterises events in general and especially those that concern us in the social sciences. However, this does not mean giving up on method per se. Instead we can adopt the complementary methods of eventalisation and dramatisation developed by Foucault and Deleuze, respectively. Both of these methods attune the researcher to the singularity of events and their multiple causes. They also offer ways in which these two dimensions can be brought out at the same time. For that to be the case, however, method cannot be divorced from politics or critique more generally. The 'theoretico-political function' of method is established on the basis of a dual conception of the time of the event and the twofold processes of intensification and concept creation. Events, understood in an evental way, are real world dramas that can only be approached through their dramatisation. The methods we need to adopt are not, therefore, those of the scientist or the interpreter, but of the artist.

All of which has led us some way from the opening assumption, that events are *at least* as ontologically basic as things. If we are to truly grasp how we should approach events in an evental way then it is necessary to make a more radical ontological gesture: events are ontologically prior to things. The challenge of the more critical turn in event studies is the challenge of thinking the event 'all the way down' and, therefore, thinking that our approaches to the study of events must be evental 'all the way down'.

References

Bowden, S. (2011) *The Priority of Events: Deleuze's Logic of Sense*. Edinburgh: Edinburgh University Press.

Conover, M. D., Davis, C., Ferrara, E., McKelvey, K., Menczer, F. and Flammini, A. (2013) 'The geospatial characteristics of a social movement communication network', *PLoS ONE*, 8: 3.

Davidson D. (1980) *Essays on Actions and Events*. Oxford: Clarendon Press.

Deleuze, G. (1990) *The Logic of Sense*. New York: Columbia University Press.

Deleuze, G. (1994) *Difference and Repetition*. New York: Columbia University Press.

Deleuze, G. (2004) *Desert Islands and Other Texts 1953–1974*. Los Angeles: Semiotext(e).

Deleuze, G. and Guattari, F. (1994) *What Is Philosophy?* London: Verso.

Foucault, M. (2002) 'Questions of method', in J. Faubion (ed.), *Power: Essential Works of Foucault 1954–1984*, Vol. 3. London: Penguin Books, pp. 223–38.

Getz, D. (2012) *Event Studies: Theory, Research and Policy for Planned Events*, 2nd edn. London: Routledge.

Lang, A. S. and Lang/Levitsky, D. (eds) (2012) *Dreaming in Public: Building the Occupy Movement*. Oxford: New Internationalist Publications.

Langman, L. (2013) 'Occupy: a new new social movement', *Current Sociology*, 61: 510–24.

Lowe, E. J. (2002) *A Survey of Metaphysics*. Oxford: Oxford University Press.

MacKenzie, I. (2008) 'What is a political event?', *Theory and Event*, 11 (3): 1–28.

MacKenzie, I. and Porter, R. (2011a) 'Dramatization as method in political theory', *Contemporary Political Theory*, 10: 482–501.

MacKenzie, I. and Porter, R. (2011b) *Dramatizing the Political: Deleuze and Guattari*. Basingstoke: Palgrave Macmillan.

Pickerill, J. and Krinsky, J. (2012) 'Why does Occupy matter?', *Social Movement Studies: Journal of Social, Cultural and Political Protest*, 11: 279–87.

Ricœur, P. (1981) *Hermeneutics and the Human Sciences: Essays on Language, Action and Interpretation*. Cambridge: Cambridge University Press.

Ricœur, P. (1992) *Oneself as Another*. Chicago: University of Chicago Press.

Williams, J. (2008). *Gilles Deleuze's Logic of Sense: A Critical Introduction and Guide*. Edinburgh: Edinburgh University Press.

Žižek, S. (2014) *Event*. London: Penguin Books.

Zourabichvili, F. (2012) *Deleuze: A Philosophy of the Event*. Edinburgh: Edinburgh University Press.

3 Eventification

Framing the Ordinary as the Extraordinary

Temple Hauptfleisch

Introduction

Drama, theatre, spectacle, performance, carnivals and festivals have all been an integral part of the social fabric of human existence for as long as we know. Today, they are among the multitude of more recognisable social activities we have come to refer to as *events* (social events, sports events, theatrical events, political events, hallmark events, public events and so on) and they form a core focus of the new disciplines broadly referred to as 'event studies' and 'event management', as may be seen from the many handbooks that have appeared in recent years. Helped along by the enormous escalation in festival activity across the globe – by what Kaptein (1996) refers to as the 'festivalisation' of culture – events have also become a topic of intense interest in other fields of study, including communication studies, history, economics, sociology, literature and the arts.

But how does such an event actually work, and how does any event manage to have an impact on the individual member of the public (or 'consumer'), on the immediate community and/or ultimately on society at large? To answer such a question requires the kind of multi- and cross-disciplinary study that is being undertaken by this book.

In the case of drama and theatre, this particular question (though perhaps phrased somewhat differently) has long been the domain of the practitioner rather than of academics and theorists. Theatre critics and historians have apparently been content with studying the form and quality of the texts, the histories and biographies of actors and companies, and perhaps the nature of the 'acting' as a theoretical idea, rather than considering theatre-making as an inclusive process. When the late nineteenth century and especially the twentieth century saw the gradual advent of anthropological, social, psychological, economic and systemic studies of social structures and processes, including social impact and effect, we saw this transferred to sociological and systemic studies of theatre-making as process as well. In many ways it has become the stuff of semiotics and semiology as well as of cultural and performance studies.

The interest in context and impact has since also been explored by a number of influential arts theorists interested in the processes of performing for, and interacting with, audiences and society in general. On the one hand there were, for example, the interesting but bewildering array of theories and practices inevitably beginning with Konstantin Stanislavsky's system and the Method school of acting in America, on to the experimental work of Joan Littlewood, Peter Brook, Jerzy Grotowski and others, the political theatre of Bertolt Brecht, the interventionist work of Paulo Freire and Augusto Boal, plus a plethora of theories and methodologies for the pedagogical uses of theatre and performance, etc. On the other hand, there was the appearance of numerous sociologically, psychologically and/or anthropologically inspired histories and theories about theatre and festival culture, including the ideas of Irving Goffmann (1959, 1974), Elizabeth Burns (1972) and others about frame analysis, 'theatricality' and the presentation of self in everyday life, Richard Schechner and Victor Turner's radical but useful theories of performance and performance studies, Eugenio Barba's ideas on theatre anthropology, and so on.

It is in this context that a small group of academics was invited to a colloquium in Stockholm by Wilmar Sauter, to discuss ideas proposed in his position paper 'Approaching the Theatrical Event' (read in Japan, 1995; published in *Theatre Research International*, 22 (1), 1997) and the issue of the 'eventness' of theatre. From this discussion, led by Henri Schoenmakers and Wilmar Sauter, came the proposal to establish a formal new Working Group on the Theatrical Event, under the auspices of the International Federation for Theatre Research (IFTR) in Puebla, Mexico in 1997 (hereafter referred to simply as 'the Working Group').

The aim of the group was to study what they referred to as 'the theatrical event' (or 'the performance event' by some authors), and it tended to consist of individuals with a specific interest in the nature of theatre as a *performed* art form and a social event, rather than as an aesthetic and/or literary form. Many of the members had a strong interest in the demography and societal impact of theatrical events and a number worked in the broad field one might call 'the sociology of theatre'. Some of the members, I believe, were also reacting to the growing influence of Richard Schechner's intriguing but somewhat alarmingly open and arcane field of performance theory, which had by then spawned many books and courses at training institutions, as well as an international association and journal *Performance Studies International* (PSi) (also founded, interestingly enough, in 1997).

The Working Group has since published three books on the subject and are working on a fourth, while members of the group have also published individually on this theme over the past two decades. (For more on the initial history of the Working Group, see Jacqueline Martin's 'Preface' in Cremona *et al.*, 2004).

In a 1999 draft contribution to the initial working sessions for the first book (*Theatrical Events – Borders Dynamics Frames*; Cremona *et al.*, 2004), I introduced two new terms, *eventify* and *eventification*, as short-hand descriptors for a particular process I was discussing, one I had originally identified as the *eventification of the ordinary*. The terms soon became part of the vocabulary of the Working Group. The contribution was reworked for the next IFTR conference, held in Lyon in 2000, and since then the tentative ideas expressed there have been expanded in a number of articles and book contributions, including the second book published by the Working Group (*Festivalising! Theatrical Events, Politics and Culture*; Hauptfleisch *et al.*, 2007). The current chapter is an attempt to draw on those earlier publications (notably Hauptfleisch, 2004 and 2007), to outline my current thinking about the concept of eventification and to consider a few new questions that have occurred to me since, as well as some implications the concept may have for event studies in general.

In the spirit of multi-disciplinarity championed by the current book, and to provide myself and the reader with some specific examples of eventification for this discussion, I shall largely maintain my focus on the context best known to me, namely the world of theatre and performance. In the original studies, I tended to use many extensive discussions of concrete examples to make my initial points, the case studies largely drawn from my own more specific environment and field of expertise: the theatre and performance history of South Africa. In this particular discussion of eventification as a theoretical tool, I wish to undertake an overview and perhaps occasional re-evaluation of the theory underlying the previous studies and publications. I will therefore usually only refer to some illustrative examples from the world of international performance, where they appear instrumental for the argument, and largely eschew any in-depth discussion of the South African case studies, since many such discussions and analyses (by myself and by others) are readily available in various publications.

The theatrical event

While the term 'theatrical event' is often used simply to point to a particular production of a play as a specialised form of a general social event, the Working Group has tended to go somewhat further and view it as an independent phenomenon, with its own particular characteristics and conventions, i.e. as a complex, subjective process of framing, enacting and performance, which takes place in a specific venue and in a particular context, over a defined length of time, under unique conditions and involving a specific group of participants (see, for example, Wilmar Sauter's introduction to the 2004 IFTR volume).

The notion itself is, thus, a complex and highly elusive thing, its key attributes in some ways being its ephemerality on the one hand, and its artificiality on the other. Susan Bennett (1990: 114), for instance, refers to it as a 'culturally constructed product'. However, it is of immense importance in any consideration of the history of theatre and performance – as much for theatre practitioners as for theatre researchers and students. To me, there would appear to be four closely interrelated ways in which term the *theatrical event* has been used over time, and they all seem to have some bearing on what follows:

- First of all, it can refer to the entire complex of processes occurring in and around a performance space at a particular time (i.e. a single performance of a theatrical work, which includes performers, text, audience and the greater context – historical, social, political, cultural and economic). Richard Schechner terms this 'theatre' in his publications.
- An equally interesting interpretation would refer to more than a single performance or event (e.g. the published text or the opening night), and

rather to what one might previously have referred to as a 'production', i.e. the entire run of a play, seen as a composite event. This is more general than the first interpretation, but also a little more complicated, for in such cases the emphasis is more on the *event* and on its broader socio-cultural and artistic impact, with the entire performance history of the work becoming part of its *eventness*.

- By contrast there is the complementary notion, suggested by Bennett's comment quoted above, that the theatrical event is simply a specialised form of societal (social and cultural) event, with a (set of) general and particular societal function(s), like any other event. Important for the argument here is the possibility that neither these social functions nor the shape and impact of the event itself are determined solely by the creators (producers, writers, directors, performers, etc.) of the particular event, but that they are abetted and possibly limited by external conditions that apply during the event itself (i.e. the specific place, time and context of the occurrence, the latter including such matters as the physical, political, economic, social, cultural, psychological and other circumstances of performance). Stated otherwise: the venue and context shape the performance event as much as the 'creators' do.
- Finally, there is the intriguing suggestion that 'life events' may also constitute 'theatrical events' under certain circumstances, where circumstances or onlookers tap into the latent theatricality or *eventness* inherent in all human activity, to redefine such events in dramatic (theatrical) terms – i.e. 'dramatise' or 'theatricalise' it. This is in part what Schechner (1977, 1985) refers to as 'performance' and implies a process of what Irving Goffmann (1959) called 'framing', i.e. where the particular life event is placed in/viewed through a dramatic/theatrical frame, and shown and interpreted as if it were a scripted ('theatricalised') event.

Putting a frame of any kind around a human event naturally has some very specific relevance in fields such as documentary and news reportage, for the frame isolates and turns a momentary fragment of an incident or occurrence in the (ordinary/extraordinary) flow of human life into a defined and singular 'event'. One need but think of the old newsreels shown in the cinema or of contemporary TV news coverage of wars, sporting events, public events such as funerals, weddings, carnivals, pop concerts, awards ceremonies and the like to get a sense of the impact of framing on our sensibilities and view of the world. Some version of frame analysis constitutes a fundamental analytic tool for semioticians, theatre anthropologists and performance theorists, including many members of the Working Group.

The title and focus of this chapter flows directly from the foregoing points, but especially the implied suggestion that the theatrical event can, and often does, serve as a framing device, able to turn what one might call an (everyday, ordinary) *event* into an (exceptional, extraordinary) *Event*. And it is this process that I have termed *eventification*.

Eventification

We have all known the experience of watching some great ceremonial, tragic and/or historic event unfold before our eyes, often viewed through and interpreted for our eyes by the media. Fed to us through the various communication channels, these images fill our minds with unforgettable and even iconic images, which often become an indelible part of our collective cultural memory. It is accepted as one of the ways in which we experience the world, and share in the experiences of our global community. (Or, at least, that has long been the argument for the existence and importance of such things as the newspapers, the broadcast media, publicity campaigns, Hollywood-style celebrity occasions and – for better or worse – the flood of so-called 'social media' that has come to dominate our share of the twenty-first century.)

However, as media, marketing and communications research has so often shown us, this experience, this 'way of seeing', is far from the simple or innocent activity suggested by the paragraph above, for we are never fed an unedited, unenhanced and/or unbiased 'message' or 'image'; it is *always* a mediated version of the 'reality' we get to see and hear about, specifically, expertly and more often than not consciously enhanced and edited for our consumption. Not even something apparently so gut-wrenchingly 'real' as the brief, but compelling, images of two passenger planes smashing explosively into the Twin Towers in New York on Tuesday, 11 September 2001, came to us unmediated.

Processes of eventification

At the most elementary level, the images from 9/11 were manipulated to slow the planes down and the images enlarged, not only to make the incident observable, but also to allow the onlooker/viewer to take it in and respond to it. Then the new images were repeated, hundreds of times, on all news channels throughout the world. In an instant, almost before any commentary or information could be added, the images had become a global possession, and thus ideal material for widescale and varied forms of interpretation, reaction and manipulation.

The 9/11 experience is only one of many such examples one might choose from the recent past alone to illustrate the idea of a great event 'theatricalised' or, more correctly I suppose, 'mediatised' – and thus in my terminology 'eventified'. Sometimes, as in the above example, the images are shocking, forced on us by the reality of the moment; at other times they are images that develop (or are manufactured) more deliberately and, on occasion, are even cynically, planned and orchestrated over time to attain a specific effect or outcome.

Of course the images can also be created by a combination of the two processes. A familiar example of this is provided by the brief, but luminescent, arc described by the very public life of Britain's popular Princess Diana: the coverage of the courtship and the spectacular presentation of her fairytale wedding on the one hand, and the public outpouring of grief at her tragic death and funeral on the other, both owed a great deal to a spontaneous reaction from an enamoured public of course, but also to a strategic use of the potent mass media exposure the events elicited. A combination of the formal Buckingham Palace and government publicity machines and the public media used the storybook quality of the events themselves, not only to create the iconic 'Princess Di' and to transmit an image of a popular and united royal family, but to begin setting up a fertile context for the incredible outpouring of grief that would follow her unexpected and tragic death, and the huge public event that accompanied her funeral. This was true eventification, tapping into the circumstances to compel a resurrection, and in many ways a 'canonisation', of Diana's image.

Another rather telling example of such potent, and to my mind far more cynical and calculated, use of eventification through mediation and theatricalisation is to be found in our original exposure to the so-called 'Gulf War' of 1991. What we have in this case is a regional squabble in the Gulf region, framed as what might be termed an 'International Event' for consumption by the entire world, through blatant 'cinematisation' of the actual military operations, in addition to prolific and repetitive use of symbolic imagery (courtesy of CNN, Sky News, Baghdad radio *et al.* of course). In the case of CNN, for example, each evening's 'episode' was framed like a Hollywood epic by Cecil B. De Mille (complete with monumental title sequences very reminiscent of those he had employed for *Ben Hur*), or in the case of Sky News, like a serialised, modern version of the BBC's illustrious series *The World At War* (again with similar title sequences). In both cases, we are invited to see what is really a regional stand-off as a threat to humanity with the potential of unleashing World War III. *How* this was done and by whom is a most interesting case of media-based eventification in its impact on people's thinking and perceptions of international politics on a par with the more successful propaganda exercises of the Second World War. But consider the comparison: a genuine, five-year-long struggle for European domination involving whole nations being equated to a rattling of arms and a baring of teeth around Baghdad – which we are made to view as (and come to believe to be) the potential 'mother of all wars'. The only things that have really changed are the weapons employed and the nature, reach and abilities of the media – more specifically their influence over our perceptions of the events. (The 'War on Terror' announced by George W. Bush on 20 September 2001 as a response to the 9/11 tragedy is another example we could have considered – especially as it has since been called off – but the propaganda machine and eventification processes in this case are far less structured and creative.)

The examples I have cited so far tend to be the obvious, public ones, but the magnitude and scope of the particular happening being dramatised makes no real difference and the same thing occurs at all levels of human experience: natural and human disasters (floods, earthquakes, sinking ships, train collisions, etc.), social occasions (birthday parties, awards ceremonies, weddings, funerals), domestic quarrels, touching stories involving animals, etc. Many such examples exist in the public domain, especially the thousands of poignant images of the everyday happening, place or person, caught (or in some cases set up) by photographers over the years. One need but think of such enduring examples as Henri Cartier Bresson's

Breughelesque documentation of urban life, Ansell Adams's unique dramatisations of the landscape in the American West and Steve McCurry's haunting cover picture for National Geographic (*Afghan Girl*, 1985). The same is true of stories of ordinary people, picked up, noted and retold in a dramatised form, hence eventified, by writers, film makers and journalists. (Photography as an eventification process can, of course, be a whole fascinating field of study on its own.)

The larger, public events are normally more easily recognised and, hence, they often become the model for the way the less famous less public event may be approached. Marvellous examples are provided by the world of sport, for instance the various 'world championships' and 'world cups' alone provide endless examples of how celebrity and significance can be artificially manufactured. Almost more interesting to me in this respect are such pseudo sports as professional wrestling on the one hand – i.e. sport tending to theatre – and game shows like *Gladiators* – theatre (television) tending toward sport – on the other. Both forms utilise choreographed mayhem and a hyped-up and hysterical style of media-presentation, the first to suggest that the outcome is wholly unpredictable and fortuitous, hence a genuine sport, the second that the contrived, sanitised competitive games played are serious matters of life and death. One could go on in this vein of course – what about so called 'Reality TV'? It can almost be seen as the *reverse* of normal eventification: a complicated attempt to somehow 'de-eventify' an obviously mediated, artificially set-up and theatricalised event, and present it as an 'ordinary' event (or series of ordinary incidents perhaps).

Eventification and socio-cultural systems

A key aspect of all the examples I have noted thus far has been that, irrespective of how and why they were conceived and set up, the images and enthusiasm generated have by now become part of our collective cultural memory, having been 'planted' in there by the specific set of processes set in motion when what is (theoretically at least) an ordinary or 'everyday' incident, occurrence or process is framed (even mythologised) and presented to us ready-made, in specifically dramatic and public terms, by the strategic use of the media and hype and thus turned into a (dramatised, mediated, theatricalised) *public event* and/or iconic image.

As we have seen, the process of eventification is not necessarily driven and effected by individual creators/manipulators and/or performers alone, but is also significantly stimulated, enhanced and supported by the nature of the event itself and by its socio-cultural context. In other words, it is driven by a cultural and/or social *system* or *systems*, which are constantly looking for and developing specific framing situations which would allow the processes to take place. Eventification (and the profit, enhancement and celebrity it generates) is thus a core process at the heart of such varied domains or social systems as politics, high finance, organised religion, even education and the academic enterprise – and always has been. The very existence of many formal systemic structures in contemporary society testify to this.

For instance, Neil Postman (1983) has argued that schools are a relatively recent development in general human development, and were *inter alia* introduced as systemic structures by which children were taken out of everyday life and were then moulded in ways that would benefit society before returning them to it. In this way, an almost unnoticed, natural process of learning by example, learning by doing in everyday life, was replaced by 'instruction': a process whereby selected aspects of everyday life are chosen to be objects of study and are then specifically framed and simulated in a space and situation (the classroom) specially created for the purpose, in order to make them memorable and significant. In short, supposedly important aspects of the real world are *eventified*, using an array of framing, marketing and theatricalising devices, to enhance their meaning and to convey the fundamental facts and principles involved to the young people *in abstracto* rather than by experience.

Other systemic structures that exist to supply a variety of forms of mutual support, focused activity and/or leisure activities for defined subcultures within communities, range from relatively open and simply structured charity organisations, social societies and sports clubs to the more complex organisational structures one finds with trade organisations, secret societies, political parties and the like (i.e. systemic structures to obtain power by harnessing the support of people sharing similar values). Perhaps the most clearly defined of these would be the numerous formal religions that have evolved over the millennia and their respective creeds and liturgical practices. The point is that all these organisational structures provide systems and ceremonial processes by which everyday human actions and interactions may not only be regulated but, more importantly, be eventified and given special significance – leading to power, influence, wealth, fame, eternal life perhaps, and other desirable outcomes.

It is obvious that, given the notions of framing, theatricalisation and cinematisation referred to in the foregoing discussions of public experiences, the concept of eventification could be particularly apt as a key to discussing the impact of the various art forms (theatres and theatre companies, galleries and museums, film and television companies), which all have strongly defined systemic structures, even more overtly committed to the eventification of their products as an end result. And 'drama' and 'theatre' have long been used as metaphors for the process.

Eventification and the theatre

Let us begin in somewhat traditional fashion by considering the formally written and produced stage play. Based on the introductory outline of the four general ways of looking at the theatrical event per se, I would postulate that there are also two (contrasting yet fundamental) ways of looking specifically at the notion of eventification in relation to a play or performance (= theatrical event).

The first, possibly more conventional, way is to view the play, play-text and/or performance as a (specific) mechanism whereby the ordinary may be eventified within society. (All arts, literature and media do this of course – theatre and the theatrical event is but one form of it.) In other words, making a play happen (writing or evolving a text and performing it), constitutes *one* of the means whereby the *ordinary* may be eventified. By selecting incidents, issues and/or personalities from everyday life and recasting and framing them in a 'dramatic' or performance mode of some kind, theatre-makers use theatrical events as powerful and pervasive eventifying mechanisms or media for presenting such everyday matters to audiences as something extraordinary – as 'reality' with enhanced stature and meaning.

One must, to follow this line of reasoning, accept that the very act of putting on the play in front of an audience in a space of some kind constitutes a 'performance' or a 'theatrical event' in the general sense, no matter where, by whom and for whom it is done. Indeed the *where*, *by whom* and *for whom* already establish some kind of triangulated frame for a particular event, for which both producers, performers and audience have prepared in some way, and to which each one brings a certain amount of 'baggage' – emotional, intellectual, experiential, etc., as well as some measure of value and/or celebrity. In other words: the particular evening's performance becomes an 'event' in itself, and when the play is repeated, so does the extended run of all the performances become an 'event' from another perspective.

The foregoing is pretty much the usual way of looking at theatre and its aesthetic function nowadays, one that has been discussed from various perspectives in many articles and books, as well as the publications and discussions of the Working Group. The second, perhaps less conventional, way of looking at the theatrical event and the processes involved in making it happen is to view it essentially as an *everyday societal process*. By doing this, we think of it as comparable and equal to any of the other daily rituals, ceremonies and social usages that guide and enhance our lives and the public and private interactions we have with our fellows. The 'theatrical' or 'performative' nature of formal and informal meetings and social gatherings is accepted as a given by many theorists and practitioners today and has been much studied. (See, for instance, Richard Schechner's many publications and more specifically his notion of 'performance'.) In this interpretation, any gathering of people, in the drawing rooms, pubs, churches, council halls, the office, concert halls and so on, in any community, involves all the processes we have mentioned so far – framing, sets, costume, performing, dramatisation, ritual and so on, and is therefore potentially a vehicle for the eventification of life incidents, people and issues. This is especially true of the more formal and emblematic rituals that drive society, and give meaning and stature to moments of birth, marriage, investiture, death, burial and so on, rituals and ceremonial events from which the concept of theatre really arose in most societies (see, for example, Schechner, 1985; Southern, 1964; Turner, 1982).

The significance of viewing the theatrical event itself as an 'ordinary' event, i.e. as a normal (though distinctive and significant) part of the fabric of our lives, no different from the myriad of other 'events' which constitute the sum of human social life, is that it suggests that the theatrical event may, in its turn, become amenable to eventification itself. By (re)framing a *theatrical event* as a *societal event of significance*, one may perhaps plausibly speak of the *eventification of the theatrical event*, despite the apparent tautology. The process activated would then entail the (conscious) exploitation of the latent *eventness* in the original theatrical event, by making use of the full range of (theatrical, but especially non-theatrical) eventifying processes, in order to alter and enhance perceptions of the theatrical performance or the play (as a vehicle for eventifying a social issue or event), turning its image into another level of event – transcendental, memorable, profitable or even artistic – with its own (added) meaning, impact and/or value.

At the most elementary level, this is what marketing processes (posters, interviews, adverts, etc.) and opening nights are intended to do; to make an 'Event' of the first performance of a play and thus focus attention on its presence, suggests that it is somehow extraordinary and worth the price of a ticket. The old circus custom of a parade through the streets of a town by the cast and the animals, to announce that the circus is in town (a strategy that has often been copied by play-makers as well), is another wonderful example, as are the opening nights of art exhibitions of course (which often seek to find controversy and notoriety enough to draw attention to the art work). These processes are all part of a secondary or adjacent 'event' generated by an original theatrical or artistic event.

What it often boils down to, then, is the art of eventifying the production by tapping into, appropriating and marketing the power of the already eventified image. This is something individual performers, writers and directors (or their publicists) have seemingly always been aware of, for they utilise eventification processes consistently as part of their craft, seeking to distinguish their products from the total work on offer, often in creative and even bizarre ways. (Indeed, to many, the twinned notions of 'publicity and marketing' have become synonymous with these processes, as has the much touted notion of 'celebrity'.) The fact is, they cannot do otherwise, for this is a natural part of the process of theatre-making. The point is that eventification per se may not be an *optional* matter at all, but rather a fundamental and defining part of the process of creating art, of making theatre. The very decision to write, produce and perform a play is itself an irreversible decision to participate in an act of eventification, a commitment to eventify a moment or aspect of ordinary/everyday life in theatrical terms, and then to *Eventify* your representation of that eventification in order to make it noticeable and of significance (eventification of the ordinary, but applied to the theatrical event *as societal event*).

The foregoing kind of eventification can, of course, offer immediate and pragmatic benefits for play-makers: the turning of (yet another) drawing room comedy into a vehicle for a celebrated performer from the movies or TV soaps, or the utilisation of controversy (nudity, vulgarity, sensational content) not only as material (or decoration), and marketing material, but as a way to provide an identity for the theatre and/or the company doing the play (one need only think of the advent of *Oh! Calcutta!*) – both have repercussions at the box-office or in the columns of critics. Similarly, tapping into the fervour and fury of a specific political situation may turn an ordinary narrative into a political event and hence a clarion cry for action and change – which then elevates a modest theatrical event to the status of Theatrical Event, with the accompanying critical and monetary rewards.

Secondary eventification can also work in other ways, as a number of the examples suggest. For instance, it sometimes does not accompany but rather follows on the performance, becoming part of the response to a work. Obvious examples here would be subsequent performances (which in a way must inevitably reference the original production), and 'contemporary' versions of successful plays or productions (translated, adapted, revisited). In some cases, such eventification may carry over into longer-term celebrity, even canonisation, which may turn virtually any following production into an event per se. Examples would include such money-spinning events as *Charley's Aunt*, *The Mouse Trap*, *The Rocky Horror Show*, *West Side Story* and *The Phantom of the Opera*, as well as the more profound works of Shakespeare, Molière, Ibsen, Chekhov and the like, which appear to have acquired and shown immense and enduring eventification potential in their critical celebrity.

Another version of secondary eventification occurs in the form of what are sometimes termed 'metatheatrical plays' – works that comment self-referentially on the original, its production or the players, thus eventifying the original. *Oedipus Rex* and *Hamlet*, for example, have both been the source and inspiration of a whole series of adaptations and staged (re)interpretations over the centuries. Film and television, too, have a strong inclination to exploit this kind of practice. There are interesting cinematic examples of film being used to eventify stage productions, for example *Shakespeare in Love* (1998), the Tom Stoppard and Marc Norman fantasy about the origins and first performance of *Romeo and Juliet*; *Topsy-Turvy* (1999) about the creation and first production of *The Mikado*; and *Alceste à Bicyclette* ('Bicycling with Molière', 2013), about a modern-day production of *Le Misanthrope*. The world of experimental theatre, film and performance abounds with this kind of work.

It is thus clear that any form of secondary eventification is achieved by tapping into and using the entire polysystem of intertwined and interdependent subsystems that make up the larger, more encompassing theatrical system of the particular society, thereby setting up longer-term processes of persuasion and eventification by the particular artistic or cultural grouping/system/structure responsible for the specific project.

What the general notion of *eventification* therefore provides is a way of understanding the extreme importance of the way plays, productions, performances and 'theatrical events' are *displayed* (framed and presented) in a particular context. As we have seen, it is done not only to establish them as 'theatrical events' (i.e. 'plays', 'performances', 'theatre') as outlined at the start of this section, but specifically to *enhance* their meaning, value, impact and celebrity, as well as their marketability, as societal events, and possibly make them available for further exploration and exploitation.

However, there are also aspects of the eventification process which are clearly *not* always in the control of the individual theatre-makers themselves, but may be imposed on the theatricalisation process (or provided for it) by a larger, complex and dynamic context or system enfolding the theatrical event as such.

Eventification as a systemic process

I would contend that a fundamental imperative for the development and maintenance of any theatrical system anywhere in the world may be the need to provide the necessary subsystems, facilities and processes which would enable the eventification of the theatrical event to take place. The key elements required here seem to be a system for *legitimisation* on the one hand (the public's need to have their tastes ratified, or their choices made for them, by some kind of external vetting system – the reviewer, the selection panel for a festival) and a system of *commodification* on the other (the performer's need to 'sell' his/her product to the public for gain – financial, emotional, artistic, whatever, and the resultant packaging of the offering). Naturally, as times and circumstances change, so do all the eventifying processes utilised. Hence, even the system *itself* must constantly change or adapt to the new context.

When I refer to a 'theatrical system' or a 'societal system', I am not talking about a simple and singular structure or process at all, nor of something consciously and purposely set up and planned by some government department or business venture. What I am referring to is a complex, naturally evolved (and constantly evolving and adapting), range of interrelated yet separate and dynamic subsystems, which in their turn are imbedded in (and form part of) an even more encompassing cultural, social, political, economic and other set of systems and processes. While numerous authors from a variety of theoretical perspectives have sought to build theoretical models to explain the systemic nature of theatre and performance (and its social, cultural, political and economic roots) over the years, I have found that a useful way of trying to understanding this *complexity* of social structures, systems and processes, is to think of it in terms of Itamar Even-Zohar's notion of an overall 'polysystem' made up of dynamic, interlinked and mutually supporting 'subsystems' (Even-Zohar, 1979; see also the models proposed by, *inter alia*, Carlson 1990; Elam, 1980; Hauptfleisch, 1997; Sauter, 2007; Schechner, 1977, 1985; Schoenmakers, 2007; Styan, 1975; Van Maanen, 2004).

I believe that such a 'polystemic' description of the theatre system is useful for virtually any and every human society or community, though the details of individual forms, processes and systems may differ from context to context. Each of the subsystems that make up the larger polysystem makes its own demands on and creates its own opportunities and artistic spaces for theatre-makers, and each has its own ethos, conventions and reputation through which it may even be said to make its own *meaning*. In this way theatrical companies, venues, repertory circuits, festivals, competitions, radio stations, television channels and film companies all constitute subsystems within the larger entertainment industry/system and serve as *eventifying frames* into which individuals and companies can slot their work as I have argued above. By doing so, the creators (and their work) are not only given a platform and exposure, but are also identified with (and helped and/or constrained by) the inherent history, values, conventions and ethos that pertain in that subsystem. Let us conclude this chapter by considering one such subsystem for a moment.

Festivals as eventifying systems

The *festival* (in its various forms, and there are many) has always been a distinctive phenomenon in the history of humankind, and has long been closely related to the religious, artistic and cultural life of a particular community. It has played a considerable role in the history of dance, drama and music (*vide* the classic Greek theatre festival of Dionysus, the medieval Cycle plays of Europe, the development of the Noh theatre, the Ogungun Festival in Nigeria). Not always respectable or perceived to be a subject worthy in its own right, the festival has nevertheless always been an extremely important element in the theatrical system and in the processes of making theatre, as well as a distinctive cultural event in society at large.

Originally, and primarily one supposes, the majority of festivals must have come into being as subsystemic elements of the broader cultural polysystem aimed at enhancing the reputation of the organisers by providing very specific and effective mechanisms and processes for the eventification of particular plays and/or presentations. The way they work and can be made to work is the core theme of countless books in recent years, in many ways the present one as well. Not only is a festival a site or venue where the work is to take place, it is where the artistic output of the actor, director, choreographer, etc. is *displayed* and *eventified*. It is where the everyday *life event* (performing a play, a concerto, a dance, exhibiting a painting, a sculpture, an installation) is turned into a significant *Cultural Event* with socio-cultural, socio-political and possibly even socio-economic significance, framed and made meaningful by the presence of an audience and reviewers who will respond to the celebrated event. They thus become a means of retaining the event in the cultural memory of the particular society.

As I have argued elsewhere (Hauptfleisch, 1997), this process – if successful – may give the single performance (i.e. theatrical event) or the exhibition a life *after* the festival, and an important aspect of this is its association with the celebrity attached to that particular festival event – all this bearing in mind the essential unpredictability and instability of the theatre as business, of course.

But this brings us to another aspect of festivals, namely the potential of their own innate 'eventness'. As I have mentioned above, festivals *may* be created by and for the benefit of the playmakers (writers, actors, directors, etc.), but also for a host of other reasons, and very often the motivation and aims may lie elsewhere, arising from one or more local, community-driven need, aspiration or vision. The theatrical (and musical, artistic, cultural and other) events drawn into the programme of a festival thus become tools and attributes of the festival as an event in itself, with its own aims, which may but do not necessarily correspond with the aims of the individual 'acts'. If successful, the festival may soon attain an independent and longer-term life and/or identity of its own, a kind of polysystemic mega-event, independent of the subsystemic items that make up the programme of each successive presentation of the festival. This pattern may be discerned throughout the history of performance, whether it be in the competitions of Aristotle's Greece, the mystery and miracle plays of the Middle Ages, the glory and pageantry of the Renaissance or the slick and competitive entertainment industry we have today.

As Martin *et al.* (2004) point out, considerable attention has lately been paid to festivals, carnivals, pageants and other celebratory events, often using a performance theory or theatrical event perspective to look at the festivals *as performances* or *as theatrical events* in their own right. Such studies focus on the important, though often less consciously conceived, ideological imperatives that lie behind particular festivals and other composite events. And as these scholars then show, some festivals are not only pre-eminently the occasions on which a series of plays and performances are each eventified, but the festival itself, as an event, may be the vehicle or medium of expression for a specific point of view, a means of exploring socio-cultural and other issues, or may even become a metaphor or symbol for an attitude, a belief or a value system.

There are a number of marvellous contemporary examples of this kind of success when we consider the major international festivals. For instance, the Edinburgh Festival's ever increasing status as one of the more significant annual international *Events* (hence an important element in the City of Edinburgh's claim to international cultural status and a useful spur to increased cultural tourism and income) is obviously intimately entwined with the influential *eventifying* function the festival has for theatre-makers from across the globe. Being able to say that one's play has been performed at or was a success at Edinburgh is a marvellous addition to the play's reputation and hence a boon for its marketability and potential life. The same may, of course, be said of so many of the world's most prominent festivals, from Avignon to Woodstock.

To illustrate the tightly integrated nature of this double role of the arts festival, I have over the years considered a number of relevant South African examples. Among them have been historically based celebratory events such as the annual Van der Stel Festival in Stellenbosch and the vibrant Cape Coon Carnival in Cape Town, as well as a number of national arts festivals, particularly the National Arts Festival in Grahamstown and the Klein Karoo Nasionale Kunstefees in Oudtshoorn. In addition there have been a large number of once-off celebratory events which have received attention from researchers over the years, including the symbolically re-enacted 1938 ox-wagon 'Great Trek', the 1952 Van Riebeeck Festival, the 1994 inauguration of President Nelson Mandela, the 1995 Rugby World Cup, the 2010 Football World Cup and so on (in this regard see also Hauptfleisch 2001, 2003; Kitshoff, 2004a, 2004b; Kruger, 1999; Martin, 1999; Merrington, 1999).

However, this time around I would like to shift my focus a little, and conclude the chapter by briefly comparing two similarly contrasting international twentieth-century examples from the field of popular music culture. As should be clear from the discussion so far, some of the most suitable and least complicated examples of influential public events are the more tightly focused one-off occurrences, from public and/or political assemblies (protest marches, riots, political gatherings) to celebratory occasions (pageants, centennials, inaugurations, weddings and funerals, and so on). In the case of festivals, for example, the legendary Woodstock festival of 1969 (or 'The Woodstock Music & Art Fair' as it was officially called) is almost a prototype for an explosive, even 'seismological', public event. It had spontaneously erupted into an enormous 'happening' (with 32 acts performed outdoors before an audience of 400,000 young people played out over three days) and immediately sent shockwaves rippling through society, and continued to do so for decades afterwards. It was an effect greatly enhanced (eventified) by the film that followed. While the festival was not repeated and thus never became a regular or annual event, those magical days on a common near Bethal, New York, had a profound and lasting impact on America and the world at many levels.

By contrast the well-established Glastonbury Festival in England, which also began in that era, did so much more quietly, starting as a one-day event on Worthy Farm near Pilton, Somerset, attended by 1,500 people (and originally called the 'Pilton Pop, Blues & Folk Festival'). Revived periodically in the 1970s, it eventually became the massive annual, five-day music festival we know today. Nowadays, it draws an average of 175,000 festival-goers and hosts not only contemporary music acts, but also a whole slew of events, including dance, comedy, theatre, circus, cabaret and other arts.

An interesting aspect of these events is that films have been made of both and did much to spread the image of the events around the globe. The original Woodstock film was perhaps the most obvious case in point – an *Extraordinary Event* in its own right, in many ways. In addition there are the many other side-events that took place: controversial – even tragic – occurrences during the events themselves, vociferous opposition and public response not only to the festivals but even to the *idea* of the festival or celebratory event (and, as so many satirists and artists know by now, your harshest critics are often your best publicity agents, particularly those who have not even seen the play or read the book).

However, as in the case of Edinburgh, the undoubted impact of the Glastonbury experience on contemporary music and performance was not (and is not) as immediate and noticeable perhaps as that of Woodstock and is, thus, far more difficult to determine and describe, being something that has accrued over time, *inter alia* through the festival's eventification of its constituent 'acts' rather than as an event per se with a single message and/or single metaphoric meaning. But it is possibly no less important, certainly not in the long run.

Conclusion

The point made above really applies to a number of the theatrical and other examples we have briefly considered in this chapter. Once a specific 'event' (play, film, public celebration, festival) has taken place and has subsequently been reframed, eventified and accepted as an 'Extraordinary Event' in its genre, it often embarks on a totally new life. In such a case not only does the image, message and meaning of the original event become part of a longer-term process of secondary eventification and re-evaluation but so, too, does some (or all) of its accrued body of marginalia, reputation and commentary, all of which leads to participation in the global network of events and our cultural memory. In this way, any current version of an event is also an indelible part of the eventified and mediated reality and existence of the theatrical event as a social event.

Which once more confronts us with what has always been a fundamental challenge for researchers working on our ephemeral art form, and somehow it can also be one of their greatest sources of fascination: if what we have before us today are only a few remnants of an original cultural event, and perhaps some received impressions of its original impact, anything we study now will almost certainly not be anything near like the 'true' or 'authentic' version of the original production or theatrical event at all. We really only have an eventified (framed and interpreted) *version* of the previous incarnations of an ephemeral and fleeting event from a specific time and place, and the current version cannot reflect the original impulses and issues that drove the creation of that original event in the first place. Yet, it is an indelible part of the longer-term, eventified and mediated, reality and existence of the original theatrical event as a social event. The search for that impossible 'ideal' performance thus implies an almost unique understanding of not only the seismology governing the dissemination of the images of and impressions made by an event, but also an ability to follow through on an evidence-driven archaeological study of the event and its impact.

References

Bennett, S. (1990) *Theatre Audiences: A Theory of Production and Reception*. London: Routledge.

Burns, E. (1972) *Theatricality*. London: Longman.

Carlson, M. (1990) *Theatre Semiotics: Signs of Life*. Bloomington, IN: Indiana University Press.

Cremona, V. A., Eversmann, P., Van Maanen, H., Sauter, W. and Tulloch, J. (eds) (2004) *Theatrical Events – Borders Dynamics Frames*. Amsterdam: Rodopi.

Elam, K. (1980) *The Semiotics of Theatre and Drama*. London: Methuen.

Even-Zohar, I. (1979) 'Polysystem theory', *Poetics Today*, 1: 287–310.

Goffman, E. (1959) *The Presentation of Self in Everyday Life*. New York: Doubleday Anchor.

Goffman, E. (1974) *Frame Analysis: An Essay on the Organization of Experience*. Cambridge, MA: Harvard University Press.

Hauptfleisch, T. (1997) *Theatre and Society in South Africa: Reflections in a Fractured Mirror*. Pretoria: J. L. van Schaik.

Hauptfleisch, T. (2001) 'The eventification of Afrikaans culture – some thoughts on the Klein Karoo National Arts Festival', *South African Theatre Journal*, 15: 169–77.

Hauptfleisch, T. (2003) 'The cultural bazaar: thoughts on festival culture after a visit to the 2003 *Klein Karoo Nasionale Kunstefees (KKNK)* in Oudtshoorn', *South African Theatre Journal*, 17: 258–75.

Hauptfleisch, T. (2004) 'Eventification: utilizing the theatrical system to frame the event', in V. A. Cremona, P. Eversmann, H. van Maanen, W. Sauter and J. Tulloch (eds), *Theatrical Events – Borders Dynamics Frames*. Amsterdam: Rodopi, pp. 278–302.

Hauptfleisch, T. (2007) 'The seismology of theatre: tracing the shock waves of a theatrical event in society', *South African Theatre Journal*, 21: 253–71.

Hauptfleisch, T., Lev-aladgem, S., Martin, J., Sauter, W. and Schoenmakers, H. (2007) *Festivalising! Theatrical Events, Politics and Culture*. Amsterdam: Rodopi.

Kaptein, P. (1996) 'De beginperiode van het Holland Festival. Festivals en festivalisering', in R. L. Erenstein (ed.), *Een theater geschiedenis de Nederlanden*. Amsterdam: Amsterdam University Press, pp. 672–80.

Kitshoff, H. (2004a) 'Claiming cultural festivals: playing for power at the Klein Karoo Nasionale Kunstefees (KKNK)', *South African Theatre Journal*, 18: 64–80.

Kitshoff, H. (2004b) 'Klein Karoo Nasionale Kunstefees (KKNK)' ['A review of the 2003 festival'], *South African Theatre Journal*, 18: 235–9.

Kruger, L. (1999) *The Drama of South Africa: Plays, Pageants and Publics Since 1910*. London: Routledge.

Martin, D.-C. (1999) *Coon Carnival: New Year in Cape Town – Past and Present*. Cape Town: David Philip.

Martin, J., Seffrin, G. and Wissler, R. (2004) 'The festival is a theatrical event', in V. A. Cremona, P. Eversmann, H. van Maanen, W. Sauter and J. Tulloch (eds), *Theatrical Events – Borders Dynamics Frames*. Amsterdam: Rodopi, pp. 91–110.

Merrington, P. (1999) *The 'New Pageantry' and Performance Studies*. Paper read at the SASTR Conference, 11–12 September, Stellenbosch, South Africa.

Postman, N. (1983) *The Disappearance of Childhood*. New York: Delacorte Press.

Sauter, W. (1997) 'Approaching the theatrical event: the influence of semiotics and hermeneutics on European theatre studies', *Theatre Research International*, 22 (1): 4–13.

Sauter, W. (2004) 'Introducing the theatrical event', in V. A. Cremona, P. Eversmann, H. van Maanen, W. Sauter and J. Tulloch (eds), *Theatrical Events – Borders Dynamics Frames*. Amsterdam: Rodopi, pp. 3–14.

Sauter, W. (2007) 'Festivals as theatrical events: building theories', in T. Hauptfleisch, S. Lev-aladgem, J. Martin, W. Sauter and H. Schoenmakers (eds), *Festivalising! Theatrical Events, Politics and Culture*. Amsterdam: Rodopi, pp. 17–26.

Schechner, R. (1977) *Essays on Performance Theory 1970–1977*. New York: Drama Book Specialists.

Schechner, R. (1985) *Between Theater and Anthropology*. Philadelphia: University of Pennsylvania Press.

Schoenmakers, H. (2007) 'Festivals, theatrical events and communicative interactions', in T. Hauptfleisch, S. Lev-aladgem, J. Martin, W. Sauter and H. Schoenmakers (eds), *Festivalising! Theatrical Events, Politics and Culture*. Amsterdam: Rodopi, pp. 27–38.

Southern, R. (1964) *The Seven Ages of the Theatre*. London: Faber & Faber.

Styan, J. L. (1975) *Drama, Stage and Audience*. London: Cambridge University Press.

Turner, V. (1982) *From Ritual to Theatre: The Human Seriousness of Play*. New York: PAJ Publications.

Van Maanen, H. (2004) 'How contexts frame theatrical events', in V. A. Cremona, P. Eversmann, H. van Maanen, W. Sauter and J. Tulloch (eds), *Theatrical Events – Borders Dynamics Frames*. Amsterdam: Rodopi, pp. 234–78.

Websites consulted

http://www.firt-iftr.org/working-groups/methodologies/the-theatrical-event
http://www.glastonburyfestivals.co.uk/
http://www.psi-web.org/page/about
https://en.wikipedia.org/wiki/Gulf_War
https://en.wikipedia.org/wiki/Woodstock

4 The creative guerrilla

Makers, organisation and belonging

Welby Ings

This chapter considers guerrilla maker-community collectives and the events they generate. It discusses the nature of free exchange in recent community arts practices like 'yarn bombing', 'zine fests' and 'maker faires'. Normally, the events generated by these groups are not predicated on hierarchical models of facilitation. Instead, they grow in a rhizome-like manner, building cultures of practice, facilitation and dissemination by interfacing online and maker-oriented physical communities. In so doing, their events reconceive space as local within the global, while simultaneously empowering practice, distribution and a sense of belonging.

The maker-oriented guerrilla

Unruly natures

In this chapter, I use the adjective 'guerrilla' to describe certain irregular, collaborative, maker-oriented initiatives, developed outside of mainstream art and craft conventions. Often, they operate from the political, legal, economic or social margins. The events they engender contribute to networks that are highly responsive. Their pop ups,[1] workshops, faires, and festivals are neither managed by nor answerable to a central constituted body. Despite this, they can be hugely influential, with initiatives often catalysing at both local and international levels. Because such communities and the events they organise can morph, accumulate and grow at exponential speed, they can sometimes be seen as unruly, unstable or subversive. Yet the examples I discuss in this chapter have significantly changed not only local conditions but, in some cases, global economies, politics and cultural understandings.

What differentiates these communities is their propensity to oscillate between maker-oriented physical events and online environments. They engage in unique forms of collaboration that operate not only at a creative level but also in political, social, artistic and economic dimensions. In their local manifestations they all function as physical, workshop-based community initiatives. People cooperate with other people to make things. Because they are guerrilla in nature, the events they engender generally fall outside of mainstream concerns, so they rarely have access to the financial support (funding grants or sponsorship) afforded to more conventional projects. However, this arguably enables such communities and the events they engender to circumvent many of the restrictions posed by the governing values of mainstream organisations.

Rhizomatic structures

The empowering network

Maker-oriented guerrilla initiatives normally function as rhizomes. In using this term I draw on the writings of Deleuze and Guattari (1972, 1980),[2] who describe rhizomatic organisations as those where parts are connected in reciprocal, multiple relations. Being non-hierarchical, these organisations are not fixed but are able to expand in different dimensions, growing and forming increasingly rich and more complex networks. Unlike the manifesto-proscribed nature of many twentieth-century modernist art practices, rhizomatic initiatives are resourced and built in an endless process of rethinking and restructuring. Ideas, initiatives and values transform within an expanding network. In these open systems, power and decision-making are not confined to one place.

Web 2.0

In this century, advances in the capabilities of online environments have had considerable influence on maker-oriented guerrilla initiatives. Cumulative changes in Web 2.0 environments have enabled dynamic connections beyond the static (and arguably passive) nature of earlier websites. These newer environments (social networking sites, blogs, web applications and hosted services) have enabled significant user-generated content where individuals are able to interact, discuss and demonstrate as creators and collaborators in both virtual and physical communities.

Relinquished individual ownership

Events, Pernecky (2014) suggests, are 'deployed purposefully as tools for communicating and disseminating ideological messages, and they feature directly in the processes of ideological conditioning' (p. 28). Thus, although maker-oriented guerrilla events may differ in emphasis, certain ideological messages around democratisation, individual and small community empowerment, and non-hierarchical structures remain central and predicate how they function.

Notably, these networks feature distinctive ideologies relating to ownership and collaboration. Within them, an individual operates as a creative member of a supportive, multidimensional and accumulating whole. Ideas, designs and events are not framed as intellectual property. A free exchange exists; for example, as uploaded software applications (often designed by members) become available, they are rapidly integrated into maker cultures (Richardson *et al.*, 2013). Similarly, documentations of events are rapidly disseminated, initiatives are shared and local communities generate further physical events like workshops, exhibitions and faires in response to these.

The handmade

Finally, these networks share a conjoint concern with manual craft and the social support that small, local collectives can offer. The events they generate emphasise the sharing of physical and collegial space. What is produced is seen as valuable both in itself and in terms of its contribution to something socially meaningful. Within this mix are values like support for individuals, political empowerment and renegotiations of what it means to be part of a community.

The 1985 quilt initiative

Alternative grieving

There have, of course, been maker-oriented guerrilla initiatives prior to the advent of Web 2.0. Perhaps one of the most graphic and politically successful was the *NAMES Project AIDS Memorial Quilt* initiated in 1985. At the time when Cleve Jones conceived the idea of quilt-making as a form of political agency, many people who died of AIDS did not have funerals. This was due partly to their families' anxieties around the social stigma of AIDS or to the refusal of many funeral homes and cemeteries to process victims' remains (Gross, 1987; Laderman, 2003). Because there were often no memorials or gravesites, the Quilt became a way that survivors could navigate the complex grieving process that stigma at the time made difficult in the public domain (Epstein and Friedman, 1989; Kerewsky, 1997; Yardley and Langley, 1994).

Origins

In an interview in 2006, Cleve Jones described the political and medical climate in the period that the Quilt initiative took form.

> There was no response of any kind from the government, from the medical establishment. We were completely on our own. What I did was I tried to fill the vacuum left by the government's response. It was ordinary people, ordinary folks, men, women, children … But the government did nothing … President Reagan could not even say the word until more people had died of this disease than died in the Vietnam War.
>
> (Frontline, 2006, para. 21)

Transformative political pressure was brought to bear on the United States government in 1987 when a major event was organised in which 1,920 quilt panels were displayed across the National Mall in Washington, DC. Half a million people visited the initiative and the subsequent media coverage meant that the issue could no longer be ignored. The event also acted as a catalyst for a four-month, 20-city, National Quilt Tour. This raised nearly $500,000 for AIDS service organisations (many initiated, like the Quilt, from inside gay and lesbian communities).[3]

The Quilt project was individually initiated, community activated and rhizomatic in its development. Perceiving how invisibility was being used politically to mask a lack of funded support, Jones and a small number of friends asked people at a candlelit march to commemorate the assassination of the gay activist Harvey Milk to write onto a piece of cardboard the name of one person they knew who had been killed by AIDS. Jones and his friends scaled three stories of the San Francisco Federal Building and taped the cards on to the grey stone facade. Thousands of people watched in silence. He recalled:

> I was just overwhelmed by the need to find a way to grieve together for our loved ones who had died so horribly, and also to try to find the weapon that would break through the stupidity and the bigotry … and all of the cruel indifference that even today hampers our response. I … looked back at that patchwork of names on the wall, and I thought, it looks like a quilt … I thought, what a perfect symbol; what a warm, comforting, middle-class, middle-American, traditional-family-values symbol to attach to this disease that's killing homosexuals and IV drug users and Haitian immigrants.
>
> (Frontline, 2006, para. 21)

Rhizomatic growth

During the period of the project's gestation, Jones learned that he was also infected with the virus. Instead of hiding the condition he went public with his diagnosis on *60 Minutes*. He used the disseminating power of the media to talk about the pandemic and its effect in San Francisco. As a consequence he received death threats and was eventually attacked and stabbed by a group of neo-Nazis.

Jones' first quilts were made from stolen bolts of fabric, assembled in a basement and decorated with spray paint. As people became aware of the initiative, small groups formed in the other US cities most affected by AIDS: Atlanta, Los Angeles and New York. They sent panels to San Francisco in memory of their friends and loved ones. Others donated sewing machines, office supplies and volunteers to the increasing numbers of small maker-workshops. The first 40 quilts were hung from the Mayor's balcony at San Francisco City Hall on 27 June during the 1985 Lesbian and Gay Pride Parade.

Impact

In the years that followed, the Quilt's initiative grew rhizomatically, not only in America but also in other countries.[4] In making their quilts, bereaved partners, friends and families continued to operate in small groups, sewing, collaging and painting (Howe, 1997; Yardley and Langley, 1994). Once a quilt was finished it

Figure 4.1 AIDS Memorial Quilt for Ian Booth (1953–86)

The author made the quilt from his partner's farm clothes. These materials and Ian's painted portrait were sewn on to heavy calico. The memorial became part of the New Zealand Quilt Project in 1988. As with the American and Australian initiatives, volunteers organised and resourced local display events and also ran maker-workshops that helped grieving friends and partners learn the craft skills necessary to realise their commemorations. Photograph by Welby Ings (New Zealand Quilt Project).

was attached to other quilts.[5] The resulting blocks were displayed at events in schools, community centres and parks. This visibility of hitherto marginalised voices was used as a means of fund-raising, educating and elevating and maintaining the presence of AIDS in the public/political domain.

In 1989 the Quilt was nominated for a Nobel Peace Prize and by 2010 it had become the largest piece of community folk art in the world (McKinley, 2007). Significantly, the project and events it spawned were catalysts for a number of subsequent projects including the KIA Memorial Quilt, the 9/11 Quilt project (9/11 Memorial, n.d.), breast cancer activism (Riter, 2014) and quilt projects for Huntington's disease (Davis, 2010) and congenital heart disease (Sivasubramanian, 2011).

The AIDS Memorial Quilt projects, as local, maker-oriented activism, became part of a globally disseminated idea. Based in an environment predicated on the sharing of resources, skills and stories, these projects used strategically documented events to move the disempowered local into the global consciousness. In the United States today, the AIDs Memorial Quilt consists of more than 48,000 individual memorial panels and weighs an estimated 54 tons (Williams, 2012). However, its legacy of empowering rhizomatic, maker-oriented communities to use events as a means of globally disseminating ideas has developed into the twenty-first century. Three current examples are useful to consider.

The Maker Movement

Origins

The term 'Maker Movement' is normally attributed to Dale Dougherty (O'Reilly Media) who in 2005 used it to describe digital and physical collectives that create artefacts using the Web. Within one year of publishing his flagship magazine *Make*, the publication was instrumental in launching a nationwide series of events called Maker Faires. Drawing on the concept of the traditional art and craft fairs of the 1960s, Dougherty's Faires not only publicised the idea of social making but also profiled the local innovator as a viable economic construct. Anderson (2013) suggests that the movement and the events it has spawned may be attributed to three phenomena.

Firstly, as increasing numbers of factories worldwide began advertising space and facilities on the Web, small collectives were able to access hitherto unaffordable resources. In certain cities, small groups began to develop small specialist orders, sharing skills and knowledge, and outsourcing manufacture. The second phenomenon was the increasing democratisation and availability of affordable digital tools for design and manufacturing. These include 3-D scanners and printers, laser cutters, milling machines and CAD software that are now available in dimensions and at a cost that means they can be comfortably integrated into domestic living spaces. The third factor was the use of digital means for collaboration. Maker-designers currently tap into open source and online social environments. Utilising crowd funding sites they can finance initiatives that might not have attracted conventional economic support. In addition, they can access systems that link what might hitherto have been isolated individuals with global networks of expertise. Anderson (2013: para. 7) notes that these factors have resulted in 'a bottom up transformation of manufacturing that is following the similar democratised trajectories of computing and communications'.

Ideological shift

However, the Maker Movement is not simply a technological phenomenon. Viewed in the context of wider, maker-oriented guerrilla initiatives, it may also be understood as social and political. Its events, either the increasingly populated maker faires or workshops that happen in makerspaces, demonstrate the power of peer-initiated and controlled environments that place emphasis on empowered, critical, co-construction.[6] Events become agents for demonstrating and promoting an ideological shift towards a new type of cultural production, where the passive consumer transitions through making practice and peer support towards being an informed, socially engaged consumer-maker (Goldense, 2013; Richardson *et al.*, 2013).

Social spaces

Within this shift, we increasingly encounter a diversity of local makerspaces. These are peer-initiated, collaborative environments for people who share tools and ideas. They might make robotics or utensils, automatic dog feeders or idiosyncratic toys, or they may sew circuits connecting LED sensors into textiles. Makerspaces may occupy church basements, vacated buildings, homes, museums, libraries, schools and online environments. Lahart (2009) notes that members and fees from classes they offer normally independently fund these spaces and the events they generate. Sharples *et al.* (2013: 5) suggest that they offer a distinct form of 'informal, shared social learning' that embraces risk-taking and rapid iterative development. Skills and events grow socially and technologically through informal mentoring of activities from traditional handcrafts to advanced digitally realised concepts. These maker workshops and faires reinforce the value of the local.

Rhizomatic growth

Of course, in such systems the local exists in the context of something much larger. Events that engage social learning or exhibition at a community level also contribute (via networked technologies) to other communities with differing values, skills, needs and aspirations. Currently, makers can live stream their work in progress and concurrently receive feedback (from across the world). Video demonstrations posted online can explain skills and processes that circumvent language barriers. Most significantly, peer validation, peripheral participation, free exchange and belongingness can be sourced in 'conceptual neighbourhoods' that transcend national borders. The rhizomatic nature of maker initiatives, whether they be large public events like faires, or discreet, scheduled workshops where two people link into overseas advice and discussion, become part of a cumulative dynamic where events become part of what is shared, part of what sustains and part of what grows innovation, questioning and possibility.

Yarn bombing

Peer validation, craft workshops, free exchange and belongingness are also features of a phenomenon known as yarn bombing (or fabric graffiti). Here, vernacular urban objects like supermarket trolleys, fire hydrants, lampposts, park benches, parking meters, bicycles or park tree trunks are clandestinely 'clothed' in knitted or crocheted fabric. Yarn bombing is a socially playful form of impermanent interventionism. As a contemporary, networked and decentralised initiative it has grown into an international phenomenon.[7]

Origins

The origins of yarn bombing are disputed. Wollan (2011) suggests it began in Texas in 2005 with the work of Magda Sayeg. However, Klaasmeyer (2000) and Jahn (2002) record early iterations in the work of artists like Bill Davenport and Shanon Schollian. Carpenter (2010) traces its origins to David Medalla's 1960s collectively darned *Stitch in Time* and Germaine Koh's extended *Knitwork* performances of the 1990s.

Although yarn bombing may be seen as part of the larger DIY movement that resurrected and developed traditional handicrafts, it also operates on a socio-political level. Hemmons (as cited in Wollan, 2011) argues that being largely women activated, it renegotiates the largely 'male-oriented' arenas of street and graffiti art, and Scheuing (2010) describes it as 'a twist on a woman's touch to the urban landscape' (p. 2). Carpenter (2010) suggests that knitting as a political voice has precedents in the Calgary Revolutionary Knitting Circle, established in 2000 to carry out 'Peace Knits' as part of the anti-capitalist movement and, more recently, in Marianna Jørgensen's collective that in 2006 created a pink, knitted cover for an M.24 Chaffee tank that was exhibited in protest against Denmark's involvement in the Gulf War.

However, despite these precedents, many yarn bombers eschew claims to the political. Mollins (2011) suggests, 'these guerrilla knitters … frustrate efforts by some critics to burden their art with political overtones or diminish it with comparisons to the kind of urban graffiti made by artists such as Britain's Banksy' (para. 12).

Rhizomatic growth

Like many maker-oriented movements, yarn bombing was locally initiated but quickly distributed through Web 2.0 environments. Here, Carpenter (2010) notes, 'the stitches aren't perfect, the patterns are circulating, the politics evolving, but the correlation between craft and free libre open source culture is not always apparent' (para. 6). In these contexts, free online knitting design programs like

Figure 4.2 Photograph by Alvaro León: Bolardos en la calle Lavapies de Madrid 2011

knitPro enable collectives to translate digital images into knit, crochet, needlepoint and cross-stitch patterns.[8] Scheuing (2010: 3) suggests that such easily available, open source software 'digitally mimics the tradition of pre-industrial craft circles that freely shared patterns and passed them down from generation to generation.' Access to software applications like these means that skill levels can be built very quickly. Complementing this, shared patterns and 'tips' posted by experienced bombers contribute to an increasingly rich, democratic domain of accumulating knowledge and experience.

Mollins (2011) notes that yarn bombing events are quickly photographed or video recorded, uploaded and shared. The blogs, social networks and websites serve to preserve guerrilla interventions that fray, fade or face vandalism in their original physical contexts. As a consequence, these events are largely consumed as digital recordings of themselves. They surpass the temporal to become cumulative. They develop meaning through posted responses and the ongoing influence they have on other practitioners. When documentary material is accessed online, both the recorded event and its accumulated discourse are consumed as an integrated whole.

Pace and dissent

The process of making, recording, uploading and discussing guerrilla events establishes a high level of currency more efficient than anything traditional print publishing might achieve. Rapid access to these events has meant that, since its inception, yarn bombing has encountered wide media coverage[9] and commercial interest.[10] Perhaps more interestingly, discourse and practice within yarn bombing has faced distinct value conflicts (significantly around purpose and meaning). However, dissent within rhizomatic systems is not problematic. In fact, it may be seen as a sign of ideological health. Unlike certain event-generating organisations that produce initiatives off a shared and agreed vision, rhizomatic initiatives quickly encounter diverse social, economic and political environments that are underpinned by unique cultural histories. The flexibility this affords is one of their great strengths.

Zines

A maker-oriented guerrilla artifact that conspicuously engages with dissent is the zine. Zines are small circulation self-published works of original or appropriated texts that are normally reproduced via a photocopier. They are normally written, collaged or hand-illustrated and produced in limited edition runs of less than a hundred copies. They are rarely copyrighted because within zine culture there is a commonly held belief that material should be free or sold at a minimal cost (Piepmeier, 2009; Poletti, 2008).

Origins

Zines and zine events have surfaced from a complex history of literary marginalisation and subversion that can be traced through comic books as counterculture artefacts (Duncombe, 1997; Estren, 1994). Although Punk zines flourished in the 1970s, it was during the 1980s that publications like *Factsheet Five* began cataloguing and reviewing submitted zines. Initiatives like this also made available zine authors' mailing addresses. In so doing, they helped to establish communities where zine creators and readers were able to form a networked subculture.

Currently, zines are distributed in two forms. Print versions circulate through events like zine symposiums, festivals and faires, community stalls and exhibitions. A few zines are also distributed through distros[11] and specialist bookshops. They are also traded or given as gifts between zinesters. Online distribution occurs via websites or social networking profiles. These e-zines are normally available free to download and print.[12]

Historically the zine, its communities and events have been framed as counterculture. This is because the content of zines often falls outside of what is included in traditional media, either because of its explicitness, its personal nature, its political position or its small, specialised target demographic. The producers of zines are largely free to present whatever ideas they wish because the provision of editorial policy is removed and distribution operates rhizomatically.

Figure 4.3 Zinefest in Auckland, New Zealand

(27 July 2013; photograph by Kristin Leitch). In addition to displaying, sharing, selling and swapping zines, the event also featured free workshops on cartooning, type design and publishing, as well as a panel discussion. At these events, the sense of community and networking is physical but documentation of the event is preserved and disseminated online. (See Design Assembly: http://www.designassembly.org.nz/articles/auckland-zinefest-2013 and Auckland Zinefest: http://www.aucklandzinefest.org/.)

The nature of events

Like other maker-oriented guerrilla groups, zine communities generate events that promote and distribute not only their artefacts but also a wider culture of craft, empowerment and ideology. Like yarn bombing, there is a strong emphasis on the social context of physical craft that enables a political and personal voice to operate inside locally driven, community-generated initiatives. Zine festivals (fests) or faires are organised so producers can meet and trade their publications. These are normally free and open to the general public. Stockburger (2011) notes that such events often include 'a day-long "tabling" session where zinesters display their publications for sale, skill-sharing workshops, and round-tables where more experienced zinesters lead discussions on zine-related topics' (p. 12). In addition, zine communities sometimes generate reading events that are often organised at independent bookstores, coffee shops or other public spaces. Here, zine writers read excerpts from their work to an audience, normally comprising other zine producers and readers. These events, Stockburger suggests, reinforce zine practice as public and 'help to define and shape the community' (p. 12).

Zine events are more complex than simply the textual networking of readers and writers. Piepmeier (2009), Poletti (2008) and Stockburger (2011) suggest that they contribute to 'embodied communities' of people, social practices and ideologies. Events are predicated on a few commonly agreed tenets including shared skills and technologies, flexible distribution, freedom of speech, rhizomatic structuring and empowerment. However, within this, diverse practitioners negotiate a fluid and flexible range of opinions that reinforce the nature of zine events as non- homogenous.

Conclusion

Down the road from where I live there is a collective called Knitted Graffiti. They meet fortnightly on a Friday morning in a community centre where they share materials, skills, ideas and company. They are local. Currently they are working on a project to 'tree-cosy' a large pohutukawa tree in a nearby suburb. Knitted Graffiti, like other maker-oriented guerrilla initiatives, operates on amateur, non-specialist and democratic participation. The group's purpose is as much about guerrilla activity as it is about free exchange and belongingness.

Maker-oriented collectives like Knitted Graffiti and the events they generate share a number of features. First, they tend to function as local in an international neighbourhood. While participants meet in small maker communities to share space, materials and a sense of belongingness, connections through Web 2.0 facilities allow them to disseminate and access skills and ideas across a global platform. The events these groups generate, be they zine readings, yarn bombings, maker faires or small collective workshops, operate within and beyond the local.

Second, events generated by these groups grow out of a shared understanding that technology and ideas should be democratic. Communities utilise free software, donate time and resources and organise public events that emphasise the dissemination of ideas over the pursuit of a lucrative economic return. Thus events operate as a system of free exchange within the public domain. Third, events function and grow rhizomatically. Although individual initiatives may engage a team of coordinators, they are rarely structured in a hierarchical manner, nor are they tied to ideologically consistent outcomes. Events function as reciprocal and multi-relational. Consequently, as open systems they can expand and adapt in diverse dimensions, feeding both local and international communities with diverse populations and values. This is what enables both events and the values underpinning them to transform so responsively. Finally, maker-oriented events heighten the sense and value of craft as individual and collective agency. In this regard, they serve to empower both what is made and the idea of making. Operating outside of conventional structures they posit the maker as a politically viable phenomenon.

Pernecky (2014) suggests that events are "“worldmaking” agents that are intertwined with ideologies and, as such, hold an immense value to understanding both the processes of being and becoming and the ways in which societies are made, “re-made” and “de-made”" (p. 28). When a community re-makes what exists, they challenge convention. When they create public events that manifest this challenge they may be understood as engaging in a form of subversion. While it would be naive to assume that maker-oriented community events do not encounter the challenges of personality conflict and dissent, their predication on the tenets of free exchange and rhizomatics means that they can operate in environments where diversity, transition, empowerment and challenge function as agents for growth. This flexibility may be seen as the substrate upon which their success is built.

Notes

1. The term refers to pop-up exhibitions, based on Koster's (2010) *No Man's Gallery*. This is a form of gallery with no fixed location. Individual pop-up gallery events might occur in diverse locations like an abandoned warehouse, a temporarily vacant shop window or a luxury flat, in different countries in consecutive months.
2. The term 'rhizomatic' comes from their project *Capitalism and Schizophrenia* that was published in two volumes: *Anti-Oedipus* (1972, trans. 1977) and *A Thousand Plateaus* (1980, trans. 1987).
3. More than 9,000 volunteers across the United States supported the seven-person travelling crew to move and display the Quilt. New panels were added at community-initiated events in each city it visited. By the end of the tour, the Quilt project had tripled its size to 6,000 panels, and in October 1988, when it was laid out in front of the White House, there were 8,288 panels displayed (Williams, 2012).
4. The project prefigured similar initiatives in Australia and New Zealand, and later a range of online developments including the Southern AIDS Living Quilt, the Microsoft AIDS Quilt Touch and Project Stitch.
5. Each panel was 3ft × 6ft (the size of a human grave). In local groups these panels were sewn on to other contributions and assembled into 12ft square sections called *blocks*. Each block typically contained eight individual panels.
6. By 2014, there were 133 independently produced Maker and mini-faires in a range of cities including Tokyo, Rome, Detroit, Oslo and Shenzhen (Peppler and Bender, 2013:26).

7. Currently, its collectives have monikers as diverse as The Ladies Fancywork Society (Denver), The YarnCore Collective (Seattle), Masquerade (Stockholm), the Knitterarti (Auckland, New Zealand), Yarn Corner (Melbourne, Australia) and Knit the City (London).
8. An individual bomber or collective simply uploads a jpeg, gif or png image and the software generates a graph sizable to the intended project.
9. Significant among these was the 2013 *Time* photo essay, 'The Fine Art of Yarn Bombing': http://content.time.com/time/photogallery/0,29307,2077071,00.html.
10. Wollan (2011) notes that Fortune 500 companies paid Sayeg $20,000 to wrap their products in yarn, and she was also hired to knit a cover for a Toyota Prius as part of the company's video and accompanying website promotion. Now working full-time, she has undertaken contracts for clients like the Montague Street Business Improvement District and Insight Australia.
11. Distros are distribution sources for independent publishing initiatives. Some of the more established include Pander Zine Distro and Moonrocket. Distros are rarely economically profitable but operate as a service to support independent creative initiatives. Being 'distro'ed' involves a less formal process than what one would encounter with traditional publishers, 'sometimes zinesters can just send in a note and a copy of their zine and, if the owner of the distro likes it, they'll agree to sell any number of copies' (Urban Dictionary: http://www.urbandictionary.com/define.php?term=distro&defid=1024601).
12. Pogue (1995) notes that these are economically viable because, being authored and posted by the same individual, the publications don't have to pay for writing, editing, design, paper, ink or postage. 'True' e-zines, he suggests, aren't available in printed form.

References

9/11 Memorial (n.d.) *The September 11 Quilt Project*. Retrieved 2 March 2014 from: https://www.911memorial.org/tribute/the-september-11-quilt-project.

Anderson, C. (2013) 'Maker Movement', *Wired*, 21 (5): 106.

Carpenter, E. (2010) 'Activist tendencies in craft', *Concept Store #3 Art, Activism and Recuperation*, 3. Retrieved 2 March 2014 from: http://eprints.gold.ac.uk/3109/1/Activist_Tendencies_in_Craft_EC.pdf.

Davis, R. (2010) *Huntington's Disease Memorial Quilt*. Retrieved 2 March 2014 from: http://www.hdac.org/features/article.php?p_articleNumber=33.

Deleuze, G. and Guattari, F. (1972) *Anti-Œdipus*, trans. R. Hurley, M. Seem and H. R. Lane. London: Continuum.

Deleuze, G. and Guattari, F. (1980) *A Thousand Plateaus*. London: Continuum.

Duncombe, S. (1997) *Notes from the Underground: Zines and the Politics of Alternative Culture*. Bloomington, IN: Microcosm Publishing.

Epstein, R. and Friedman, J. (dir.) (1989) *Common Threads: Stories from the Quilt* [motion picture]. USA: Couterie, Home Box Office (HBO).

Estren, M. J. (1994) *A History of Underground Comics*. Berkeley, CA: Ronin Publishing.

Frontline (2006) *The Age of AIDS: Interview Cleve Jones*. Retrieved 2 March 2014 from: http://www.pbs.org/wgbh/pages/frontline/aids/interviews/jones.html.

Goldense, B. L. (2013) 'The maker movement spurs corporate innovation and entrepreneurship', *Machine Design*, 85 (9): 76.

Gross, J. (1987) 'Funerals for AIDS victims: searching for sensitivity', *New York Times Archives*, 13 February. Retrieved 12 March 2014 from: http://www.nytimes.com/1987/02/13/nyregion/funerals-for-aids-victims-searching-for-sensitivity.html.

Howe, L. (1997) 'The AIDS Quilt and its traditions', *College Literature*, 24 (2): 109–24.

Jahn, J. (2002) 'Salmon courage and the three-year itch', *NW Drizzle Monthly Arts, Music and Culture E-zine*, April. Retrieved 4 March 2014 from: http://www.nwdrizzle.com/drizzle/0204/ci.html.

Kerewsky, S. (1997) 'The AIDS memorial quilt: personal and therapeutic uses', *Arts in Psychotherapy*, 24 (5): 431–8.

Klaasmeyer, K. (2000) 'Art: the third dimension', *Houston Press*, 1 June. Retrieved 4 March 2014 from: http://www.houstonpress.com/2000-06-01/culture/art-the-third-dimension/full/.

Koster, E. (2010) *No Man's Art Gallery: About Us*. Retrieved 3 March 2014 from: http://www.nomansart.com/about-us/.

Laderman, G. (2003) *Rest in Peace: A Cultural History of Death and the Funeral Home in Twentieth Century America*. New York: Oxford University Press.

Lahart, J. (2009) 'Tinkering makes a comeback amid crisis', *Wall Street Journal*, 13 November. Retrieved 3 March 2014 from: http://online.wsj.com/news/articles/SB125798004542744219.

McKinley, J. (2007) 'Fight over quilt reflects changing times in battle against AIDS', *New York Times*, 31 January. Retrieved 2 March 2014 from: http://query.nytimes.com/gst/fullpage.html?res=9C01E2DE153FF932A05752C0A9619C8B63.

Mollins, J. (2011) 'Graffiti knitters to hit streets on Yarnbombing Day', 10 June. Retrieved 4 March 2014 from: http://www.reuters.com/article/2011/06/10/us-knitting-yarnbombing-idUSTRE7595JB20110610.

Peppler, K. and Bender, S. (2013) 'Maker movement spreads innovation one project at a time', *Kappan*, 95 (3): 22–7.

Pernecky, T. (2014) 'The making of societies through events: on ideology, power and consent', in M. Moufakkir and T. Pernecky (eds), *Ideological, Social and Cultural Aspects of Events*. Wallingford, UK: CAB International, pp. 28–46.

Piepmeier, A. (2009) *Girl Zines: Making Media, Doing Feminism*. New York: NYU Press.

Pogue, D. (1995) 'Mega 'zines', *Macworld*, 12 (5): 143–4.

Poletti, A. (2008) 'Auto/assemblage: reading the zine', *Biography*, 31 (1): 85–102.

Richardson, M., Elliot, S. and Haylock, B. (2013) *The Home Is Factory: Implications of the Maker Movement on Urban Environments*. Retrieved 6 March 2014 from: http://press.anu.edu.au/wp-content/uploads/2013/09/ch093.pdf.

Riter, B. (2014) *History of Breast Cancer Advocacy*. Retrieved 2 March 2014 from: http://www.crcfl.net/content/view/history-of-breast-cancer-advocacy.html

Scheuing, R. (2010) 'Urban textiles: from yarn bombing to crochet ivy chains', *Textile Society of America Symposium Proceedings*, Paper 50. Retrieved 3 March 2014 from: http://digitalcommons.unl.edu/cgi/viewcontent.cgi?article=1049andcontext=tsaconf.

Sharples, M., McAndrew, P., Weller, M., Ferguson, R., Fitzgerald, E., Hirst, T. and Gaved, M. (2013) *Innovating Pedagogy 2013: Exploring New Forms of Teaching, Learning and Assessment, to Guide Educators and Policy Makers*, Open University Innovation Report 2. Retrieved 8 March 2014 from: http://www.open.ac.uk/personalpages/mike.sharples/Reports/Innovating_Pedagogy_report_2013.pdf.

Sivasubramanian, M. (2011) *C.H.D. Awareness Quilt Project*. Retrieved 2 March 2014 from: http://www.scoop.it/t/congenital-heart-disease-awareness?page=3.

Stockburger, I. Z. (2011) *Making Zines, Making Selves: Identity Construction in DIY Autobiography*. Doctoral thesis, Georgetown University, Washington, DC.

Williams, R. (2012) *The AIDS Memorial Quilt*. Retrieved 2 March 2014 from: http://www.aidsquilt.org/about/the-aids-memorial-quilt

Wollan, M. (2011) 'Graffiti's cozy, feminine side', *New York Times*, 18 May. Retrieved 3 March 2014 from: http://www.nytimes.com/2011/05/19/fashion/creating-graffiti-with-yarn.html?_r=0.

Yardley, A. and Langley, K. (1994) *Unfolding: The Story of the Australian and New Zealand AIDS Quilt Projects*. Ringwood, Australia: McPhee Gribble/Penguin Books.

5 A mobilities approach to events

Kevin Hannam

Introduction

In this chapter I want to problematise approaches to event studies by engaging with the mobilities paradigm (Sheller and Urry, 2004). As I write this chapter, there are billions of events taking place today across the world: small, everyday events (my children are going back to school), national commemorations (let me check Facebook – on 5 September 2015 it is National Cheese Pizza Day in the USA) as well as global sporting events (the Rugby Union World Cup is commencing very soon). All these events involve various complex mobilities to make them work and lead to further events and further mobilities. People and materials have to be put in place so that events can be planned and happen. Events involve proactive planning which is shaped by the memories and disturbances of past events, management and organisation in the present, and also involve projection into the future – memories and the legacies and impact of events have become commonplace (Masterman, 2014).

However, this complexity then problematises our understandings of temporalities of events in postmodern life: events are both being done and becoming in the same moment as being remembered – refolding time and space as we wait and attend to various events. Mobilities research then also draws attention to moments of stillness and of waiting: an 'animated suspension' in 'which the event of waiting is no longer conceptualised as a dead period of stasis or stilling, or even a slower urban rhythm, but is instead alive with the potential of being other than this' (Bissell, 2007: 277).

In short, various mobilities inform events which lead to mobilities which lead to further events in a never ending process of event formation, critique and development. As a number of philosophers have noted, events and the acquisition of them have become a defining feature of contemporary life, bound up with our identities (Badiou, 2013; Žižek, 2014). The number of events as well as their different scales also leads to various stresses: in terms of transport systems through congestion, in terms of security through geopolitical systems of control as well as in terms of individuals' abilities to cope with attending multiple events at the same time (should I attend my son's birthday party or go to an international soccer match, or should I take him with me even if he isn't interested?).

These stresses then also problematise our understandings of what it means to be free. Sager (2006: 465) has argued that: 'Freedom as mobility is composed both of opportunities to travel when and where one pleases and of the feasibility of the choice not to travel.' Engaging with the freedom to do something, as Bauman (1988) has noted, ultimately leads us into various unfreedoms (Freudendal-Pedersen, 2009). For example, we can go to an event but the social nature of this event may lead us to become obligated to attend further events which we may not (really) want to attend (another friend's birthday party). Events and mobilities coexist in various foldings and unfoldings through time and space which are slippery in our attempts to control them through contemporary scheduling, as much as they are subject to national and international structures (Freudendal-Pedersen, 2009).

This chapter thus reviews and develops mobilities approaches to researching events. We begin by outlining some key concepts in mobilities. Next, we develop these concepts in terms of event mobilities specifically and discuss how event mobilities can be understood through a number of key theoretical ideas.

Conceptualising mobilities

In terms of mapping the larger-scale movements of people, objects, capital and information across the world, a mobilities perspective emphasises the complexities of a reconfigured critical geopolitics (Hannam, 2013; Hannam *et al.*, 2006). International relations can have profound effects on when, who and for what reason people are able to freely move across international borders (see Anderson, 2013; Rogaly, 2015). The current conflict in Syria, for example, has led to profound mobilities across Europe with ensuing protests for and against the admittance of refugees. Geopolitical discourses or 'scripts', as shown in any variety of institutional and popular media, are also powerful and, as they divide up the world, lead to conflicts over space and resources (O'Tuathail, 2002) and subsequent mobilities and immobilities. Global media representations are also significant in terms of the ordering of social life and the ways in which people and things move across space and borders. Tzanelli (2006), for example, has explored how the film *The Beach* was used by Internet tourist providers for the global promotion of Thailand as a travel destination.

However, the mobilities paradigm seeks to understand how such global ordering is also networked with everyday mobilities, developing the notion of performativity and the 'more than representational'. Thus conceptualising mobilities is not just about recognising the interconnections between different forms of mobility such as travel and migration, but developing a more sophisticated ontology of the movements of people, places and things. In particular, this has sought to develop the notion of 'performativity' (Nash, 2000) in relation to mobilities (Hannam, 2006).

Performativity is an attempt to 'find a more embodied way of rethinking the relationships between determining social structures and personal agency' (Nash, 2000: 654). 'More than representational' theories challenge the status of social constructionist understandings of the world by highlighting some of the limitations of representational approaches. Through insights derived from both post-humanistic theory and actor-network theory concerning the complex relationships between humans and the material worlds they encounter – often through specific events – mobilities research attempts to theorise the ways in which structures and agents become intimate (Danby and Hannam, in press).

The concept of performativity is thus concerned with the ways in which people know the world without knowing it, the multi-sensual practices and experiences of everyday life; as such, it proposes a post-humanistic approach to the understanding of social life (Hannam, 2006). As Peter Adey (2009: 149) notes:

> [t]his is an approach which is not limited to representational thinking and feeling, but a different sort of thinking-feeling altogether. It is a recognition that everyday mobilities such as walking or dancing involve various combinations of thought, action, feeling and articulation.

Mobilities research thus examines the embodied nature and experience of different modes of travel, seeing these modes in part as forms of material and sociable dwelling-in-motion, places of and for various activities (Obrador-Pons, 2003). These 'activities' can include specific forms of talk, work or information-gathering, but may involve simply being connected, maintaining a moving presence with others that holds the potential for many different convergences or divergences of global and local physical presence (Hannam *et al.*, 2006, 2014).

Conceptualising mobilities also entails an attention to distinct social spaces or 'moorings' that orchestrate new forms of social and cultural life, for example stations, hotels, motorways, resorts, airports, leisure complexes, beaches, galleries, roadside parks and so on (Hannam *et al.*, 2006). Places are thus significant for understanding the geopolitics of forms of hospitality involved in mobilities in this context (Fregonese and Ramadan, 2015). Germann Molz and Paris (2015: 173), meanwhile, have noted how the proliferation of digital devices and online social media and networking technologies has altered practices of travel landscape in recent years such that they 'are now able to stay in continuous touch with friends, family and other travellers while on the move.' This has led to a 'new sociality: virtual mooring, following, collaborating, and (dis)connecting'.

Conceptualising event mobilities

The mobilities paradigm has also recently gained greater attention within studies of tourism. Tourism mobilities have thus been conceptualised in terms of involving the interconnections of various movements: movement of people, the movement of a whole range of material things, the movement of more intangible thoughts and fantasies and the use of a range of technologies, both old and new (Hannam *et al.*, 2014; Sheller and Urry, 2006). Rather than thinking of event mobilities, it can perhaps be more useful to, conversely, conceptualise mobilities as consisting of networks or assemblages of events (Hannam *et al.*, in press).

Many approaches to event studies take, as a starting point, spectacular mega-events such as sporting occasions like the Olympic Games in London with its related security concerns (Boyle and Haggerty, 2009). Such events involve the development of complex transport systems to manage both participants and spectators as they gather and disperse (Cidell, 2014; Currie and Shalaby, 2011). However, when scholars talk about mobilities they often evoke a momentary or temporary event, or a series of memorable events: walking, driving, running, flying, cycling, commuting, busking, sailing, boating, skiing or hunting (Myers and Hannam, 2012). Here, the act of mobility can be the actual event (Cidell, 2014). Cidell argues that:

> Although running can and does take place almost anywhere, bringing together hundreds or thousands of runners at a time via an event known as a road race enables a different, transgressive occupation of space that no one runner could accomplish on his or her own.
>
> (p. 571)

Thus, by temporarily taking over a space usually devoted to motorised vehicles, the event allows 'for the pleasure of being transgressive without the risks that transgression normally entails' (p. 571).

Mobilities are articulated in relation to, and as, a series of other sorts of social functions and pursuits, from travelling to work and numerous leisure activities, to going on holiday, leaving a country in search of work or sanctuary or hopping on a bus to get to the supermarket. Mobile events might appear to serve as contexts that provide meanings and purpose to a distinct action – from frantically leaving one's home to escape from a mudslide, to embarking on a protest march (Cook and Butz, 2015; Lamond and Spracklen, 2014). Indeed, in their edited collection, Lamond and Spracklen (2014) specifically focus on activism as a leisure activity and protests as events.

On the one hand, considering mobilities as events enables mobility to be understood as much more than an undifferentiated flow and rather as a series of identifiable activities that might concern a particular organisation or institution. Weddings, for example, routinely involve complex orderings of mobility and proximity in the social, familial and religious obligations to travel to the event (Satter *et al.*, 2013; Urry, 2002). But frequently, such events also involve multiple governance assemblages – for example, when a non-EU or non-US citizen seeks to marry an EU or US citizen. This can lead to the reconfiguring of a wedding as a series of multiple events – of multiple weddings in different geographical locations in order to gain the necessary paperwork, rather than the event as a single point in time. Events of love can thus become governmentalised (Mai and King, 2009) as well as problematised in terms of their temporalities and spatialities.

'Moving is by definition an event: it begins and ends, it has a measure and a tempo, it is infused with rhythms and breaks' (Adey *et al.*, 2013). Event mobilities are a 'network in time', with turning points, hinges and eventful punctuation points (Abbott, 2001). However, although mobilities depend upon various speeds, velocities, viscosities and flows they also involve various immobilities such as blockages, congestion, turbulence, friction and disruption. Adey *et al.* (2014) therefore ask the question: 'How do different events of moving, slowing, staying, passing, pausing or rushing inform the meaning and experience of mobility?' This question may be answered in part by an engagement with the philosopher Slavoj Žižek's (2014) work entitled, *Event: Philosophy in Transit*, where he reflects on numerous events in terms of their philosophical consequences.

Significantly perhaps, Žižek (2014) begins by asking us to take a risk and board a train to understand the notion of an event. Thus, we are already on the move.

> An 'Event' can refer to a devastating natural disaster or to the latest celebrity scandal, the triumph of the people or a brutal political change, an intense experience of a work of art or an intimate decision.
>
> (Žižek, 2014: 1)

An event, he discusses, is, firstly, commonly understood at its most minimal level as something out of place, something shocking that interrupts the normal flow of things that comes out of the blue such as the events of the 'Arab Spring' – a synergy that nobody can actually explain fully. Events, then, are somewhat enigmatic and imaginative such that 'an event is thus the effect that seems to exceed its causes – and the space of an event is that which opens up by the gap that separates an effect from its causes' (Žižek, 2014: 3). Such events can also be considered as traumatic, as the 'intrusion of something New which remains unacceptable for the predominant view' (Žižek, 2014: 77). Events may be attributed a traumatic meaning collectively (Alexander, 2004; Ashworth, 2008; Eyerman, 2004). Ferron and Massa (2014: 23) have argued that

> studying how collective memories are formed, particularly in the case of trauma, is important because they persist for entire generations and they play a crucial social role, in that the interaction of the cultural elements involved can influence attitudes not only toward the past but also toward the present of current societies.

A deeply traumatic event such as the disaster at Chernobyl can lead to a multitude of subsequent events, both unplanned and planned (Yankovska and Hannam, 2014).

Secondly, an event can also be conceived as a change: a change in terms of the ways in which reality may appear to us as well as a transformation of the self. In this way, an event produces something new and heralds a symbolic transition as many social anthropologists have recognised in terms of progression through the human life course in different societies (Turner, 1969). The educational mobilities discussed below are good examples of this as students embark on gap years and study-abroad activities. Similarly, funeral events mark the social transition between life and death and are frequently conceptualised in terms of mobilities (Sebro, in press).

Thirdly, Žižek (2014) considers the motion of events as 'a change of the very frame through which we perceive the world and engage in it' (p. 10). This alludes to the ways in which films and other media commonly frame our understandings of events and the places of events, as has been demonstrated in analyses of films such as *Slumdog Millionaire* in Mumbai where tourists seek to re-perform significant events from the film while on tour (Diekmann and Hannam, 2012). Fundamentally, fiction and reality thus become blurred in events. Tzanelli and Yar (2014: 1), for example, explore the 'intersections between the consumption of mediated popular culture and the real and imagined topographies within which those representations are framed'. Through an examination of the TV series *Breaking Bad*, they examine 'the multiple modes of sensorial and embodied travel experience enjoyed by fans of the show as they consume their way around the show's sites, scenes and tastes in the city of Albuquerque' (p. 1).

Fourthly, we might also conceptualise events as 'extremely fragile moments' which may be initially memorable but which can easily be forgotten – hence an emphasis on the materialities of events through which we attempt to remember them. Time, in terms of past, present and future, then, is an important aspect of events, such that many governments and communities now think of their material legacies as much as the events themselves when planning them. Hall (2006) has written about how sports mega-events involve neoliberal strategies and policies which move events into the future in a number of ways:

> Sports mega-events emerge as central elements in place competition in at least three ways. First, the infrastructure required for such events is usually regarded as integral to further economic development whether as an amenity resource or as infrastructure. Second, the hosting of events is seen as a contribution to business vitality and economic development. Thirdly, the ability to attract events is often regarded as a performance indicator in its own right of the capacity of a city or region to compete.
>
> (p. 64)

Graham and Marvin (2001) in their book, *Splintering Urbanism*, meanwhile, have also written of how such mega-events seek to sanitise urban space through corporate branding and, through this, the voices of those who may disagree with the urban planning legacies that this entails are silenced.

Contra Žižek's (2014) philosophical reflections, events often consist of everyday, mundane mobilities (Edensor, 2007). For example, the packing of luggage for an event involves various technologies while producing worries of loss. Lightness and the use of specially designed travel materials mark the holiday as a special event, one requiring specialised 'skills, routines and reflexes'. The timing of mobility for events is equally informed by more routine moves. How and when people go to work, whether they work from home and how they use their time while commuting are all 'kinds of event-in-progress' (Adey *et al.*, 2014). In the discussion below, we explore five dimensions of the 'event in transition', namely 'interruptions', 'transitions', 'framings' and 'materialities', tempered by the acknowledgement that such mobilities are frequently grounded in the more routine aspects of social lives.

Interruptions

While event studies are generally concerned with the planning of events in the future, many other events need to be planned for, even though they may be unexpected and unwanted. Thus various planned and unplanned events can be conceptualised as interruptions in contemporary mobilities. It can be argued that scholars of event studies and those of disaster studies need to engage further in order to better ameliorate the effects of disaster events. Disaster events, for example, bring to the fore the astounding fragility of complex mobility systems (Hannam *et al.*, 2006). The attacks of 9/11 – an event which many people still find hard to comprehend – embedded into the global consciousness not only a massive loss of human life, but also a vision of the simultaneous destruction of multiple mobility systems and a disruption of the global discourse of unfettered mobility as a way of life. This event was both a significant interruption but also significantly traumatic and clearly led to a further series of events and more repercussions than could have been envisaged or imagined.

Memorials and the events associated with them may serve the needs of a community in the present connected to its collective identity in order to overcome a past trauma (Johnson, 1995). Legg (2005) has drawn attention to the ways in which such traumatic remembering is socially contested and further suggests that trauma should be understood as a collective social, political, and aesthetic condition where human agency becomes irrecoverable. Legg (2005) emphasises the embodied power relations in any form of remembering: that we remember through our bodily actions, which combine moments of stillness and movement. As Hebbert (2005: 581) asserts, 'memory and identity are rooted in bodily experiences of being and moving in material space.'

Transitions

To illustrate the notion of the event as mobile transition, we can call upon any number of anthropological studies of various rites of passage – the liminal passage from youth to adulthood, for instance. We can conceptualise students' gap years, educational exchanges or volunteering experiences as mobile events which are all concerned with transitions. Indeed, many universities and travel companies highlight the need for students to engage with such life-changing events for their future careers. To travel as part of education has been recognised by most cultures around the world and was an integral part of the Grand Tour. Brodsky-Porges (1981) noted that the French writer Montaigne in the 1500s argued that students needed 'some direct adventuring with the world, a steady and lively interplay with common folk, supplemented and fortified with trips abroad'. Holdsworth (2009: 1852) adds that '[s]tudents are constantly on the move: between halls; from place of residence (which may be halls of residence, privately rented accommodation, or parental home) to campus; as well as from 'home' to university'.

Engaging in transitional events has arguably led to new cultural forms, including new cultural identities and subjectivities as students travel as part of the

New Zealand overseas experience (OE), for example (see Conradson and Latham, 2007; Haverig, 2011; Williams *et al.*, 2011; Wilson *et al.*, 2009). Event mobilities thus become articulated as meaningful activities within the different systems that involve the production of knowledge (Hannam and Guereno-Omil, 2014). Van Mol and Michielsen (2015) explore the social interactions and shared social spaces of Erasmus students. Doherty (2015) develops the concept of 'institutional viscosity' to illustrate how Australian Defence Force families cope with their children's disrupted education given frequent forced relocations. Through these examples, we can see how educational mobilities are transitional events in themselves.

Sebro (in press) further examines the antagonisms between event transitions and mobilities in her study of necromobilities on the Thai/Burma border. She focuses on the choreographing or what she terms 'the choreomobility' of bodies through funerary events which, she argues, involve processes and performances of becoming: vibrant mobilities arise after the death of the body. Funerals as death-events may be punctures in the seemingly stable world of everyday lives but also help with social transitions even in the face of violence. Theoretically, such events again problematise the geographies of the 'more than representational' by further disturbing notions of temporality such that '[s]paces and times are folded, allowing distant presences, events, people and things to become rather more intimate' (Maddern and Adey, 2008: 292).

Framings

Contemporary events are also 'framed' by global media systems. Events are nothing without publicity, and both cinematic events and events portrayed on social media have significant effects (Hannam *et al.*, 2014). Drawing upon the concept of performativity discussed above, the relations between various media and mobilities are not determined by each other, rather they coexist as relational 'more-than representational mobilities' (Adey, 2009: 146). For instance, Spracklen (in press) takes us on a journey into the world of heavy metal music festivals, connecting ideas concerning events as transition and framing in the context of pilgrimage to the Bloodstock festival. He concludes that there are conflicting instrumental rationalities at work around music festivals where the language of global festivals works to stretch the event into a mediatised simulacrum.

In terms of mega-events, however, Rodanthi Tzanelli (2015) has recently produced a mobilities-informed analysis of the ethics and aesthetics of the Football World Cup held in Brazil in 2014. She notes that

> [t]he 2014 mega-event's opening ceremony and the Brazilian mourning of football defeat become chrono-spatial windows to the Brazilian culture's emotional and material movements in the world. Performed Brazilian-style, these movements are recorded in music, rhythm, theatrical performance and (un)choreographed protest in equally important ways …
>
> (p. 6)

She goes on to discuss the new technologies that were introduced to frame the World Cup for audiences around the world using over 37 television cameras for each match. Moreover, she further notes that the British football commentators' presentations

> were framed around discourses of travel and mobility: the slum and Carnival capital for Rio; the coastal artistic metropolis for Recife; the country's power base for Brasilia; the Amazonian beautiful but progressively industrialised Manaus; the home of African capoeira for Salvador; and the industrious, concrete but cosmopolitan São Paulo.
>
> (p. 17)

Materialities

There has been recognition of the ways in which material 'stuff' helps to constitute events. Such stuff is always in motion, being assembled and reassembled in changing configurations (Sheller and Urry, 2004). In their classic paper, Cook and Crang (1996) discuss how, rather than being spatially fixed, the material geographies of food are mobilised within circuits of culinary culture, outlining their production and consumption through processes of commodity fetishism. Cook *et al.* (1998) then examine how food geographies are the result of 'locally circulated' global flows of agents and knowledge. They suggest that the analysis of the geographies and biographies of food is a vital component of any food analysis, as it illustrates the interconnectivity between the mobilities of food paths (Cook *et al.*, 1998). And, as we know, food is a core component of the hospitality afforded at events.

However, many events are materialisations of past events – heritage – rather than current ones, and materials such as food are used to remember past events, as Marcel Proust importantly pointed out in his involuntary remembrance of taste. The mobile materialities of heritage thus involve complex 'hybrid geographies' (Whatmore, 2002) of humans and non-humans that contingently enable people and things to move and to hold their shape as they move across various regions, both physically and imaginatively. There is thus a complex materiality to being on the move, as heritage events and the things that constitute heritage itself engage with all sorts of materials that enable their movement.

The event of moving away from home is about encountering a new world, new experiences and a sense of adventure with all the accompanying anxieties that may need to be endured. For many migrant populations, there are many material things that then become heritage in the present day. Basu and Coleman (2008) emphasise the notion that heritage moves people, physically as well as emotionally and imaginatively, to think about their own pasts through different sensations which themselves can be both tangible and intangible.

Conclusions

It seems self-evident that events lead to even more events but, in an age of turbulent mobilities, this is just the case as people continuously schedule more events into their electronic calendars on their mobile phones (Urry, 2007). This chapter has sought to introduce and discuss aspects of what we have called a mobilities approach to the study of events. In doing so, I have outlined some of the key conceptual dimensions of event mobilities in terms of interruptions, transitions, framings and materialities. However, as the current events taking place across Europe in terms of the refugee crisis suggest, these dimensions are not discrete but intimately connected. The politics of the interruption of traumatic migration from Syria involves a significant transition, educational as well as emotional, for the refugees themselves. These are framed within particular geopolitical discourses and practices – governmobilities of movement – which seek to codify the materialities and memories of freedom and unfreedom. Events, planned and unplanned, are always being and becoming.

References

Abbott, A. (2001) *Time Matters: On Theory and Method.* Chicago: University of Chicago Press.

Adey, P. (2009) *Mobility*. London: Routledge.

Adey, P., Bissell, D., Merriman, P., Hannam, K. and Sheller, M. (eds) (2013) *The Routledge Handbook of Mobilities*. London: Routledge.

Alexander, J. C. (2004) 'Toward a theory of cultural trauma', in J. C. Alexander, R. Eyerman and B. Giesen (eds), *Cultural Trauma and Collective Identity*. Berkeley, CA: University of California Press, pp. 1–29.

Anderson, B. (2013) *'Us' and 'Them': The Dangerous Politics of Immigration Control.* Oxford: Oxford University Press.

Ashworth, G. J. (2008) 'The memorialization of violence and tragedy: human trauma as heritage', in B. Graham and P. Howard (eds), *The Ashgate Research Companion to Heritage and Identity*. Aldershot: Ashgate, pp. 231–44.

Badiou, A. (2013) *Philosophy and the Event*. New York: Polity.

Basu, P. and Coleman, S. (2008) 'Introduction: migrant worlds, material cultures', *Mobilities*, 3: 313–30.

Bauman, Z. (1988) *Freedom*. Berkeley, CA: Open University Press.

Bissell, D. (2007) 'Animating suspension: waiting for mobilities', *Mobilities*, 2: 277–98.

Boyle, P. and Haggerty, K. (2009) 'Spectacular security: mega-events and the security complex', *International Political Sociology*, 3: 257–74.

Brodsky-Porges, E. (1981) 'The Grand Tour: travel as an educational device, 1600–1800', *Annals of Tourism Research*, 8: 171–86.

Cidell, J. (2014) 'Running road races as transgressive event mobilities', *Social and Cultural Geography*, 15: 571–83.

Conradson, D. and Latham, A. (2007) 'The affective possibilities of London: antipodean transnationals and the overseas experience', *Mobilities*, 2: 231–54.

Cook, I. and Crang, P. (1996) 'The world on a plate: culinary culture, displacement and geographical knowledges', *Journal of Material Culture*, 1: 131–53.

Cook, I., Crang, P. and Thorpe, M. (1998) 'Biographies and geographies: consumer understandings of the origins of foods', *British Food Journal*, 100 (3): 162–7.

Cook, N. and Butz, D. (2015) 'Mobility justice in the context of disaster', *Mobilities* (advance online publication – DOI: 10.1080/17450101.2015.1047613).

Currie, G. and Shalaby, A. (2011) 'Synthesis of transport planning approaches for the world's largest events', *Transport Reviews*, 32: 113–36.

Danby, P. and Hannam, K. (in press) 'Entrainment: human-equine leisure mobilities', in J. Rickly, K. Hannam and M. Mostafanezhad (eds), *Tourism and Leisure Mobilities: Politics, Work and Play*. London: Routledge.

Diekmann, A. and Hannam, K. (2012) 'Touristic mobilities in India's slum spaces', *Annals of Tourism Research*, 39 (3): 1316–36.

Doherty, C. (2015) 'Agentive motility meets structural viscosity: Australian families relocating in educational markets', *Mobilities*, 10: 249–66.

Edensor, T. (2007) 'Mundane mobilities, performances and spaces of tourism', *Social and Cultural Geography*, 8: 199–215.

Eyerman, R. (2004) 'Cultural trauma: slavery and the formation of African American identity', in J. C. Alexander, R. Eyerman and B. Giesen (eds), *Cultural Trauma and Collective Identity*. Berkeley, CA: University of California Press, pp. 61–111.

Ferron, M. and Massa, P. (2014) 'Beyond the encyclopedia: collective memories in Wikipedia', *Memory Studies*, 7: 22–45.

Fregonese, S. and Ramadan, A. (2015) 'Hotel geopolitics: a research agenda', *Geopolitics*, 20 (4): 793–813.

Freudendal-Pedersen, M. (2009) *Mobility in Daily Life: Between Freedom and Unfreedom*. Farnham: Ashgate.

Germann Molz, J. and Paris, C. M. (2015) 'The social affordances of flashpacking: exploring the mobility nexus of travel and communication', *Mobilities*, 10: 173–92.

Graham, S. and Marvin, S. (2001) *Splintering Urbanism: Networked Infrastructures, Technological Mobilities and the Urban Condition*. London: Routledge.

Hall, C. M. (2006) 'Urban entrepreneurship, corporate interests and sports mega events: the thin policies of competitiveness within the hard outcomes of neoliberalism', *Sociological Review*, 54 (2): 59–70.

Hannam, K. (2006) 'Tourism and development III: performance, performativities and mobilities', *Progress in Development Studies*, 6: 243–9.

Hannam, K. (2013) '"Shangri-La" and the new "Great Game": exploring tourism geopolitics between China and India', *Tourism, Planning and Development*, 10: 178–86.

Hannam, K. and Guereno-Omil, B. (2014) 'Educational mobilities: mobile students, mobile knowledge', in D. Airey, D. Dredge and M. Gross (eds), *The Routledge Handbook of Tourism and Hospitality Education*. London: Routledge, pp. 143–54.

Hannam, K., Butler, G. and Paris, C. (2014) 'Developments and key concepts in tourism mobilities', *Annals of Tourism Research*, 44: 171–85.

Hannam, K., Rickly, J. and Mostafanezhad, M. (eds) (2016) *Event Mobilities: Politics, Performance and Place*. London: Routledge.

Hannam, K., Sheller, M. and Urry, J. (2006) 'Mobilities, immobilities and moorings', *Mobilities*, 1: 1–22.

Haverig, A. (2011) 'Constructing global/local subjectivities – the New Zealand OE as governance through freedom', *Mobilities*, 6: 102–23.

Hebbert, M. (2005) 'The street as locus of collective memory', *Environment and Planning D: Society and Space*, 23: 581–96.

Holdsworth, C. (2009) '"Going away to uni": mobility, modernity, and independence of English higher education students', *Environment and Planning A*, 41: 1849–64.

Johnson, N. (1995) 'Cast in stone: monuments, geography, and nationalism', *Environment and Planning D: Society and Space*, 13: 51–65.

Lamond, I. and Spracklen, K. (eds) (2014) *Protests as Events: Politics, Activism and Leisure*. London: Rowman & Littlefield.

Legg, S. (2005) 'Contesting and surviving memory: space, nation, and nostalgia in Les Lieux de Memoire', *Environment and Planning D: Society and Space*, 23: 481–504.

Maddern, J. and Adey, P. (2008) 'Editorial: spectro-geographies', *Cultural Geographies*, 15: 291–5.

Mai, N. and King, R. (2009) 'Love, sexuality and migration: mapping the issue(s)', *Mobilities*, 4: 295–307.

Masterman, G. (2014) *Strategic Sports Management*. London: Routledge.

Myers, L. and Hannam, K. (2012) 'Adventure tourism as a series of memorable events: women travellers' walking experiences in New Zealand', in R. Shipway and A. Fyall (eds), *International Sports Events: Impacts, Experiences and Identities*. London: Routledge, pp. 154–66.

Nash, C. (2000) 'Performativity in practice: some recent work in cultural geography', *Progress in Human Geography*, 24: 653–64.

O'Tuathail, G. (2002) 'Post-Cold War geopolitics: contrasting superpowers in a world of global dangers', in R. J. Johnson, P. Taylor and M. Watts (eds), *Geographies of Global Change*, 2nd edn. Oxford: Blackwell, pp. 174–90.

Obrador-Pons, P. (2003) 'Being-on-holiday: tourist dwelling, bodies and place', *Tourist Studies*, 3: 47–66.

Rogaly, B. (2015) 'Disrupting migration stories: reading life histories through the lens of mobility and fixity', *Environment and Planning D: Society and Space*, 33: 528–44.

Sager, T. (2006) 'Freedom as mobility: implications of the distinction between actual and potential travelling', *Mobilities*, 1: 465–88.

Sattar, Z., Hannam, K. and Ali, N. (2013) 'Religious obligations to travel', *Journal of Tourism and Cultural Change*, 11: 61–72.

Sebro, T. (2016) 'Necromobility/choreomobility: dance, death and displacement in the Thai–Burma border-zone', in K. Hannam, J. Rickly and M. Mostafanezhad (eds), *Event Mobilities: Politics, Performance and Place*. London: Routledge.

Sheller, M. and Urry, J. (eds) (2004) *Tourism Mobilities: Places to Play, Places in Play*. London: Routledge.

Spracklen, K. (2016) 'Framing identities and mobilities in heavy metal music festival events', in K. Hannam, J. Rickly and M. Mostafanezhad (eds), *Event Mobilities: Politics, Performance and Place*. London: Routledge.

Turner, V. (1969) *The Ritual Process: Structure and Anti-structure*. London: Aldine.

Tzanelli, R. (2006) 'Reel Western fantasies: portrait of a tourist imagination in *The Beach* (2000)', *Mobilities*, 1: 121–42.

Tzanelli, R. (2015) *Socio-cultural Mobility and Mega-events: Ethics and aesthetics in Brazil's 2014 World Cup*. London: Routledge.

Tzanelli, R. and Yar, M. (2014) 'Breaking bad, making good: notes on a televisual tourist industry', *Mobilities* (advance online publication– DOI: 10.1080/17450101.2014.929256).

Urry, J. (2002) *The Tourist Gaze*. London: Sage.

Urry, J. (2007) *Mobilities*. London: Sage.

Van Mol, C. and Michielsen, J. (2015) 'The reconstruction of a social network abroad: an analysis of the interaction patterns of Erasmus students', *Mobilities*, 10: 423–44.

Whatmore, S. (2002) *Hybrid Geographies: Natures, Cultures and Spaces*. London: Sage.

Williams, A., Chaban, N. and Holland, M. (2011) 'The circular international migration of New Zealanders: enfolded mobilities and relational places', *Mobilities*, 6: 125–47.

Wilson, J., Fisher, D. and Moore, K. (2009) 'Reverse diaspora and the evolution of a cultural tradition: the case of the New Zealand "overseas experience"', *Mobilities*, 4: 159–75.

Yankovska, G. and Hannam, K. (2014) 'Dark and toxic tourism in the Chernobyl exclusion zone', *Current Issues in Tourism*, 17: 929–39.

Žižek, S. (2014) *Event: Philosophy in Transit*. Harmondsworth: Penguin.

Part III

Towards critical capacity and methodological vigilance for the study of events

6 Critical discourse analysis

Towards critiquing the language of events

William G. Feighery

Introduction

Events are an outcome of the human desire to construct and articulate shared understandings and to mark identities within broader socio-cultural contexts. In contemporary society these 'organised acts of performance' (Raj et al., 2013: 4) are routinely deemed to be an aspect of the economy and a key component of the 'cultural industries'. With the penetration of broadcast and narrowcast media on a global scale, together with the 'democratisation of travel' (Santis, 1978), the economic implications of events are subject to a significant level of attention both within and outside the academy. Much less attention has been paid to the broader social, cultural and political implications of events. Yet, as Rojek (2013) notes, 'it is dangerous to take events at face value' and he calls for 'a more searching attitude to *who* defines events, *how* they are managed and *what* they achieve' (p. xi). In attempting to contribute to the debate, this chapter explores how critical discourse analysis (CDA) might usefully be employed to inspect what I will refer to here as 'the language of events'. In particular, the discussion focuses on facets of multimodal discourse analysis (Kress and Van Leeuwen, 1996) in the context of the textual and photographic representation of sporting events/personalities in the media.

In the increasingly 'global' context within which major events take place, they are often exploited to communicate a variety of positive messages about the host society and/or its potential as an economic resource. In these processes, events may be enlisted to legitimate political philosophies or to offer resistance to dominant ideologies (e.g. the 2008 Beijing Olympics or the 'Gay Pride' franchise as relevant examples). Events also provide a key node of representation in and through popular mediation. In the digital landscape which has developed since the dawn of the millennium, representations of events in text and talk, such as award ceremonies, film releases, concert performances, sporting events, festivals, etc., can be regarded as the 'wallpaper of popular culture' providing a fluid backdrop to the formation and articulation of the kinds of ambivalent, precarious and mutating subjectivities which have emerged from the neoliberalism that underpins globalisation (Standing, 2011).

The 'language of events', or perhaps I should say the construction of events through language, potentially reveals a raft of economic, environmental, social, cultural and political concerns which can be informed through critical discourse studies. Events associated with entertainment and sport continue to rely heavily on a combination of written and photographic representations as part of the promotion and commodification process (Hall, 1997; Julier, 2006). Indeed, it has been argued that '[v]isual symbolism has begun to rival spoken or printed words as the medium by which our sense of cultural tradition is to be carried forward' (Williams, 1997: 28). Recent developments in digital communication seem to support this contention. In this increasingly visual environment, sport is encountered largely through visual representation, whether television, still photography or, increasingly, digital media (Huggins, 2008). Such representations have important implications in terms of their broader socio-cultural influences. Representation of events, as well as of those individuals associated with events (entertainers, sports personalities, etc.), have numerous potential influences beyond the immediate leisure or media economy within which they are often conceived. Scholars have, for example, explored aspects of gender representation (Boykoff and Yasuoka, 2015; Fink and Kensicki, 2002; Levina et al., 2000; Liao and Markula, 2009; Miller, 1975; Signorielli et al., 1994; Tseng, 2015), ethnicity (Van Sterkenburg and Knoppers, 2004), stereotyping (Beasley and Collins Standley, 2002; Desmarais and Bruce, 2010) and nationalism (Militz, 2015; Tseng, 2015) by examining the ways in which events are represented in text and talk. However, there is a vast array of potential influences which remain undertheorised and which might usefully be explored through critical discourse studies. Before we consider a specific example of how CDA might be used to probe representational practice in and through sporting events, it is necessary to introduce the theoretical background to CDA and to highlight some of the diversity of approaches that have emerged in and through critical discourse studies thus far.

Critical discourse studies

Discourse is not simply what is said in text and talk but is that which constrains and enables what can be said in any given setting. Thus critical discourse studies are usually concerned with exploring the ways in which language 'in use' produces such effects. Luke (2002: 98) argues that 'conditions of global capitalism are enabled by discourse-saturated technology and environments where language, text, and discourse become the principal modes of social relations, civic and political life, economic behaviours and activity.' Part of the response to these conditions has grown out of critical theory with the emergence of critical linguistics (Halliday, 1994) and the subsequent development of CDA. There are numerous definitions of CDA all of which emphasise the relationship between language and power. Luke (2002: 100) provides the following definition:

> CDA involves a principled and transparent shunting back and forth between the microanalysis of texts using varied tools of linguistic, semiotic and literary analysis, and the macro analysis of social formations, institutions and power relations that these texts index and construct.

CDA does not seek to provide a single or specific theory or research methodology. Studies in CDA are multifarious, deriving from different theoretical backgrounds and oriented towards different data and methodologies (Wodak and Meyer, 2009). An important reflective aspect of CDA is an awareness of the social embeddedness of the researcher/activist who occupies a position within the social field and is subject to its structures. Proponents of CDA have acknowledged that this approach to research practice can never be objective: it always serves particular interests, always comes from a particular perspective and proffers insights that are always partial, incomplete and provisional (Fairclough, 1989, 2003).

While the first use of term 'critical discourse analysis' is attributed to Fairclough (1985: 739), critical perspectives on political issues of power and control had begun to gain momentum from the late 1970s (Fowler et al., 1979; Hodge and Kress, 1993). Subsequently, Fairclough published two influential volumes under the titles *Language and Power* (1989) and *Critical Discourse Analysis* (1995a). From these early works, scholars have developed and applied a variety of approaches within the broad movement of CDA. These include the discourse historic approach (Reisigl and Wodak, 2009), the corpus-linguistics approach (Mautner, 2009), the social actors approach (van Leeuwen, 1996), dispositive analysis (Jäger and Maier, 2009), the socio-cognative approach (Van Dijk, 2008) and the dialectical-relational approach (Fairclough, 1989, 1992, 1995). The approach adopted is likely to be influenced both by the theoretical background underpinning it as well as by the research context and the disposition of the researcher. In the following section, I will focus on the work of Fairclough and in particular a three-dimensional approach to CDA which he proposed as 'a guide not a blueprint' (Fairclough, 1989: 110). This non-prescriptive posture is characteristic of CDA which depends less on rigorous procedures and more on what Phillips and Hardy (2002: 75) refer to as 'interpretative sensitivities'.

As is evident from the diversity of approaches which it embraces, CDA can be conceptualised as a heterogeneous 'movement' rather than as a discrete school or method. The theoretical framework is derived from Louis Althusser, Mikhail Bakhtin and the philosophical traditions of Antonio Gramsci and the 'Frankfurt School' (Titscher and Jenner, 2000). The work of Michel Foucault has also had a major influence on scholars such as Fairclough. Another line of influence and development is the one going back to Gramsci's followers in France and the UK, most notably Hall and the work of the Centre for Contemporary Cultural Studies, Birmingham. Hall's (1997) work on 'difference' provides a particularly useful example in the context of the current discussion in that it explores the meanings constructed through the representation of events in text and image (in this case sport) and how these are implicated in perpetuating dominant stereotypes. Later in the discussion, I will revisit the work of Hall (1997) in order to illustrate how CDA might be used to highlight the continued deployment of discursive events in attempts to fix meaning in the service of ideologically determined relations of power.

Text-interaction-context

Fairclough has conceived the term 'discourse' as referring to the whole process of social interaction, identifying a discursive event as simultaneously a piece of *text*, an instance of *discursive practice* and an instance of *social practice*. This unfolding approach is also referred to as the *text-interaction-context* model. Fairclough's (1992: 92) 'social theory of discourse' consists of three interrelated processes of analysis tied to three interrelated dimensions of discourse, all of which intersect with other elements within and between texts (Figure 6.1). This approach has been widely adopted across the spectrum of social analysis and offers an accessible framework for critical studies of discourse for both the novice analyst and for more accomplished practitioners. In simplified form, the approach focuses on:

- describing 'texts' (which the analyst has selected for a given topic);
- exploring the processes by which such texts have been produced, distributed and consumed (interpreting the relationship between text and interaction); and
- considering the social implications of these texts through intertextuality and their subsequent implication in orders of discourse (explanation of the relationship between interaction and social context).

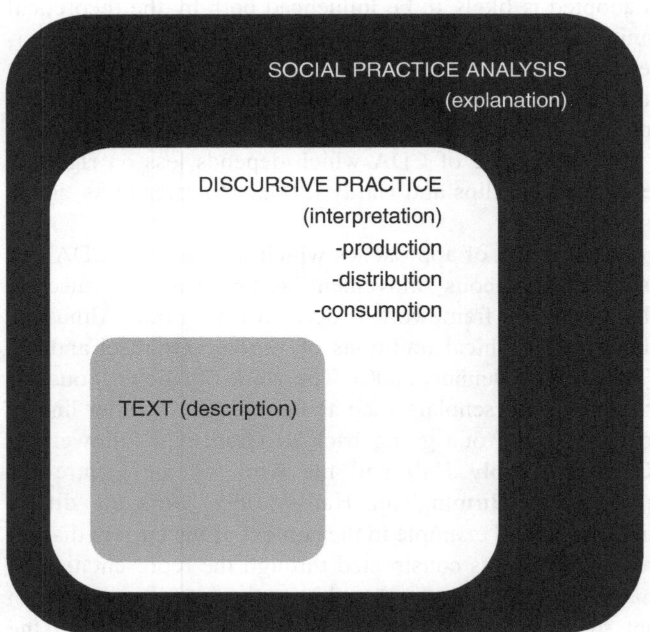

Figure 6.1 Three dimensions of discourse

Adapted from Furlough (1995: 59).

Fairclough (1989: 26) insists that

> in seeing language as discourse and as social practice, one is committing oneself not just to analysing texts, nor just to analysing processes of production and interpretation, but to analysing the relationship between texts, processes and their social conditions, both the immediate conditions of the situational context and the more remote conditions of institutional and social structures.

There is no requirement in CDA to find texts (data) that are 'representative' of a broader set of data as there is in, for example, content analysis. In CDA the analyst may be working with a single brief written text or image, or with a larger corpus of data.

Dimension 1: text (description)

According to Fairclough (1989: 24) 'a text is a product rather than a process – a product of the process of text production'. It includes the *process of production* and the *process of interpretation*, for which the text is a resource. Text analysis is, correspondingly, only a part of discourse analysis, which also includes analysis of productive and interpretative processes. At the site of the text itself one might initially ask, 'what genre has this text event emerged from?' Genres are groups of texts that share the same characteristics. They are also part of the unequally distributed symbolic capital of society, and thus, from a critical perspective, are empowering to some and oppressive to others. Such questions (and you may want to ask many more) can be used as a heuristic device which potentially aids the analyst's understanding of how any given text works to persuade and to produce effects of truth. It is also possible and desirable at this initial stage of analysis to begin to trace the text's 'natural history' (Blommaert 2001) across a range of settings and text types.

In developing a critical analysis it is essential to engage in 'close reading' in an iterative approach in which the analyst 'returns' to the text until one reaches what I have previously referred to as 'interpretative exhaustion' (Feighery, 2006: 6). To develop the analysis from an initial 'text description' (dimension 1) it is necessary to understand the context of text production and reception and this necessitates an investigation/analysis of associated discourse practices. At this stage in the analysis, the focus is expanding to embrace social interaction, highlighting CDA commitment to not just analysing texts, but broader relationships of their production and social conditions.

As our discussion here includes multimodal representations, the work of Rose (2011) is informative as she has made a significant contribution to the literature by drawing visual methods and discourse analysis closer through an articulation of a critical visual methodology. Additionally, Wang (2014) has provided a useful example of the application of Fairclough's (1989) model of CDA in the context of photographic images. For those working with visual images, text *description* involves the categorisation of visual elements which can be used to conduct a linguistic description of the visuals, with each type of presentation, process and other visual elements being presented in detail (see Wang, 2014).

Dimension 2: discourse practice (interpretation)

Discourse practice is regarded as mediating between textual practice and socio-cultural practice. In this dimension the analyst begins to 'go outside the text' (Fairclough, 2003: 129) to get a sense of its social context. Here, the analyst is urged to consider the context within which any given 'text' might have been produced, circulated and consumed – its social conditions of production. There is a 'need to locate the social site from which particular statements are made, and to position the speaker of the statement in terms of their social authority' (Foucault, 1972: 50–2, as cited in Rose, 2011: 220). For example, in a study which I conducted (Feighery, 2006) on the representation of diversity in promotional texts, following a 'close reading' of the written texts, I interviewed those writers and editors responsible for their production, thus informing the study in terms of *discourse practice*, *relexicalisation* (words or phrases which are repeated) and *intertextuality* (the practice of drawing on other texts and genres). Going 'outside the text' can also inform the analysis on what Fairclough (1989) refers to as 'member resources' (MR), also referred to as 'social cognitions' (Van Dijk, 1993). MR may include knowledge of language, representations of the natural and social worlds, values, beliefs, assumptions, and so on. As Fairclough (1989: 24) has it:

> The MR which people draw upon to produce and interpret texts are cognitive in the sense that they are in people's heads, but they are social in the sense that they have social origins – they are socially generated, and their nature is dependent on the social relations and struggles out of which they were generated – as well as being socially transmitted and, in our society, unequally distributed.

This includes the complex of socio-linguistic means and communicative skills that participants bring to a particular situation (Breeze, 2013). Such resources are important because of 'the deep relation between language and a general economy of symbols and status in societies' (Blommaert, 2001: 23). Thus we can say that interpretations are generated through a combination of 'what is in the text and what is "in" the interpreter' (Fairclough, 1989: 141). In acknowledging the socially determined nature of MR, it is important to recognise that discourses and ideologies are not simply to be found in, for example, media texts, but are produced as an outcome of the social embeddedness of the individual (including the analyst) in networks of social relations. In this sense, individuals are sign makers within their own social environments. They are part of the process through which signs are made, used and remade. Although individuals in less powerful positions may be unable to propagate discourses to the same extent as, for example, the editorial teams of major media outlets, they are implicated in 'discourse practice' in, for example, aligning themselves with, or resisting, particular discursive events. Thus we can view CDA as seeking 'to make sense of or to interpret phenomena in terms of the meanings people bring to them' (Denzin and Lincoln, 2000: 3). According to Fairclough, the stage of interpretation (*discourse practice*) makes explicit what for participants is generally implicit. What it does not do on its own, however, is explicate the relations of power and domination and the ideologies which are built into these assumptions, and which make ordinary discourse practice a site of social struggle. For this, we need the stage of explanation.

Dimension 3: social practice (explanation)

Social practice is concerned with an analysis of the macro-structural context within which the text is embedded. The objective is to portray discourse as 'part of a social process, as a social practice, showing how it is determined by social structures, and what reproductive effects discourses can cumulatively have on those structures, sustaining them or changing them' (Fairclough, 1989: 163). We might, for example, consider the ways in which 'mega-events' are represented in the media as an element in social processes at the institutional (media) and societal levels by exploring the ways in which such practice is ideologically determined by, and ideologically determinative of, power relations and power struggles. In developing analysis in the sphere of social practice (explanation), Fairclough suggests a number of useful questions which can be asked of a particular discourse under investigation, as follows:

- *Social determinants* – what power relations at situational, institutional and societal levels help shape this discourse?
- *Ideologies* – what elements of MR which are drawn upon have an ideological character?
- *Effects* – how is this discourse positioned in relation to struggles at the situational, institutional and societal levels? Are these struggles overt or covert? Is the discourse normative with respect to MR or creative? Does it contribute to sustaining existing power relations or transforming them?

For example, critical analysis of the representation of 'mega-events' in the media might consider the systems of governance and the institutional context within which media outlets operate in any given territory, the ideological position mediated in and through institutional statements, or the positions taken up by those responsible for editorial policy (the editorial gaze), etc. These are all obvious examples of the macro-structural context of text production. They are crucial aspects of the way in which the processes of production and interpretation are 'socially determined' (Fairclough, 1989: 24) within a matrix of relations of power which potentially reproduce forms of oppression, but while also offering pathways to resistance because discourses are never fixed, they are socially determined and 'mediated'.

The discourse of difference: an example

As I have already noted, there are numerous aspects of events which fall within the realm of CDA's usual concern with domination, exclusion and power, and as such are open to critical investigation. In the following example, I will explore the ways in which athletes from ethnic minority backgrounds are represented in the media. Here, I connect with Hall's (1997) work on the representation of ethnic minority athletes in and through media reporting of major sporting events. My focus here on the representation of elite athletes in so-called 'mega-events' is perhaps an obvious starting place, but analysts might equally explore the discursive contours of such practices through a local lens. In light of recent debates regarding the role of elite athletes from ethnic minority backgrounds (Andersson, 2002; Martin, 2015), it is perhaps fitting to cite an example which illustrates the discursive construction of difference in media representations of 'mega-events'. It is not difficult to find examples of stereotypical representation of 'racial difference' in coverage of, for example, elite Black sports personalities. Here, I will take just two examples from well-known magazine covers, one from the United Kingdom and one from the United States. Although these two magazine covers were published more than two decades apart, there are striking similarities in the representational practices operating within the two. Before moving to consider these two examples, I would like to acknowledge that any exploration of the representation of Black athletes in the media, such as my discussion here, is itself implicated in the social practice associated with such discursive events. Such representations are enacted within a rigid and limited grid of visibility which conforms to stereotypes of which the athletic Black body is an established trope and thus to some extent the discussion here is part of their macro-political context.

My first example is the *Sunday Times Magazine Olympic Special* published on 9 October 1988. The cover photograph depicts a number of athletes (including the Canadian sprinter Ben Johnson) in the final of the men's 100 metres at the 1988 Olympic Games. The photograph is accompanied by the caption 'Heroes and Villains' (see Figure 6.2). The caption infers both the heroic achievements of the predominantly Black field in the final, as well as Johnson's disgrace in being disqualified for a doping offence. However, the plural caption ('Heroes and Villains') is referring not just to Ben Johnson, but to all those in the image, and by extension to all athletes. In this sense, the image simultaneously shows an event and carries an underlying meaning or myth which potentially accumulates across different discursive events and within different genres. One could interpret this multimodal text as suggesting that they are all suspect, all potential villains, and in this image they all happen to be Black. Before I explore the discursive construction of Black athletes in the media further, let me turn to my second more recent example.

The 12 July 2010 cover of *Sports Illustrated* (Time Inc.) depicts the tennis player Serena Williams competing at Wimbledon during the Women's Finals at the All England Club (the cover can be viewed at Getty Images). The cover photograph, which foregrounds Williams, is accompanied by the caption 'Love

Figure 6.2 'Heroes and Villains'

Reproduced with the permission of Coloursport.

Her, Hate Her – She's the Best Ever'. The caption, taken together with the accompanying photograph, is an illustration of the caustic media coverage that this athlete has attracted over several years. She has, for example, been variously described as; 'childish', 'physically intimidating', 'masculine', 'aggressive', 'a rugby lock forward', as possessing the 'wingspan of a condor', as a 'heavyweight fighter' and a 'predator' (see Douglas, 2002). Much of the media coverage of Serena Williams has either implicitly or explicitly referred to her position as a Black female athlete in a 'White' sport (Douglas, 2002) and as such is at the intersection of discourses of race and gender.

Multimodal representations such as these 'resonate with a particular kind of racial imagery, one that always sees Black bodies as dangerous bodies' (Douglas, 2002: para. 2.6). The athletes in our two magazine covers are represented through a sharply opposite, polarised binary system: Hero/Villain and Love/Hate. Of course the binaries in operation here are not equal; in each there is a relation of power with one dominant pole (Derrida, 1981). In the Love/Hate binary, the evidence from media reports (Douglas, 2002) of numerous instances of offensive, disparaging and racist remarks suggests that 'Hate' is positioned as the dominant pole. The depiction of Ben Johnson at his moment of triumph in the knowledge that he has been disqualified for cheating positions villains as the dominant pole of the Heroes and Villains binary. These texts are part of a larger formation stretching over decades of discourse practice. Both of these magazine covers intersect with myriad representations of Black athletes in the media – 'superbly-honed athletic bodies, tensed for action, super-men and super-women encapsulating extreme alternatives which through a process of inter-textual representation act to essentialise, naturalise and fix difference' (Hall, 1997: 233).

When photographic representations of Black athletes in the media are read in context or in connection with one another, they accumulate meanings across different texts, and in this sense are 'intertextual' (Hall, 1997: 232). The combination of written text and photographic image work in concert to deploy an established multimodal device for 'making meaning'. At their *denotative* level of meaning, the photographs depict elite athletes performing at the peak of their profession. At the *connotative* level, the meaning of such photographs, together with their captions, are ambiguous and carry multiple potential messages. In attempting to discover the 'preferred meaning' of such photographs, we can 'read' the caption in conjunction with the image as an attempt anchor and 'fix' meaning (of 'belongingness' and 'otherness') in an effort to secure discursive or ideological closure, which in this example connects to a sub-theme of 'race' and difference. In order to analyse the above examples, analysts may want to explore and interpret the connotative meanings which they associate with them. I might, for example, interpret 'Love Her, Hate Her – She's the Best Ever' as suggesting that Black athletes, particularly successful ones, are not welcome in the sport of tennis, or that their presence will somehow alter the entire tennis 'culture'.

The images and their accompanying captions, like countless others associated with the planning, organising, marketing and reporting of events, are of course 'texts' and thus are part of a discourse open to critical analysis which has the potential to expose the relations of power embedded in the ideologies constructed through and circulated by language. As Wodak (2001) has noted, media texts are 'sites of struggle in that they show traces of differing discourses and ideologies contending and struggling for dominance'. Media texts are important sites for the production and contestation of competing narratives of race and ethnicity (McDonald, 2010). In the context of the foregoing discussion, we can say that as these multimodal texts are brought into play they act to retrieve past representations of 'otherness'. As Hall (1980, p. 134) suggests, preferred *meanings* become preferred *readings* when they are interpreted by audiences in ways that retain the institutional\political\ideological order imprinted on them.

In this regard, media images dissemble the extent to which they are aligned with the interests of powerful groups in society (Carter and Steiner, 2003). In the presence of such 'orders of discourse', the work of critical discourse studies is to disrupt 'the tranquillity with which they are accepted' and to 'show that they do not come about of themselves, but are always the result of a construction the rules of which must be known, and the justifications of which must be scrutinised' (Foucault, 1972: 25). When representations refer to the same object (e.g. 'difference' or 'otherness'), appear across a range of texts and at different institutional sites and share the same style or strategy, they produce what Foucault (1972) theorises as 'orders of discourse' or 'discursive formations' which in turn produce 'objects of knowledge' or subjects produced through discourse. Viewed as part of these dynamic processes, multimodal 'texts' are indeed a significant component of the language of events.

Developing critical discourse studies

The above examples have only briefly touched on aspects of 'discourse practices' associated with representations of Black athletes in sporting events. There are numerous other elements which would need to be addressed in any comprehensive analysis of the two images referred to here. However, in simple terms it is possible to develop research projects in which the analyst draws selectively on, for example, Fairclough (1989, 1995). Whatever the target of analysis, the analyst should first provide a text *description* posing questions such as those noted above.

In the *interpretation* stage the analyst could begin to ask questions relating to the production of the original text: (1) when was the text produced; (2) where, by whom and who was it produced for; (3) for what purpose; and (4) what are or were the social identities of the maker, owner and subject of the text? One could also investigate the editorial processes resulting in its selection (the editorial gaze), as well as its distribution, or the processes by which the texts are disseminated to audiences and the subsequent consumption or take-up of texts. I have already noted the importance of intertextuality in the accumulation of meaning and relations of power associated with any given text, and in the digital era the prevalence of intertextuality and its effects are likely to increase.

Moving to the dimension of social practice, explanation could include an analysis of the potential influences of the texts on, for example, social attitudes: (1) how is it shaped by institutional or societal power relations; and (2) is it deployed to sustain such relations or towards transforming them? These are just some of the processes through which the text enters discursive practice and circulates in and through social practice. As already noted, there are always an extensive number of potential leads which one could follow in conducting discourse analysis and ultimately there can never be a complete analysis. For many analysts, the available resources will determine the extent to which they continue an analysis in any given setting.

This brief exploration of media representations of elite sporting events/personalities through multimodal 'texts' provides an example of the constitutive role of discourses 'which are determined by social structures and which have effects upon social structures, thus contributing to the achievement of social continuity or social change' (Fairclough, 1989: 37). Of course, *event studies* analysts could also include less high-profile events, but which nonetheless may produce highly contested discourses within the socio-political arena. Likewise, through the prism of discourse, analysts could find countless sources of data dealing with social, economic and environmental aspects of events. One only has to review media outlets such as TV, newspaper, radio and websites in order to engage with the bourgeoning volumes of useful data which one might subject to CDA. In fact one of the difficulties the analyst is likely to face is an oversupply of potentially useful data (text and talk). In developing critical discourse studies scholars have, to date, analysed a wide variety of data including, but not limited to, political speeches, leaflets, posters, TV broadcasts, job advertisements, promotional videos, policy documents, interviews, university prospectuses, etc. The language of events is at different times and in different contexts filtered through such discursive events and thus provides a vast array of potential action agendas for event studies researchers/activists.

Discussion

This chapter has introduced CDA as an accessible and potentially productive research method in the field of Event Studies. While there are numerous schools within the broad 'movement' of CDA the discussion here has focused on Fairclough's (1989, 1995) interactional approach in the context of multimodal representation. The key characteristic of this approach, and one which is shared among CDAs diverse schools, is its commitment to working across *texts*, to exploring the broader *social interactions* within which they are embedded and the *social conditions* which influence, and are influenced by, their production and consumption. In considering the representation of racial stereotypes in and through the genre of sports journalism, I have noted how multimodal texts work to communicate 'preferred meanings' in seeking to fix difference.

In exploring an example of multimodal representation of Black athletes in sporting events, I have only briefly discussed aspects of text 'description' (dimension 1) within Fairclough's approach. There is much more work to do in order to conduct an analysis across all three interpenetrating dimensions of *text*, *discourse practice* and *social practice*. Yet I hope readers will begin to appreciate the potential of CDA as an approach to researching the discursive construction of events and the broader socio-political implications of such practice. As the modes of communication associated with events are increasingly characterised by participation and content curation, CDA offers the possibility of conducting critical research on complex socio-political currents through the discourses which both shape and are shaped by them.

It would be remiss of me to close a discussion of CDA as an approach to researching the meanings and role of events in society without reference to the productive potential of discourses. If CDA is concerned with the transformation of society and the empowerment of the oppressed, analysts will inevitably be confronted with the challenge of enabling constructive social action alongside the more common activity of 'deconstructing texts' in order to expose their ideological workings. As Martin (2004: 186) has argued in his call for a positive discourse analysis, 'we need a complementary focus on community, taking into account how people get together and make room for themselves in the world – in ways that redistribute power without necessarily struggling against it.' Because CDA takes an explicit socio-political stance, its practitioners must confront changing objects of study in and through blended and heteroglossic forms of representation and identity in the semiotic economy (Luke, 2002). In the academy, critical scholars/activists are often inhibited by dominant/established practices of governance pushing them to rethink how and what they research, how they write and where they publish. In the conduct of such moves, they may also produce spaces in which to examine the relationship between discourse and society, between the micro-politics of text and its macro-political context. Language and the social world are mutually shaping and, in this regard, events are both a catalyst for and an outcome of the kinds of constructive social action which is at the core of the CDA movement. In this sense, the performance of events provides a ground upon which scholar/activists have the opportunity to practise research which is both critical and positive.

References

Andersson, M. (2002) 'Identity work in sports: ethnic minority youth, Norwegian macro-debates and the role model aspect', *Journal of International Migration and Integration/ Revue De l'Intégration et de la Migration Internationale*, 3: 83–106.

Beasley, B. and Collins Standley, T. (2002) 'Shirts vs. skins: clothing as an indicator of gender role stereotyping in video games', *Mass Communication and Society*, 5: 279–93.

Blommaert, J. (2001) 'Context is/as critique', *Critique of Anthropology*, 21: 13–32.

Boykoff, J. and Yasuoka, M. (2015) 'Gender and politics at the 2012 Olympics: media coverage and its implications', *Sport in Society*, 18: 219–33.

Breeze, R. (2013) 'Critical discourse analysis and its critics', *Pragmatics*, 21: 493–525.

Carter, C. and Steiner, L. (2003) *Critical Readings: Media and Gender*. London: McGraw-Hill International.

Denzin, N. K. and Lincoln, Y. (eds) (2000) *The Handbook of Qualitative Research*. London: Sage.

Derrida, J. (1981) *Positions*, trans. A. Bass. London: Athlone Press.

Desmarais, F. and Bruce, T. (2010) 'The power of stereotypes: anchoring images through language in live sports broadcasts', *Journal of Language and Social Psychology*, 29: 338–62.

Douglas, D. D. (2002) 'To be young, gifted, black and female: a meditation on the cultural politics at play in representations of Venus and Serena Williams', *Sociology of Sport Online*, 5 (2): 1–23.

Fairclough, N. (1985) 'Critical and descriptive goals in discourse analysis', *Journal of Pragmatics*, 9: 739–63.

Fairclough, N. (1989) *Language and Power*. Harlow: Pearson.

Fairclough, N. (1992) *Discourse and Social Change*. Cambridge: Polity press.

Fairclough, N. (1995a) *Critical Discourse Analysis*. New York: Longman.

Fairclough, N. (1995b) *Media Discourse*. London: Edward Arnold.

Fairclough, N. (2003) *Analysing Discourse: Textual Analysis for Social Research*. London: Psychology Press.

Feighery, W. (2006) 'Reading tourism texts in context: a critical discourse analysis', *Tourism Analysis*, 11: 1–11.

Feighery, W. (2009) 'Tourism, stock photography and surveillance: a Foucauldian interpretation', *Journal of Tourism and Cultural Change*, 7 (3): 161–78.

Fink, J. S. and Kensicki, L. J. (2002) 'An imperceptible difference: visual and textual constructions of femininity in sports illustrated and sports illustrated for women', *Mass Communication and Society*, 5: 317–39.

Foucault, M. (1972) *The Archeology of Knowledge*, trans. A. M. Sheridan Smith. London: Tavistock.

Fowler, R., Hodge, R., Kress, G. and Trew, T. (1979) *Language and Control*. London: Routledge and K. Paul.

Hall, S. (1980) *Culture, Media, Language*. London: Routledge.

Hall, S. (1997) *Representation: Cultural Representations and Signifying Practices*. London: Sage.

Halliday, M. A. (1994) *An Introduction to Functional Grammar*. London: Routledge.

Hodge, R. I. V. and Kress, G. R. (1993) *Language as Ideology*. London: Routledge.

Huggins, M. (2008) 'The sporting gaze: towards a visual turn in sports history – documenting art and sport', *Journal of Sport History*, 35: 311–29.

Jäger, S. and Maier, F. (2009) 'Theoretical and methodological aspects of Foucauldian critical discourse analysis and dispositive analysis', in R. Wodak and M. Reisigl (eds), *Methods of Critical Discourse Analysis*, 2nd edn. London: Sage, pp. 34–61.

Julier, G. (2006) 'From visual culture to design culture', *Design Issues*, 22 (1): 64–76.

Kress, G. R. and Van Leeuwen, T. (1996) *Reading Images: The Grammar of Visual Design*. London: Psychology Press.

Levina, M., Waldo, C. R. and Fitzgerald, L. F. (2000) 'We're here, we're queer, we're on TV: the effects of visual media on heterosexuals' attitudes toward gay men and lesbians', *Journal of Applied Social Psychology*, 30: 738–58.

Liao, J. and Markula, P. (2009) 'Reading media texts in women's sport: critical discourse analysis and Foucauldian discourse analysis', in P. Markula (ed.), *Olympic Women and the Media: International Perspectives*. London: Palgrave Macmillan, pp. 30–49.

Luke, A. (2002) 'Beyond science and ideology critique: developments in critical discourse analysis', *Annual Review of Applied Linguistics*, 22: 96–110.

Martin, J. R. (2004) 'Positive discourse analysis: solidarity and change', *Revista Canaria de Estudios Ingleses*, 49: 179–200.

McDonald, M. G. (2010) 'The whiteness of sport media/scholarship', in H. Hundley and A. Billings (eds), *Examining Identity in Sports Media*. Thousand Oaks, CA: Sage, pp. 153–72.

Martin, L. L. (2015) *White Sports/Black Sports: Racial Disparities in Athletic Programs*. Santa Barbara, CA: ABC-CLIO.

Mautner, G. (2009) 'Checks and balances: how corpus linguistics can contribute to CDA', in R. Wodak and M. Meyer (eds), *Methods of Critical Discourse Analysis*, 2nd edn. London: Sage, pp. 122–43.

Militz, E. (2015) 'Welcome to paradise: the construction of the Azerbaijani nation in visual representations during the Eurovision song contest 2012', in R. Isaacs and A. Polese (eds), *Nation-building and Identity in the Post-Soviet Space: New Tools and Approaches*. Lanham, MD: Ashgate.

Miller, S. H. (1975) 'The content of news photos: women's and men's roles', *Journalism and Mass Communication Quarterly*, 52 (1): 70–5.

Phillips, N. and Hardy, C. (2002) *Discourse Analysis: Investigating Processes of Social Construction*. London: Sage.

Raj, R., Walters, P. and Rashid, T. (2013) *Events Management: Principles and Practice*. London: Sage.

Reisigl, M. and Wodak, R. (2009) 'The discourse-historical approach (DHA)', *Methods of Critical Discourse Analysis*, 2: 87–121.

Rojek, C. (2013) *Event Power: How Global Events Manage and Manipulate*. London: Sage.

Rose, G. (2011) *Visual Methodologies: An Introduction to Researching with Visual Materials*. London: Sage.

Santis, H. (1978) 'The democratization of travel: the travel agent in American history', *Journal of American Culture*, 1: 1–17.

Signorielli, N., McLeod, D. and Healy, E. (1994) 'Profile: gender stereotypes in MTV commercials: the beat goes on', *Journal of Broadcasting and Electronic Media*, 38: 91–101.

Silk, M. (2014) 'Neoliberalism and sports mega-events', in J. Grix (ed.), *Leveraging Legacies from Sports Mega-events: Concepts and Cases*. Houndsmills: Palgrave Macmillan, p. 50.

Standing, G. (2011) *The Precariat: The New Dangerous Class*. London: A & C Black.

Titscher, S. and Jenner, B. (2000) *Methods of Text and Discourse Analysis: In Search of Meaning*. London: Sage.

Tseng, Y.-H. (2015) 'Reproduction of the female image and nationalism in Taiwanese sport documentaries', *International Review for the Sociology of Sport*, 10 February. Advance publication at DOI: 10.1177/1012690214568732.

Van Dijk, T. A. (1993) Principles of critical discourse analysis. *Discourse and Society*, 4 (2): 249–283.

Van Dijk, T. A. (2008) *Discourse and Context: A Sociocognitive Approach*. Cambridge: Cambridge University Press.

Van Leeuwen, T. (1996) 'The representation of social actors', *Texts and Practices: Readings in Critical Discourse Analysis*, 1: 32–70.

Van Sterkenburg, J. and Knoppers, A. (2004) 'Dominant discourses about race/ethnicity and gender in sport practice and performance', *International Review for the Sociology of Sport*, 39: 301–21.

Wang, J. (2014) 'Criticising images: critical discourse analysis of visual semiosis in picture news', *Critical Arts*, 28, 264–86.

Williams, P. J. (1997) *Seeing a Color-blind Future: The Paradox of Race*. London: Macmillan.

Wodak, R. (2001) 'The discourse-historical approach', in R. Wodak and M. Meyer (ed.), *Methods of Critical Discourse Analysis*. London: Sage, pp. 63–94.

Wodak, R. and Meyer, M. (2009) *Methods for Critical Discourse Analysis*. London: Sage.

7 Visual methods in event studies

Dennis Zuev

Introduction

Visual methods such as photo-elicitation interviews, visual ethnography, participatory videos, visual critical analysis and visual documentation can considerably increase our understanding of the dynamics, interaction orders and institutional settings related to different public cultural events. While visuality is a prominent part of many events, the front stage of the spectacle often eclipses the larger context of the visual sphere and the backstage in which it has been produced. This chapter aims to provide a comprehensive view of how events can be approached from a visual sociological perspective. The chapter will give a brief overview of the main theoretical premises provided by sociology. Due to the limitations of space, it will not be possible to review in detail the theoretical and methodological foundations for visual sociology or event studies in this chapter.

Many events have found their way into films, videogames, cartoons and popular imagery. Protest events, disasters, celebrations and mega-events have all been represented in mass media, observed and recorded by billions of people, including bystanders, professional photojournalists and amateur photographers, and reproduced on the Internet. Events make people visualise them and, in an attempt to keep a memory of them, create multiple reproductions of different interactions that texturise these events. Most cultural events are laden with politics (Zuev and Virchow, 2014) and may be comprised of rituals with multiple meanings not normally visible to outsiders, common observers or tourists.

Visual knowledge about events

Standard social science methods are not perfectly adapted to the analysis of events as phenomena with complex interactions, actors and meanings. As Law and Urry (2004) suggest, social scientists have yet to develop methods that resonate well with important reality enactments. The multiple sensory, emotional and kinaesthetic elements of events elude traditional social scientific methods of inquiry. In visual anthropology, cinematographic language, in particular, has allowed us to delve into fields that have previously escaped academic research: emotions and feelings, relativity of behaviour and values, cultural meanings of body and cultural forms of expression, among others (Piault *et al.*, 2015). Visual anthropologists were the first social scientists to experiment with employing photography and film-making as another way of registering data to complement verbal forms of knowledge (Bateson and Mead, 1942). Photography, the most democratised and accessible visual practice, enables researchers to understand the politics around the images by viewing the photographs as relational, social objects and understanding what the photographers and subjects desired from the photos (Piault *et al.*, 2015).

Anthropologist documentary film-makers, such as Jean Rouch and David MacDougall, made their academic statements via visual narratives, pointing out that the nature of the social is complex, dynamic and ambiguous and can be a paradoxical site of cultural practice and experience (MacDougall, 1995). The tradition of visually registering the 'other' customs of indigenous societies has helped to further the use of visual media as a means of exploring indigenous aesthetics (Worth and Adair, 1972), investigating the properties of visual knowledge and considering the theoretical contributions. Visual methodology can also be used for studies of modern, urban landscapes and events in the home culture.

Visual methods, if used singularly, can hardly provide a panacea, but combined with other methods such as interviews (Harper, 2002), socio-historical analysis (Nathansohn and Zuev, 2013) or content analysis (Vergani and Zuev, 2011) provide a valuable tool for revealing the often missed patterns of human behaviour and the meanings of social interactions. The majority of academics employing visual methods suggest images need to be placed in the broader social and political context of the event (Doerr *et al.*, 2013; Margolis and Pauwels, 2011; Nathansohn and Zuev, 2013).

In this chapter, I suggest that a variety of events can be approached and studied through the application of visual methods, including the fine-grained visual analysis of interactions or interaction ritual chains (Collins, 2004) and various ceremonial events or rituals that also comprise festive events (religious and secular festivals). Depending on the attention of the media, an insignificant happening can become a media event and, at this junction, it is the responsibility of the visual sociologist to intervene and reveal the network of meanings attached to such an event.

Studying public events visually: capturing and analysing visual moments

Before getting to the visual analysis of public events, I would like to distinguish between several schools of studying them. Dayan and Katz (1992) suggest a media studies approach that describes media events as one-time events which celebrate not only solidarity but also pluralism and, thus, public displays are representative of social diversity. The anthropological stance, proposed by Don Handelman (1990, 1997), advocates public events as having two distinct metalogics. One is that of ritual, which he terms as 'transformation', and the other being that of spectacle, which is called 'presentation'. Sociologists, starting from Émile Durkheim (1912), have described the social significance of rituals. Erving

Goffman (2005) in his studies of interaction rituals in public and Randall Collins (2004) in his study of interaction ritual chains continued to use Durkheim's notion of ritual. The legacy of Goffman is of particular importance in the analysis of public events, as he pays major attention to the micro-interactions of individuals and displays. He suggested looking at public displays from a dramaturgical perspective, distinguishing between presentations of self at front stage and back stage, and described experience organisation being subject to dramatic scriptings. Goffman, without a doubt, offered a rich conceptual apparatus for the visual analysis of public events and public behaviour. He honoured the analysis of the face-to-face domain, which revealed large institutional forces behind micro-interactions. Distinguishing analytically various *interaction orders* (Goffman, 1982) allowed the researcher to deal with the various ways in which individuals cope with the bodily presence of others. Instead of speaking about eventful and routine interactions, Goffman (1982) proposed a different division of focused and unfocused interactions. In most everyday life-contexts, including tourist encounters or face-to-face encounters during cultural and other mass events, there is no fixed stage setting, as compared to a conventional theatre where the stage is redecorated for each successive act. Instead, social actors move through different settings that are organised and bound by specific socially construed rules of engagement or 'frames' (Goffman, 1974) or, as argued by Picard and Zuev (2014: 103), 'plots'. Plots are the sequence of events and settings experienced by tourists, rather than a specific moment of the trip or any specific attraction that tourists encounter (Goffman, 1974; Zuev and Picard, 2015). Plot refers to a socially construed narrative structure that allows social actors to frame their participation in social life through socially held scenarios, stories and cosmologies. One can argue that participants in very concrete *focused encounters* – for instance during a carnival in Cologne, a nationalist demonstration in Leipzig or during an Antarctic tourist cruise – despite the seeming difference and variety of their experiences, existences and motifs, follow, to a very large degree, the same 'plot'. It can be of particular value for a visual sociologist to reveal an underlying mythological or interactional order or an *interactional plot* of the event or, in Goffmanian terms, of a particular *focused encounter*.

Festivals, mega-events and national imaging

Anthropologists have contributed greatly to the study of cultural public events. Getz (2010) compiled a comprehensive literature review of more than 450 academic articles dedicated to festival studies within the strand of festival tourism, identifying nine major themes of festival experiences and meanings. Some of Getz's (2010) themes relate directly to visual aspects of festivals, such as carnivalesque and spectacle (Cavalcanti, 2001; Favero, 2007; Foley and McPherson, 2004; Knox, 2008) and lie on the periphery of the academic interest in 'hallmark events' (Getz, 2010). MacAloon's (1984) theory of spectacle is important when considering a cultural performance, with the risk that larger-than-life visual spectacles will replace or render insignificant the more fundamental purposes and expressions of festivity. Foley and McPherson (2004) analysed Edinburgh's Hogmanay Celebration from the perspectives of authenticity, festivity and televised spectacle, while Knox (2008) studied the process by which Scottish song traditions evolved to become public spectacles and tourism performances, in the context of assessing their authenticity. A part of festival studies is the study of carnivals; some of them, such as Rio's Carnival, are some of the greatest spectacles in the modern world, which have become transnational events and represent the place where they are held. The highlights of the carnival celebrations are the samba parades and bodily displays (DaMatta, 1991). Although the rules for bodily display, rhythm and spectacle are not very strict (Queiroz, 1985), carnival has transformed from a disorderly, uncontrolled celebration into highly regulated spectacle of great magnitude.

Picard (2015) in his study of festivals in Reunion, argues that the Goffmanian concept of frame has been underutilised by social scientists in the analysis of events. He proposes five basic analytical elements for investigation of the 'festive frame': context, narrative, dramaturgy, circulation and play (Picard, 2015). This argument

Figure 7.1 Carnival in Lisbon

(photograph by D. Zuev, 2010), a staged skirmish between the bourgeoisie (wearing black cylindrical hats) and working-class people (*povo*), represented by the figure of Ze Povinho (see http://ensina.rtp.pt/artigo/o-ze-povinho-de-rafael-bordalo-pinheiro/). The carnival is an event that provides a venue for non-violent protest through short political performances. The costumes associated with the event carry meanings. In some settings, carnival is still a rather non-hierarchical festival. The frame of the carnival is breaking the order and transgressing the boundaries by means of costumes and masks.

shifts the focus to the practices that comprise a certain event, the event's interactional order and the visualisation practices of this event. Visualisation practices can be of the immediate context and can be produced by an astonishing variety of actors: state media, police, academics, sympathisers, participants and spectators, among others. Different political frames or ideological codes become apparent in the visualisation of certain mega-events that have a wide international audience, have become political vehicles themselves and, thus, influence global politics and human lives. As has been contended by Frost (2015), festivals and carnivals are 'inevitably subjective, embodied and *lived*' (p. 2), which means that there is a whole galaxy of elements and particular details that can elude the attention of the most watchful observer (see Figures 7.1, 7.2 and 7.5 below). Thus the visual recording of events and subsequent detailed analyses can reveal underlying meanings associated with the event.

Olympic Games, expos and World Cups are rather ambiguous public events as they celebrate the host nation as much as they celebrate internationalism and the

Figure 7.2 Victory Day Parade

(photograph by D. Zuev, 2009). Celebrations not only allow commoners to participate in the festive frame, but also provide an annual site where common people can see the ruling-class elite make a public appearance, a ritual that serves to display the unity of the political elite with common citizens. Often, the main actors in the procession, the veterans, have their honorary role emphasised by being driven in open-top cars. In the photograph, the front-row leaders of the parade are the representatives of the political elite in the Krasnoyarsk region, Russia (*from centre-left to right*: the governor, the mayor and the speaker of the regional parliament).

universal human spirit in sports competition. Additionally, they are displays of sociability (Roche, 2000); however, they can also show breaches of contact between states. The 2014 Olympic Games in Sochi where some world leaders ignored the Games and the 1980 Olympic Games in Moscow are two such cases. These examples demonstrate that mega-events are not necessarily stages for display of universal human unity but are instead a convenient platform for protest. Mega-events, as defined by Roche (2000), 'are large scale cultural events which have a dramatic character, mass popular appeal and international significance' (p. 1). Mega-events, through series of set ceremonies and rituals (such as the opening and closing ceremonies of the Olympics), create a discourse of national identity (Chen *et al.*, 2012; Hogan, 2003; Puijk, 2000) and national sentiment (pride or shame; Traganou, 2010). Olympic Games, in particular, become paramount representations of nation, where patriotism is broadcast by means of opening and closing ceremonies (MacAloon, 1984).

Olympic Games, as much as festivals or carnivals, are large commercial ventures and tourist commodities and, thus, are subject to control, carefully planned public relations, advertising displays and marketing (Waitt, 1999), as they eventually function as vehicles for national image construction (Alekseyeva, 2014). To a great extent, provisional advertising and promotion of an event can contribute to a heightened sense of emotions (Mock, 2012) and create a visual political struggle. It is here that we deal with a crucial issue of the visual design and visual production of an event. To illustrate this, I will refer to the promotional images used during the 2014 Winter Olympics in Sochi. The male and female figures that were commissioned by the visual design studio Doping-Pong, were likened to (and thus criticised for) being representative of the mythical Aryan race, used by Leni Riefenstahl (1935) in the heroic visual narrative of the Berlin Olympics in *The Triumph of the Will* (Parfitt, 2011). The event and its visual surrounding became a target for political attack giving the dominant media the power to interpret the event to suit their broadcasts. For instance, an NBC broadcast showed an abridged version of the opening and closing ceremonies in Sochi (Sasson, 2014), while an article in *The Guardian* newspaper simply stressed that the event 'lacked soul', focusing on the figure of President Putin who was behind the whole project of bringing the Olympic Games to Sochi (Gibson, 2014). Apart from the politically grounded selective focus on the mega-events, the media may selectively dramatise particular sports or disciplines within the mega-event. For instance, Whannel (2006) used film-analysis to show the mythologisation of particular sporting events. Among these events, the mile offers particularly good material for drama as it is neither too long (e.g. the marathon) nor too short (e.g. the 100m); the story is easy to understand and the tactics simple enough to perceive and comprehend. Whannel (2006) shows that athletic events have a powerful hermeneutic structure with strong dramatic potential that is demonstrated through iconic narrative.

Apart from the Olympics and other sports events, a number of international contests have attracted the attention of researchers. One example is the Eurovision Song Contest (ESC), which has become a major cultural opportunity for statements of nationality and national self-assertion. Some researchers observe that the ESC has evolved to integrate Central and East European countries and the former Soviet republics (Iglesias, 2015; Ismayilov, 2012). In the recent past, the ESC has transformed from a mere singing contest to a national performance or spectacle, with some of the performances becoming associated with the countries that the singers represent. The contest, as with the other mega-events mentioned above, is a stage for banal nationalism (Billig, 1995) and national branding. As Fricker and Gluhovic (2013) contend, the ESC has become a symbolic contact zone between European cultures, an arena in which both national solidarity and participation in a European identity are confirmed, and a site where cultural struggles over the meanings, frontiers and limits of Europe are enacted. The ESC, as an event, gives us an interesting setting for the visual analysis of artistic ways to question racial, national and sexual boundaries, as well as to raise questions about inclusion and exclusion. The 2014 performance was marked by some right-wing groups condemning the performance of the bearded drag queen from Austria, Conchita Wurst, who went on to win the contest. Consequently, in Russia, Wurst's song 'Rise Like a Phoenix' topped the Internet download chart two days after the competition, prompting activist groups to organise a march of bearded women. At the same time, Vienna's tourist board used Wurst's image on the Facebook page 'Gayfriendly Vienna', to encourage more gay holidaymakers to visit the city. Wurst also became the front-stage actor for the 2014 annual London Gay Pride parade. The performance of Conchita Wurst, to some extent, illustrated that the ESC is not only an imaging event, but also an *iconogenic* (icon generating) event. Similar to expo and sports events, a single performance at the Eurovision Song Contest (as demonstrated by the Conchita Wurst case) helped a country gain international visibility and attention.

In addition to the backstage politics of the mega-event and the spectacle potential, there are several stages of mega-event organisation and visualisation. As Zuev (2010) demonstrated, it may be important to analyse the *pre-event*, *event* and *post-event* visual production stages, while the event itself can be successfully visually analysed in terms of its immediate spatial organisation and the roles that its participants play. In the case of the nationalist demonstration in Moscow, it was apparent that much of the pre-event visual persuasion to participate was organised online through video-interviews of the organising committee, event posters and flyers available for free download, as well as event merchandise (e.g. T-shirts, badges) that could be bought without attending the event. The immediate event visualisation was not only conducted by professional photographers (see Figure 7.3), but also by ordinary observers who posted their visual reports online after the event was over.

It is common for a single contentious photograph to become an iconic image of an event. Such a photograph may continue to spark online discussions, memes and Photoshop play well after the event is over (Zuev, 2010). Askanius (2013) demonstrated that much activity, organisation and planning of key events takes place online. Protest events not only have a lengthy online trajectory that runs prior to mass direct action, but also take on an afterlife in the trails of audiovisual documentation they leave behind in online settings (e.g. YouTube). YouTube helps

Figure 7.3 The 2007 Annual Russian March in Moscow

(photograph by D. Zuev, 2007). The visualisations of the event can be contrastingly different, as different visual codes (e.g. optical code (lens angle), colour, composition) are used to represent the event (note the photographers' selection of an elevated position over the crowd of marchers).

decentralise the reading of a single event. It challenges the hegemony of state media coverage of controversial events (e.g. events associated with violence and/or death). YouTube, as a globally available media (with the exception of a few states that block its use), has becomes a global channel for streaming the unedited versions of events, both violent and festive and tragic and celebratory. YouTube constitutes a key arena for the distribution and mobilisation of images to support and sustain political activism (Askanius *et al.*, 2013: 127).

Public protest events

A visual approach is instrumental in addressing events of national identity and nationalism issues: national days, national ceremonies (Uzelac, 2010), cultural and political events (Zuev and Virchow, 2014), particular protest events (Garret, 2013; Zuev, 2013) and political rituals in collective action (e.g. demonstrations, protest events) (Casquette, 2003). National days present us with an opportunity to analyse the often contesting displays of patriotism and national pride (Zuev, 2013). Parades and organised rallies during national days are convenient windows through which to investigate the 'theatre of power' (Leong, 2001), 'visual poetry'

(Kuever, 2012) or commercialisation of memory (Norris, 2011). In the case of National Day in Singapore and Victory Day in Russia, events have both a sacred and a commercial consumerist touch. Such events also serve as an interface of power display, and create a particular interaction order between common citizens and the political elite (see Figure 7.2). National holidays as annual celebrations are comprised of rituals that often need to be unravelled in their immediate context and seen at the particular place and time (see Figure 7.4).

National days, as much as Olympic Games ceremonies, provide a front stage for nations that have deep-layered tensions between their ethnic majority and

Figure 7.4 Some of the commemorative events and celebrations have a number of staple ritual interactions, such as this flower giving act between the Great Patriotic War veteran and a schoolgirl on Victory Day in Russia.

To interpret this photograph (by D. Zuev, 2009), one has to know not only the exact setting where the act takes place, but also the tradition of flower giving that has been in effect since the Great Patriotic War ended. Flower giving is an act of generational exchange, of nurturing gratification, an expression of patriotism and a practice of keeping historical memory alive. Visual documentation is often best if a sequence of images of the same situation is presented, thus better facilitating the process under question (see Zuev, 2012) ethnic minorities. Through days linked to nationalism, ethnic minorities are allowed a legitimate channel in which to display their pride and to celebrate their cultural differences (through music, dance and costumes). The St Patrick's Day celebration, as a transnational event of celebrating 'Irishness' (Scully, 2012) or Celtic culture, is a far less contested performance of national identity than the Orange Parades which celebrate religion, class and ethnic rifts and often become vehicles of sectarianism. As Bryan (2000) argued, parades as a form of visual display provide a window for investigating how diverse class interests attempt to control rituals and how this control is exercised through the contestation of the meanings of symbols. Consequently, by analysing visual displays and their visual politics, researchers can gain insights into power relations in the given society.

In his study of the protests centred on Hong Kong identity and the confrontations between Hong Kong and the Chinese mainland, Garrett (2013) used a visual approach to analyse the visual narrative of resistance as well as to reveal the major expressive equipment of the Hong Kong protesters. He observed that protests in Hong Kong are very different from aggressive protests elsewhere and are often a family affair. The visualisation practices of protesters in Hong Kong also have peculiar features, such as the use of iPads to display protest materials. This visualisation practice is demonstrative of the social composition of the protest crowd. The visualisation of some everyday moments as 'incidents' of cultural differences between Hong Kongers and Mainland Chinese ignited a wider protest. Visual documentation of the expressive equipment of the protesters and their display techniques allow us to recreate the context and symbolic narrative of protest events, as well as to see how a protest event is embedded in a city space and thus how it may be viewed by passers-by. Protest events provide a valuable venue to see a rather opposite process to icon generation: the process of iconoclasm, or when the political authority and its images are not simply questioned and opposed but transformed in a comical or destructive way in order to attack and damage their subject.

Doerr *et al.* (2013) made a key contribution in addressing the large gap in the visual study of social movements and protest events by focusing on the visual expressions of social movements through images and other visual artefacts, the visual representation of social movements by actors external to social movements and the visibility of social movements in larger social contexts. As the authors contend, commercial and public mass media no longer have a monopoly over the visual representation of events. This is symptomatic of what Guattari termed the post-media era (Brunner *et al.*, 2013), where a multitude of diverging visual narratives of one event are produced, shared and contested. These diverging narratives, produced by post-media activists with their portable media devices, have questioned the traditional dichotomy of online-offline, stressing that with portable visual media one can be continuously online and, thus, visualisation can be instantaneous and relatively devoid of control by media editors. Progress in visual media technology has made technology such as digital cameras, smartphones, Go-pro cameras and mini drones equipped with cameras readily available to many audiences, thus enabling a qualitative leap forward in the visual representation of events, in particular facilitating qualitatively different vertical visualisation of events.

The visual sphere becomes an important site of power struggle (Nathansohn and Zuev, 2013). Thus the goal of the visual analysis is to identify different frames of an event, why these specific images of the event are used, what they signify for different kinds of audiences and what kind of audiences are being targeted. An example of such a protest event or *moment* (rather than movement) in the wave of social mobilisation was the occupation of Zuccotti Park in New York in 2011 (Calhoun, 2013). As Calhoun defined, movements are '... relatively long-term collective engagements in producing or guiding social change' (2013: 29). The case of the Zucotti Park occupation demonstrated how a brief act of symbolic occupation of public space could become a brief event, a moment at a point in the continuum of the protest. The nature of this public claim of a space which is normally controlled by government and police, its briefness, contention and conflictuality in the public sphere, make it a relevant object for a visual interrogation. This brief occupation of space by common citizens is a process that can be well registered and analysed visually. The space is open and accessible, and participants create their own accounts of the event and share them via social media. Thus a visual researcher has not only his/her version of the event, but also a universe of official and informal accounts representing diverse ideological codifications or *visual keying* of the event. Goffman's (1974) concept of visual keying was applied by Luhtakallio (2013) in her study of the reproduction and change of dominant gender framings created by activists in their own visualisation of protest events. As Luhtakallio demonstrates, visual analysis combined with ethnographic observation of visual representations of political struggle make the bodily and gendered groundings of contention more transparent (Luhtakallio, 2013).

As demonstrated by the Zucotti Park occupation, a protest event often has to do with the claiming or reclaiming of space. Political demonstration as an event has spatial and temporal limits which have to be negotiated with the authorities. Understanding the relational dynamics between event organisers and the municipal authorities is crucial in addressing the question of what sort of public visibility the authorities will allow for a particular event (Zuev, 2013). Negotiations over the central location of the performance and the specific route to be taken became the central conflict point between activists and city authorities during the Russian Marches in Moscow between 2006 and 2013, which demonstrates that activists are not always satisfied with being granted permission to perform a ritual and may further seek a wider audience and visibility in the public space. Sanctioned protest events take place in a locality easily controlled by police and often in one not conducive to giving the performance a high level of visibility. The question of visibility is closely related to the main communicative function of the demonstration marches, as perceived by the leaders of the movement. As Virchow (2007) noted, marches are used '... as a tool to expand the movement and disseminate the political ideas and self-perception of its activists' (p. 299). It makes a big difference to the visual politics if the march can be organised in a central location rather than in marginal residential districts. At the same time, a marginal location may allow for wider expressive equipment otherwise not allowed in the city centre. Communications prior to the nationalist marches in Russia between 2006 and

2013 took place in the 'third place' of the Internet, and continued in the shape of visual memories (e.g. video and photo-blogs, user comments) long after the event.

As the case of the nationalist day celebrations in Moscow demonstrate, the sanctioned demonstration also has to be maximally expressive and symbolically condensed, as occupation of public space is restricted in time (Zuev, 2010, 2013). The march not only provides a spatial focus for the nationalist movement's visual self-presentation, but also a place for informal encounters, fairs, recruitment and entertainment, thus providing a break in routine life and creating backstage micro-arenas for visual sociological inquiry. In spontaneous, one-time events, such as visits by famous personalities or the celebration of victories, a visual researcher has to be very careful in the analysis of how spontaneous interaction order is maintained, and how people interact when claiming the city (see Figure 7.5 – a photograph of celebrations on the occasion of the Portuguese football team Benfica winning the national championship title).

Figure 7.5 Celebration following the national league championship

(photograph by D. Zuev, 2010). This photograph was taken during the celebration of the Benfica football team victory in the national league championship. The streets and the central square of Marques de Pombal were occupied by celebrating crowds with the Benfica insignia. Red scarves became objects with transcendental value. The poster held by the woman shows the iconoclastic process of such popular celebration (e.g., the statue of Jesus Christ (Cristo Rei) in Lisbon wearing a red T-shirt/cloak with Benfica emblem). The red colour, and the emblem and epithets of the team (SLB *'Sport Lisboa e Benfica'*, glorious, the eagles) became markers of the *in situ* constructed group. The worship and emotional solidarity across class and ethnic boundaries demonstrated the permeating emotion invested in the spirit of football fandom.

A visual moment is a singular event, but it can be a spectacle event that triggers great change, even making the main character of such an event an iconic person. For instance, the self-immolation of a Tunisian vendor, Muhammad Bouazizi, sparked the Jasmine Revolution in Tunisia. The act of Bouazizi's self-immolation, although not recorded visually, has been widely circulated in the media as a poster and caricature (Zuev, 2012). Many events organised by activists and covered by the media take place in the city. Thus the city becomes the central stage and central actor in the staging of events. Cities are selected due to their aesthetic, political and economic appeal. They are further prepared, decorated and reimagined for the event, and they and their inhabitants are transformed by this event. The urban changes and the urban textures that weave into the event are perhaps one of the most interesting areas of inquiry for a visual sociologist, as they inevitably touch upon a number of larger social conflicts and issues. These details are best grasped by fine-grained visual analysis and observation.

Visualising the context of the event: seeing the invisible city

As Jon Wagner and Marcus Banks have stated, visual studies are nothing more and nothing less than a study of material culture (Margolis and Pauwels, 2011). Cities, in this respect, are the concentration of material culture and changes in the city help us to follow the transformation of materiality (Krase, 2013). But what can and should one see in the city to deepen one's analysis of events? I argue that the city, or urban space, in the analysis of the events remains an invisible entity, despite being the stage or even multiple stages on which various events are played out. The invisibility of the urban design and planning, and multiple connections between the materiality of the city, the public and private spheres, mobile and static subjects, and ethnic and racial boundaries in the city are some of the themes that visual researchers can successfully interrogate when studying events. The meta-narratives within a city are produced by media, infrastructures, design of the city and the urban grid or planning. Any of these components may facilitate or impede certain events. The key architectural topographical or historical features, which may be used by event organisers to emphasise their claims, enhance identity and enforce ideological statements sometimes making the event more commercially successful and memorable. These features may elude non-visual analyses; however, they are the ones on which the visual scientist should focus. A visual researcher should be capable of registering both the vernacular and festive rhythms of the city that contribute to the visual regimes of city life. This can be achieved through a combination of longitudinal visual documentation and different scales of observation of the locale of the event (Desjeux, 1996).

Often, due to their sensational character, visualised events will provide insightful and useful evidence of the material culture of the cities. In this respect, visuals of events not only help to reconstruct the event itself, but also the surrounding material culture of an event. Traganou (2010) made an insightful study of Olympic stadiums, which have become perfect vehicles for the anesthetisation of politics.

Often stadiums are commissioned from foreign designers, who are tasked with incorporating national ideals in the construction project of a stadium. For example, Athens' Calatrava Stadium resurrected the lofty ideals of Hellenism, symbolically stressing the Greek entrance into the twenty-first century. Likewise, an Olympic stadium in Beijing designed by Herzog and Meuron was based on the ideas of a public vessel, and its construction was influenced by the ideas of Chinese ceramics. The Sochi Olympic Games Fisht Stadium was commemorated by the Central Bank of Russia on a 100-rouble banknote and initially was planned to be reminiscent of a Fabergé Easter egg. Olympic stadiums, the main setting for national propaganda during an Olympic mega-event, become national icons even before the games begin. They represent the nation not only at the event, but also after the event has taken place. In some cases, these structures become underutilised and expensive 'white elephants' after the spectacle is over (Weissmann, 2012), or even ghosts, as was the case with the Sarajevo Winter Olympics facilities (Walker, 2012). Mega-events, as argued by Roche (1994), are short-term events that have long-term consequences for the cities that host and stage them. And often infrastructures have to be created from scratch causing major protests and struggle (as was the case with the opposition to the 2014 Football World Cup in Brazil). Some mega-events lead to comprehensive urban redesign, when several residential areas can be razed in order to create space for the event facilities. Such was the case with the World Expo, 1998, in Lisbon, Portugal, where several thousand dwellings of predominantly underclass urban residents (e.g. ethnic minorities of Roma and African origin) had to be relocated to the fringes of the city. These kinds of urban changes that lead to transformations of the urban visual texture need to be addressed by visual researchers to better understand how the urban landscape is visually redesigned along the lines of class, ethnicity and income.

One important methodological point to consider in the visual approach to studies of events is the consideration of the scale of the events that are being visualised and the importance of alternating the scale of observation between macro and micro (see Figures 7.6 and 7.7). Doing so allows for the consideration of macro elements, such as plot and context, but also the face-to-face domain related to micro-interactions and practices.

In contrast to the large-scale national or global encounters – mega-events – the underlying plots and visual politics serve as an excellent starting point for analysis of the practices and events that are part of the domestic cult, part of the private family life (Peixoto, 2008). As Bourdieu (1990) argued, the photographic practice of a family solemnises and eternalises the most important events and moments of family life. A simple look at a family photo album can reveal the events that reaffirm the affective unity of the family as a group. Such events may include profound rites of passage in the formation of the family (e.g. weddings, births, family trips) (Haldrup and Larsen, 2003) or unfocused interactions and vernacular events. It is no longer necessary to access private photo albums for the visual analysis of private events as Facebook and other social networking sites have opened many such events to the public through the service of photo-sharing. Indeed, a Facebook user may feel obliged to post, edit and comment on photos of

Figure 7.6 Photograph of the 2011 May Day Rally after the march in Alameda Square, Lisbon (by D. Zuev, 2011). The aerial photograph gives the scale of the event, the urban context which conditions the event and elements of expressive equipment, as well as illustrating the interaction order during the rally.

their everyday life moments, thus demonstrating the eventfulness of their personal life. Alternatively, the failure to post photos of ongoing life events can signify a decrease in popularity or social networking site (SNS) oblivion. Photographic activity on Facebook is a way to stay alive socially, reaffirm one's agency and maintain or grow an extensive social network. Facebook and other SNSs provide researchers with a new data repository for exploring events of varying scale.

The following section focuses on the nature of visual data production and collection. I raise the two questions: (1) what are the units of visual analysis; and (2) what are the basic principles of visual analysis in the context of event studies?

The nature of visual data collection and visual data analysis

It is beyond the scope of this chapter to cover in detail the various methods and techniques of visual analysis and data collection. However, it is crucial to note that visual analysis and data collection in anthropological tradition has two dominant strands: film-making and the analysis of still images. The intricacies of film-making and the issues related to it have been extensively covered (see Banks and Morphy, 1997; Hockings, 2003; MacDougall, 1995, 2011). The principles of using photography as a method have also been covered in the literature (see

Figure 7.7 Photograph of the 2011 May Day demonstration

(by D. Zuev, 2011). This image is from the same May Day demonstration (see Figure 7.6 Photo 2) in Lisbon, but with a different scale of observation and focus. In this photograph, the emphasis is on individual participants, or rather interactions in a group of participants in the same march, and their different modes of address and communication. There is a distinct choreography in the mass events and emotional management, for example the symbol of the Carnation revolution. At the same time other participants diversify the symbolic order by adding new meanings, as exemplified by the young man in the photograph climbing up the monument to hoist the flag of Palestine.

Collier and Collier, 1986; Harper, 2012). Film-making as a research practice has long been a subject of debate, but, as argued by MacDougall (2011), it is an important way of focusing on details and the experiences of individuals, thus providing a close-up and detail-rich narrative of dynamic happenings and social situations. As MacDougall (2011) remarked: in anthropological film-making one should strike a balance between being an anthropologist, who wants to cover everything, and being a film-maker, who is eager to create a conventional dramatic structure in order to attract an audience. MacDougall has been one of the proponents of collaborative film-making, whereby a film-maker allows his subjects to include a more interior perspective. One of the greatest assets of a film, according to MacDougall (2011), is 'its ability to reach across cultural boundaries through those aspects of life that are common to many societies' (p. 111).

Visual sociologists have largely employed still images often in combination with traditional qualitative data collection techniques such as interviews (Harper, 2002; Schwartz, 1989) or surveys (Corrigall-Brown and Wilkes, 2012). It is also relevant to note that visual data can be produced by the researcher (photo and video documentation), the researcher can analyse existing visual data or data can be (co) produced by both the researcher and the research subjects (Milne *et al.*, 2012). Photo-elicitation interviews provide a particularly useful method of incorporating visual data in the study of events. Lapenta (2011) detailed four approaches to photo-elicitation. Epstein *et al.* (2006) synthesised the following main questions related to photo-elicitation interviews: (1) who is going to make or select the images to be used in the interviews; (2) what is the content of the images going to be; (3) where are the images going to be used and how? As was noted previously, the images of events are produced by multiple actors and often the suggested readings of them are conflicting. One solution is to combine participant-generated, researcher-generated and media-generated images. Participant- or respondent-generated image production, often known as reflexive photography, was introduced by Harper (1988). Reflexive photography implies that respondents elaborate on the content and meaning of photographs they have produced themselves, instead of being presented with photos taken by a researcher. Photo-elicitation interviews with participants at one-time events can be problematic (but not impossible) since one may not have access to the group, which is often created *in situ*. With protest events and other organised events (e.g. celebrations) a researcher will require similar social skills and serendipity in gaining access to the informants as in other types of research. The clear advantage of photo-elicitation is that it may stimulate a much deeper discussion of the event beyond the photo itself, thus making a photo a valuable material stimulus. With the increasing popularity of amateur film-making, videos may be even more accessible for photo-elicitation focus group interviews when the video is discussed and that discussion is moderated by a researcher.

Without a doubt, photojournalistic accounts remain as useful visual data for studying events. One of the advantages of using photojournalistic accounts is their neutrality in that they do not reflect the position of the researcher or the respondent. It is also possible to study an image's impact through content analysis of the viewers' comments (if this feature is enabled online). This is particularly important when studying the impact of the videos on YouTube. At times, photographs produced during significant events become iconic and are later used as murals, stencil graffiti and/or as propaganda material. Such images may become decontextualised, with the link to the original event becoming obscure. However, it is also true that some events become associated with a particular photo that was produced by a photojournalist. One single moment captured by a photojournalist is transformed into an event as it becomes an iconic image for something larger. For example, a photo of a self-immolating monk by Malcolm Browne (1963) has become a staple photo of silent anti-war protest. 'Ulster's boy petrol-bomber' by Clive Limpkin (1969) became a symbol for violent resistance and identity politics. The death of a protester in Genoa captured by Dylan Martinez (2001) during an anti-globalisation protest became a metonym of the anti-globalisation movement (Perlmutter and Wagner, 2001).

The annual World Press Photo contests demonstrate that the winners are often photojournalists covering sensational events, natural disasters, crises or war conflicts. At the same time, some of the photographs become iconic representations of global events and can be important avenues through which to analyse the different ways of representing these events (Barcelos, 2009). Visualisation of death or 'about to die' moments are an integral part of studying events (Zelizer, 2010; Yang, 2011). Visualisation of pain, suffering and death, as well as disclosing the identity of the people in the events, are some of the key ethical issues that researchers have to consider when relying on their own visual material (Grønstad and Gustafson, 2012). A visual researcher must subject his/her work to self-censorship and make moral judgments about the publication of the material and people's potential perceptions (MacDougall, 2011).

Some analytical caveats

In this section, some caveats for the visual analysis of events are suggested. The first point is that a researcher should try to get a holistic, systemic view of the event in visual sociological perspective. This means that a visual analysis should encompass various types of data, which are not necessarily photographs or videos. Data may include three-dimensional material objects, which often go overlooked by visual researchers (see Emmison and Smith, 2007). Second, after a systemic collection of data related to the event has occurred, the analysis should focus on eliciting dominant themes and narratives, as well as tensions and inconsistencies. The second point should include not overloading the analysis with too many visuals (images). An overabundance of photos, for instance, may detract from the analysis as the images are seen as mere illustrations and thus remain under-analysed. Instead, it is recommended that the research use a smaller number of visuals and analyse each in detail (as Becker (1974) suggests to beginners in visual sociology). The selection of visuals must be grounded and carefully argued; the rationale behind choosing the images becomes an important part of the visual analysis itself. It may happen that some of the visuals are low quality (not commercially suitable); nevertheless, they carry very important data and, therefore, need to be explained in detail. Photographs or visuals do not have to be beautiful pieces of art to be valid visual data. When analysing images the researcher might need to conduct a brief socio-historical analysis to better contextualise the images being used. Perhaps even provide an etymology of the image, in order to uncover the 'rhizomic'[1] structure of it; for example, an image with hypertext may include a citation of some previous iconic photograph, poster or image.

As I have already mentioned above, the analysis of the event in totality, provided that the researcher can participate in the event, should comprise *pre-event visualisation* (in the Internet, in other media and in the street and public space) and *the immediate observation and documentation of the event* by the researcher or people assisting the researcher in other places. During the immediate observation and documentation stage, images can be already made according to a shooting script (Suchar, 1997), thus answering particular questions posed by the researcher. Visuals or observations in this case become evidence for the theoretical claims.

The final stage is *post-event visualisation* where visual politics are again occupying media and alternative media space, thus creating a new channel for visual politics, distortion and reproduction of the frames of the event. In the analysis of post-event visualisation, it can be instrumental to employ the framework suggested by Pauwels (2005) for the hybrid cultural analysis of websites, or his multimodal framework for the analysis of websites (Pauwels, 2012) which implied six stages. Nowadays, a significant part of event coverage happens due to social media users who not only consume images, but also produce them, hence becoming *prosumers* (Vergani and Zuev, 2015). One important source for event visual analysis is the visual data repository and social networking site YouTube. As some researchers suggest in their YouTube analysis (Vergani and Zuev, 2013, 2015), researchers must be flexible in the analysis of YouTube videos, as they are a relatively heterogeneous type of data in terms of genre and structure. Two techniques can be employed: narrative analysis and the construction of inventories of verbal and visual symbols. Narrative analysis best suits the continuous real-life videos and this inventory technique is suitable for slideshow videos. Many people watch YouTube videos and move on, without spending much time on the site; yet, others spend hours watching YouTube videos. YouTube has many mechanisms for drawing people in to the 'video vortex' of watching (and commenting on) videos.

Finally, images ideally should help to contribute theoretical knowledge about the issue in question. It is a question of choosing which images to focus on and one must ground the selection of the photographs. Often, the process or community that is being researched can be summarised and investigated with the provision of a few single images, produced by the author or collected from other sources (in this case copyright issues will arise). Documentation of social processes often gains from the presentation of a sequence of images that are accompanied by thick-description and contextualisation. It is more difficult to use films as data, especially when using YouTube videos, but often the technique of analysing the whole video and then its parts can be employed. Screenshots from the videos help to illustrate the concepts in the video that is being analysed (for an example, see Vergani and Zuev, 2015).

Conclusion

The purpose of this chapter was threefold: first, to give a taste of how events can be approached visually; second, to describe which theoretical approaches are best suited to analyse particular features of these events; and third, to identify the potential thematic lines of inquiry that visual research can help to develop within event studies. When researching events, the researcher need not be a professional photographer or film-maker; instead, they may reimagine an event and use visual data in a way that questions the dominant readings of this event.

The potential of visual methods is constantly being reassessed as new media provide new affordances which raise new questions of self-censorship, ethics and data-sharing. Without a doubt, as in any other field where visual methods have been used up to now, the thrust of the visual analysis will be most effective in combination with other methods. However, the iconic turn in the social sciences may imply that visual methods are in no way subservient to other approaches and indeed carry their own weight; they can be applied at the exploratory stage, while the decisions about which other methodologies to use for research projects are still emerging. The huge number of images available cannot be used as an excuse for under-theorising the visuals selected, despite their aesthetic and technical quality. Images may speak more than a thousand words but are even more valuable when they are shown to advance theoretical arguments.

Note

1. Here, I refer to the definition of rhizome by Deleuze and Guattari (1980).

References

Alekseyeva, A. (2014) 'Sochi 2014 and the rhetoric of a new Russia: image construction through mega-events', *East European Politics*, 30 (2): 158–74.

Askanius, T. (2013) 'Protest movement and spectacles of death: from urban places to video spaces', in N. Doerr, A. Mattoni and S. Teune (eds), *Advances in the Visual Analysis of Social Movements*, Research in Social Movements, Conflicts and Change, Vol. 35. Bingley: Emerald Group, pp. 105–33.

Banks, M. and Morphy, H. (1997) *Rethinking Visual Anthropology*. London: Yale University Press.

Barcelos, J. D. (2009) 'Fotojornalismo: dor e sofrimento: estudo de caso do World Press Photo of the Year 1955–2008'. MA thesis, Universidade de Coimbra.

Bateson, G. and Mead, M. (1942) *Balinese Character: A Photographic Analysis*. New York: New York Academy of Sciences.

Becker, H. S. (1974) 'Photography and sociology', *Studies in the Anthropology of Visual Communication*, 1: 3–26.

Billig, M. (1995) *Banal Nationalism*. London: Sage.

Bourdieu, P. (1990) *Photography. A Middle-brow Art*. Stanford, CA: Stanford University Press.

Brunner, C., Nigro, R. and Raunig, G. (2013) 'Post-media activism, social ecology and eco-art', *Third Text*, 27 (1): 10–16.

Bryan, D. (2000) *Orange Parades: The Politics of Ritual, Tradition and Control*. London: Pluto Press.

Calhoun, C. (2013) 'Occupy Wall Street in perspective', *British Journal of Sociology*, 64 (1): 26–38.

Casquette, J. (2003) *From Imagination to Visualization: Protest Rituals in the Basque Country*, Discussion Papers. Retrieved 12 May 2014 from: http://www.ssoar.info/ssoar/

bitstream/handle/document/11177/ssoar-2003-casquete-from_imagination_to_visualization.pdf?sequence=1.

Cavalcanti, M. (2001) 'The Amazonian Ox Dance Festival: an anthropological account', *Cultural Analysis*, 2: 69–105.

Chen, C. C., Colapinto, C. and Luo, Q. (2012) 'The 2008 Beijing Olympics opening ceremony: visual insights into China's soft power', *Visual Studies*, 27 (2): 188–95.

Collier, J. and Collier, M. (1986) *Visual Anthropology: Photography as a Research Method*. Albuquerque, NM: University of New Mexico Press.

Collins, R. (2004) *Interaction Ritual Chains*. Philadelphia: University of Pennsylvania Press.

Corrigall-Brown, C. and Wilkes, R. (2012) 'Picturing protest: the visual framing of collective action by first nations in Canada', *American Behavioural Scientist*, 56 (2): 223–43.

DaMatta, R. (1991) *Carnivals, Rogues, and Heroes: An Interpretation of the Brazilian Dilemma*. Notre Dame, IN: University of Notre Dame Press.

Dayan, D. and Katz, E. (1992) *Media Events: The Live Broadcasting of History*. Cambridge, MA: Harvard University Press.

Deleuze, G. and Guattari, F. (1980) *A Thousand Plateaus*, trans. Brian Massumi. London: Continuum, 2004. Volume 2 of *Capitalism and Schizophrenia*, 2 vols, 1972–80, trans. of *Mille Plateaux*. Paris: Les Editions de Minuit.

Desjeux, D. (1996) 'Scales of observation: a micro-sociological epistemology of social science practice', *Visual Studies*, 11 (2): 45–55.

Doerr N., Mattoni, A. and Teune, S. (2013) *Advances in the Visual Analysis of Social Movements*, Research in Social Movements, Conflicts and Change, Vol. 35. Bingley: Emerald Group.

Durkheim, E. (1912) *Les Formes élémentaires de la vie religieuse: le système totémique en Australie*. Paris: E. Alcan. (English trans., 2008, as *The Elementary Forms of Religious Life*, trans. Joseph Ward Swain. Mineola, NY: Dover.)

Emmison, M. and Smith, P. (2007) *Researching the Visual*. London: Sage.

Epstein, I., Stevens, B., McKeever, P. and Baruchel, S. (2006) 'Photo elicitation interview (PEI): using photos to elicit children's perspectives', *International Journal of Qualitative Methods*, 5 (3): 1–9.

Favero, P. (2007) 'What a wonderful world! On the "touristic ways of seeing", the knowledge and the politics of the "culture industries of otherness"', *Tourist Studies*, 7 (1): 51–81.

Foley, M. and McPherson, G. (2004) 'Edinburgh's Hogmanay in the society of the spectacle', *Journal of Hospitality and Tourism*, 2 (2): 29–42.

Fricker, K. and Gluhovic, M. (2013) *Performing the 'New' Europe. Identities, Feelings and Politics in the Eurovision Song Contest*. Basingstoke: Palgrave Macmillan.

Frost, N. (2015) 'Anthropology and festivals: festival ecologies', *Ethnos: Journal of Anthropology*. Advance online publication at: http://dx.doi.org/10.1080/00141844.2014.989875.

Garrett, D. (2013) 'Visualizing protest culture in China's Hong Kong: recent tensions over integration', *Visual Communication*, 12: 55–70.

Getz, D. (2010) 'The nature and scope of festival studies', *International Journal of Event Management Research*, 5 (1): 1–47.

Gibson, O. (2014) 'Sochi 2014: for all the nagging concerns the legacy will be the thrills', *Guardian*, 22 February. Retrieved 8 August 2015 from: http://www.theguardian.com/sport/blog/2014/feb/22/sochi-2014-winter-olympics-legacy.

Goffman, E. (1974) *Frame Analysis. An Essay on the Organization of Experience*. Boston: Northeastern University Press.

Goffman, E. (1982) 'The interaction order', *American Sociological Review*, 48 (1): 1–17.

Goffman, E. (2005) *Interaction Ritual: Essays in Face-to-Face Behaviour*. New Brunswick, NJ: Transaction Publishers.

Grønstad, A. and Gustafson, H. (2012) *Ethics and Images of Pain*. New York: Routledge.

Haldrup, M. and Larsen, J. (2003) 'The family gaze', *Tourist Studies*, 3 (1): 23–46.

Handelman, D. (1990) *Models and Mirrors: Towards an Anthropology of Public Events*. Oxford: Berghahn Books.

Handelman, D. (1997) 'Rituals/spectacles', *International Social Science Journal*, 49 (153): 387–99.

Harper, D. (1988) 'Visual sociology: expanding sociological vision', *American Sociologist*, 19 (1): 54–70

Harper, D. (2002) 'Talking about pictures: a case for photo-elicitation', *Visual Studies*, 17 (1): 13–26.

Harper, D. (2012) *Visual Sociology*. London: Routledge.

Hockings, P. (ed.) (2003) *Principles of Visual Anthropology*. The Hague: Mouton de Gruyter.

Hogan, J. (2003) 'Staging the nation: gendered and ethnicized discourses of national identity in Olympic opening ceremonies', *Journal of Sport and Social Issues*, 27 (2): 100–23.

Iglesias, J. D. (2015) 'Eurovision song contest and identity crisis in Moldova', *Nationalities Papers: The Journal of Nationalism and Ethnicity*, 43: 233–47.

Ismayilov, M. (2012) 'State, identity, and the politics of music: Eurovision and nation-building in Azerbaijan', *Nationalities Papers: The Journal of Nationalism and Ethnicity*, 40: 833–51.

Knox, D. (2008) 'Spectacular tradition: Scottish folksong and authenticity', *Annals of Tourism Research*, 35 (1): 255–73.

Krase, J. (2013) *Seeing Cities Change: Local Culture and Class*. London: Ashgate.

Kuever, E. (2012) 'Performance, spectacle, and visual poetry in the sixtieth anniversary National Day Parade in the People's Republic of China', *Studies in Ethnicity and Nationalism*, 12 (1): 6–18.

Lapenta, F. (2011) 'Some theoretical and methodological views on photo-elicitation', in E. Margolis and L. Pauwels (eds), *The Sage Handbook of Visual Research Methods*. London: Sage, pp. 201–13.

Law, J. and Urry, J. (2004) 'Enacting the social', *Economy and Society*, 33 (3): 390–410.

Leong, L. W.-T. (2001) 'Consuming the nation: National Day Parades in Singapore', *New Zealand Journal of Asian Studies*, 3 (2): 5–16.

Luhtakallio, E. (2013) 'Bodies keying politics: a visual frame analysis of gendered local activism in France and Finland', in N. Doerr, A. Mattoni and S. Teune (eds), *Advances in the Visual Analysis of Social Movements*, Research in Social Movements, Conflicts and Change, Vol. 35. Bingley: Emerald Group Publishing, pp. 27–54.

MacAloon, J. (1984) 'Olympic Games and the theory of spectacle in modern societies', in J. MacAloon (ed.), *Rite, Drama, Festival, Spectacle: Rehearsals Towards a Theory of Cultural Performance*. Philadelphia: Institute for the Study of Human Issues, pp. 241–80.

MacDougall, D. (1995) 'The subjective voice in ethnographic film', in L. Devereaux and R. Hillman (eds), *Fields of Vision*. Berkeley, CA: University of California Press, pp. 217–55.

MacDougall, D. (2011) 'Anthropological filmmaking: an empirical art', in E. Margolis and L. Pauwels (eds), *The Sage Handbook of Visual Research Methods*. London: Sage, pp. 99–113.

Margolis, E. and Pauwels, L. (eds) (2011) *The Sage Handbook of Visual Research Methods*. London: Sage.

Milne, E.-J., Mitchell, C. and De Lange, N. (2012) *Handbook of Participatory Video*. Lanham, MD: AltaMira Press.

Mock, S. J. (2012) '"Whose game they're playing": nation and emotion in Canadian TV advertising during the 2010 Winter Olympics', *Studies in Ethnicity and Nationalism*, 12 (1): 206–26.

Nathansohn, R. and Zuev, D. (2013) *Sociology of Visual Sphere*. New York: Routledge.

Norris, S. M. (2011) 'Memory for sale: Victory Day 2010 and Russian remembrance', *Soviet and Post-Soviet Review*, 38 (2): 201–29.

Parfitt, T. (2011) 'Russia's Winter Olympics slips into controversy over "Nazi images"', *Guardian*, 16 May. Retrieved 19 September 2015 from: http://www.theguardian.com/world/2011/may/16/russia-winter-olympics-nazi-images.

Pauwels, L. (2005) 'Websites as visual and multimodal cultural expressions: opportunities and issues of online hybrid media research', *Media, Culture and Society*, 27 (4): 604–13.

Pauwels, L. (2012) 'A multimodal framework for analyzing websites as cultural expressions', *Journal of Computer-Mediated Communication*, 17 (3): 247–65.

Peixoto, C. E. (2008) 'Family film: from family registers to historical artifacts', *Visual Anthropology*, 21 (2): 112–24.

Perlmutter, D. and Wagner G. L. (2001) 'The anatomy of a photojournalistic icon: marginalization of dissent in the selection and framing of "A Death in Genoa"', *Visual Communication*, 3 (1): 91–108.

Piault, M. H., Silverstein, S. M. and Graham, A. P. (2015) 'Where indeed is the theory in visual anthropology?', *Visual Anthropology*, 28 (2): 170–80.

Picard, D. (2015) 'The festive frame: festivals as mediators for social change', *Ethnos: Journal of Anthropology*. Advance online publication at: DOI: 10.1080/00141844.2014.989869.

Picard, D. and Zuev, D. (2014) 'The tourist plot: Antarctica and the modernity of nature', *Annals of Tourism Research*, 45 (1): 102–15.

Puijk, R. (2000) 'A global media event? Coverage of the 1994 Lillehammer Olympic Games', *International Review for the Sociology of Sport*, 35 (3): 309–30.

Queiroz, M. I. P. (1985) *The Samba Schools of Rio de Janeiro*. Paris: Diogenes.

Roche, M. (1994) 'Mega-events and urban policy', *Annals of Tourism Research*, 21: 1–19.

Roche, M. (2000) *Mega-events and Modernity: Olympics and Expos in the Growth of Global Culture*. London: Routledge.

Sasson, E. (2014) 'Why did bit about tolerance get cut from Olympic Broadcast?', *Wall Street Journal*, 8 February. Retrieved 19 August 2015 from: http://blogs.wsj.com/speakeasy/2014/02/08/why-did-bit-about-tolerance-get-cut-from-olympic-broadcast/.

Schwartz, D. (1989) 'Visual ethnography: using photography in qualitative research', *Qualitative Sociology*, 12 (2): 119–54.

Scully, M. (2012) 'Whose day is it anyway? St. Patrick's Day as a contested performance of national and diasporic Irishness', *Studies in Ethnicity and Nationalism*, 12 (1): 118–35.

Suchar, C. S. (1997) 'Grounding visual sociology research in shooting scripts', *Qualitative Sociology*, 20 (1): 33–55.

Traganou, J. (2010) 'National narratives in the opening and closing ceremonies of the Athens 2004 Olympic Games', *Journal of Sport and Social Issues*, 34 (2): 236–51.

Uzelac, G. (2010) 'National ceremonies: the pursuit of authenticity', *Journal of Racial and Ethnic Studies*, 33: 1718–36.

Vergani, M. and Zuev, D. (2011) 'Analysis of YouTube videos used by activists in the Uyghur Nationalist Movement: combining quantitative and qualitative methods', *Journal of Contemporary China*, 20 (69): 205–29.

Vergani, M. and Zuev, D. (2013) 'Production of solidarities in YouTube: a visual study of Uyghur nationalism', in R. Nathansohn and D. Zuev (eds), *Sociology of the Visual Sphere*. New York: Taylor & Francis Group.

Vergani, M. and Zuev, D. (2015) 'Neojihadist visual politics: comparing YouTube videos of the North Caucasus and Uighur militants', *Asian Studies Review*, 39 (1): 1–22.

Virchow, F. (2007) 'Capturing the streets: demonstration marches as a political instrument of the extreme right in contemporary Germany', in M. Reiss (ed.), *The Street as Stage: Protest Marches and Public Rallies Since the Nineteenth Century*. Oxford: Oxford University Press, pp. 295–310.

Waitt, G. (1999) 'Playing games with Sydney: marketing Sydney for the 2000 Olympics', *Journal of Urban Studies*, 36: 1055–77.

Walker, J. (2012) 'Olympic ghosts in a former warzone: what the legacy of 1984 means for Sarajevo today', *Visual Studies*, 27 (2): 174–7.

Weissmann, J. (2012) 'Empty nest: Beijing's Olympic stadium is a vacant "museum piece"', *The Atlantic*, 31 July. Retrieved 19 August 2015 from: http://www.theatlantic.com/business/archive/2012/07/empty-nest-beijings-olympic-stadium-is-a-vacant-museum-piece/260522/.

Whannel, G. (2006) 'The four minute mythology: documenting drama on film and television', *Sport in History*, 26 (2): 263–79.

Worth, S. and Adair, J. (1972) *Through Navajo Eyes: An Exploration in Film Communication and Anthropology*. Bloomington, IN: Indiana University Press.

Yang, M. M. (2011) 'Still burning: self-immolation as photographic protest', *Quarterly Journal of Speech*, 97 (1): 1–25

Zelizer, B. (2010) *About to Die. How News Images Move the Public*. New York: Oxford University Press.

Zuev, D. (2010) 'Visual dimension of protest: analysis of ritual interactions during the Russian March', *Visual Anthropology*, 23 (3): 221–53.

Zuev, D. (2012) *Self-immolation and the Use of Fire in Protest Action: Examining the Spectacle of the Flaming Objects*. Presentation made at the 40th Congress of the International Institute of Sociology, New Delhi, 16–19 February.

Zuev, D. (2013) 'Russian March: investigating symbolic dimension of the political performance in modern Russia', *Europe-Asia Studies*, 65 (1): 102–26.

Zuev, D. and Picard, D. (2015) 'Reconstructing the Antarctic tourist interaction ritual chain: visual sociological perspective', *Polar Journal*, 5 (1): 146–69.

Zuev, D. and Virchow, F. (2014) 'Performing national identity: the many logics of national(ist) spectacle', *Nations and Nationalism*, 20 (2): 191–9.

8 Tourism and new collective effervescence

The encoding of 'Aboriginality' – a worldmaking critique of special events and special places[1]

Keith Hollinshead and Rukeya Suleman

Introduction

My, how quickly can cultural scenarios change! In 1991 (in Australia) we were authoritatively told that the mandates and necessary practices of the tourism industry *are fundamentally incompatible* with the interests and capacities of the Aboriginal populations of Australia (Altman and Finlayson, 1991: 23). In that Commonwealth (i.e. Federal) sponsored document, we were decidedly informed that it would simply never be possible for Aboriginal groups and communities (on the dry continent) to meaningfully engage in or with the global tourism/travel industry (industries). Yet roll on one mere decade. In 2001 the Lonely Planet company produce *Aboriginal Australia and the Torres Strait Islands: Guide to Indigenous Australia* by Singh *et al.* – a monstrous 450-page handbook for tourists closely delineating the myriad fashions in which Black 'Australian' populations have fast become engaged in various *active* ways in the development of travel ventures, interpretive activities and (dare it be said) 'tourism product'! Whoa! Where did this Lonely Planet Publications handbook come from? In one short decade we have moved away from seemingly secure *primitive-environmentalist standpoints* which see tourism and travel as powerful and corrosive agents of Western or non-Indigenous infiltration (after Bodley, 1982: 192) and as lead forces of endogenous rationality (see Hollinshead, 1996: 317). We have seemingly moved towards a whole new whirlpool of operating public culture perspectives predicated on *liberal-political views* (which appear to encourage Aboriginal groups towards substantive local community involvement in appropriate forms of tourism (again after Bodley, 1982: 192; see also, again, Hollinshead, 1996: 316). Or perhaps we have even moved towards public culture engagements based upon *conservative-humanitarian outlooks* (Bodley, 1982: 192; Hollinshead, 1996: 316) which see tourism as an important and an immediately available/attainable source of material, symbolic and rhetorical reward for Indigenous groups. In ten short years, in Australia, we have moved from sage, governmental judgments that 'tourism marketing' and 'Aboriginal culture' are chalk-and-cheese phenomena, to a whole new imaginative ball game where all sorts of Aboriginal interest groups are decidedly involved or highly engaged in not only the 'national' but the 'global' travel marketplace.

These apparent sudden cultural developments, these apparent changes of outlook on the possibilities of sustainability through self-representation and these apparent changes of heart towards tourism all demand attention. It is imperative that a critical inspection is made of not only what an emergent international guidebook like the Lonely Planet handbook actually says literally and explicitly, but what it inherently says and implicitly means for Indigenous populations in Australia and beyond. This chapter, therefore, seeks to explore what is revealed in the 2001 Lonely Planet handbook about the ways in which Black Australian groups and communities are variously mobilising (or are being mobilised?) via the unfolding imaging identifications of tourism. It thereby seeks to inspect *Aboriginal Australia and the Torres Strait Islands: Guide to Indigenous Australia* (hereafter the *LP Aboriginal Australia Guide* or *LPG*) as a conceivable vehicle declarative of a new counter-politics of place, identity and hope through tourism and through the projective agency of the festivals and events industry. The aim of this chapter is therefore to explore directly and indirectly what the *LP Aboriginal Australia Guide* makes clear about the ways in which the workings of the international tourism industry and the life-force/life-forces of Indigenous Australia actually influence each other. This chapter therefore goes beyond Bhattacharyya's (1997) helpful study of the manner in which a particular Lonely Planet guidebook – or any such travel handbook – can mediate the experiences tourists have. While Bhattacharyya's inspection covered the semiotics involved within *The Lonely Planet Guide to India*, this current chapter seeks to examine the representational influence of the Lonely Planet discourse from a broader spectrum of socio-political outlooks and human-communication perspectives. The aim is to uncover how the new public or 'national' culture of Indigenous Australia is being represented as Black 'Australia' is variously drawn into the global travel marketplace – or as it, otherwise, draws itself into that same industrial milieu and transnational space.

Hence, the objective in this 'New collective effervescence' chapter is to see just what the *LP Aboriginal Australia Guide* states or infers about the ways in which the conceptual structures and the held cosmologies of Black 'Australia' tally with understandings which are prevalent within the global/transnational tourism and events industry. To this or these ends, the Lonely Planet handbook will be inspected to see what it says about the role of international tourism in opening up new identities for Aboriginal groups. It will be examined to see what it says about the ways in which exposure to international tourism conceivably helps the Indigenous past, Indigenous culture and/or Indigenous being to be rediscovered, retold and/or reinvented on the new sorts of 'stage' that international tourism constitutes. Hence the *LP Aboriginal Australia Guide* will be scrutinised to distil the degree to which it says anything new about the emergent subjectivities of Aboriginality. Thereby, critique will be given of the extent to which its very sudden appearance on international travel bookshelves just after the turn of the century attests to the existence of new sorts of non-static *positional identification* (Hall, 1997: 33) for Aboriginal groups and communities. Conceivably, the new publication can shed light on the degree to which many elements of traditional Aboriginality are, in many important senses, becoming transitionalised through tourism, in part.

And we have simply have had too little of these kinds of inspections of the culturally transformative force of tourism – conceivably the world's largest industry (Goeldner et al., 2000: 434–6). We learn from Brown (1998) and Meethan (2001) that little attention has been paid to the place and role of tourism vis-à-vis other industries and realms of consciousness in the wider world. We learn from Crick (1988) that while all cultures are known to be 'invented', there have been few Tourism Studies researchers who have sincerely inspected the function of tourism in cultural invention. It is thus the function of this critique to scrutinise how tourism is being used by various different Aboriginal populations not only to re-project themselves, but to reimagine themselves.

The worldmaking issues involved: the encoding of homeland culture – the decoding of drawcard culture

The inspection of the projections and interpretations contained in this chapter constitutes a scrutiny of *worldmaking* authority and agency at work in the delineation of what is seen to exist in a given culture. The chapter thereby critiques what is seen to be 'there' to encounter in the sites and settings in which Indigenous populations reveal certain aspects of their inheritance(s) and presence(s). These homeland people/host population declarations of being and becoming are commented upon vis-à-vis what the external tourism/hospitality/events industry (industries) has (have) encroached upon to either work collaboratively upon *with longstanding/local Aboriginal populations* or otherwise upon what is *conceptually and operationally appropriate* in terms of narrative, landscape, symbolic icon, whatever. It thus comprises a critique of the worldmaking 'scopic drive' (Hollinshead and Kuon, 2015) of the sometimes compossible tourism and events industry (see Venn, 2006, on 'compossibility') or the sometimes invasive tourism and events industry (see Meethan, 2001: 53–5). In this critical light, thereby, the chapter inspects not only the power of *representations* of peoples, places, pasts and presents but also the consequentiality of *misrepresentations* and *derepresentations* (either consciously engaged in or not!) of these cultural and cosmological storylines (see Hollinshead, 2009a, for a primer on 'worldmaking', *ipso facto*). Thus the chapter services a worldmaking critique of the social cum political production of Indigenous being/Indigenous place/Indigenous spirituality as 'it' is reified by the tourism and events industry and thus served up as 'active discourse', 'interpreted narrative', 'mediated vision' (see Hollinshead, 2009b, for these forms of social and political articulation) either through the representational repertoires of newly emergent Aboriginal entities/newly confident Aboriginal enterprises, or otherwise through the representational regimes of tourism and events industry operations. Hence those reading this chapter are asked to determine for themselves in worldmaking matters of normalisation and naturalisation (see Hollinshead *et al.*, 2009) just what Aboriginal groups/communities/organisations tend to inculcate about their received traditions and their contemporary transitionalities in contrast with what partner or invasive non-Aboriginal bodies and corporations tend to inculcate when they project or inscribe 'Aboriginalia' (see Hollinshead *et al.*, 2009, on the ordinary/everyday/banal worldmaking act of *inculcation*). Thus for any given tourism attraction or event exhibit, where does the non-Indigenous decoding of Indigenous culture or cosmology just not tally with, not lie spiritually consanguine with or otherwise disrespect/hurt/damage inherited Indigenous beliefs and/or hailed Indigenous aspirations? (For a fast exordium on these dialectical matters of encoded standpoints and decoded interpolations, please refer to 'encoding' and 'decoding' in Chapter 11 by these authors in this book.)

Description of the text

The *LP Aboriginal Australia Guide* (2001) has had a very short gestation period. Commencing as a bright idea as recently as 1998 (*LPG*, p. 14), the project was funded in part by the Regional Tourism Programme of the (Commonwealth, i.e. Federal) Department of Industry, Science and Resources in Australia. Conceived as a text that would present the views of individual writers from the Indigenous presses of Australia, the publication project evidently sought to embrace a diversity of voices. Indeed, a number of production training sessions were held to instruct many of those 'Indigenous voices' in the intricacies of guidebook writing. Their submissions were then supplemented by both a handful of 'experienced' Lonely Planet writers and experienced commentators on Aboriginal society (*LPG*, p. 14).

The *LP Aboriginal Australia Guide* is a text which does not just seek to cover areas of Australia where Aboriginal people live in a high proportion to the non-Aboriginal population, such as in the Kimberley region of northern Western Australia (where Aboriginal people compose over 50 per cent of the 28,000 population; *LPG*, p. 411), it constitutes an attempt to embrace all of the Aboriginal communities of today. The publication thereby serves as a testimony to the 600 to 700 'distinct [Indigenous] nations' which existed in Australia prior to the European invasion of 1788 (*LPG*, p. 46). To this end, the Lonely Planet handbook appears to pay particular attention to what it suggests – in its turn-of-the-century coverage – are the following (among other) principal drawcards for tourists and 'cultural-experience seekers':

- key interpreted settings such as Nitmiluk (Katherine Gorge) National Park in the Northern Territory (*LPG*, p. 209), Manyallaluk (the former Eva Valley Station) at the south-western edge of Arnhem Land in the Northern Territory (*LPG*, pp. 210–12) and the Brambuk Aboriginal Cultural Centre in Gariwerd (the Grampian Mountains), Victoria (*LPG*, pp. 371–2);
- key rock-art locations in the Quinkan (Spirit Being) Reserve of Kokowarra Country (near Laura, Cape York Peninsula, North Queensland; *LPG*, pp. 258, 282–3) and in the Carnarvon Gorge area of Garingbal Country/ Carnarvon National Park in Central Queensland (*LPG*, pp. 269–71);
- key tourist resorts like Yulara – adjoining the Uluru-Kata Tjuta National Park at the Southern base of the Northern Territory – which itself 'has effectively turned

[this arid area of central Australia,] one of the world's least hospitable regions, into an easy and comfortable place to visit' (*LPG*, p. 253). [Yulara was principally built to service 'Uluru', of course, the huge and ancient monolith known as 'Ayers Rock' in appropriative Euro-historical terms, and still unhelpfully termed as such in uninformed spheres of the tourism and events industry.];

- key new interpretive developments like Tjapukai Aboriginal Cultural Park north-west of Cairns (*LPG*, pp. 277–8) and Bunjilaka (Melbourne; *LPG*, p. 362) which are situated near to/within city-scapes of today;
- the galleries of key Indigenous communicators such as the 'Jabiru at the Pier' gallery or artist-musician David Hudson in Cairns (*LPG*, p. 276), the one-man-show 'bush experiences' of Bill Harney in Wardaman Country of the wider Katherine Area of the Northern Territory (*LPG*, p. 212) and the Yeddonba 'Country' tours led by Eddie Kneebone in the Wiradjuri/Duduroa/Yiamathang country of the Victoria–NSW border zones (*LPG*, pp. 375–6); and
- Indigenous 'sites-of-interpretation' being established through the dedicated present-day persistence of non-Aboriginal individuals or non-Indigenous companies, such as the Jowalbinna Bush Camp of Percy and Steve Trezise in Cape York (*LPG*, p. 283), or alternatively through the noted past deeds of significant Europeans in nineteenth- or twentieth-century Australia, namely 'the William Buckley Discovery Trail' from the You Yangs (i.e. the low-rise mountains south-west of Melbourne/north of Geelong) to Airey's Inlet in Victoria (*LPG*, pp. 366–7).

As may be judged from the list above, the *LP Aboriginal Australia Guide* runs the gamut from informing readers about the importance of traditional *cultural keeping places* like that of 'The Tribal Place' of the Kalkadoon (in and around Mt Isa in western Queensland; *LPG*, pp. 284–5) and that of the 'lost' rock art Martu country (in the Western Pilbara tracts of the north of Western Australia; *LPG*, p. 409), to the more casually available interpretation of Indigenous life that may be absorbed while cruising Geikie Gorge in the Fitzroy River Area of Bunuba county in Western Australia (*LPG*, p. 423), or while at ease on Waiben (Thursday Island) in the Torres Straits (*LPG*, pp. 335–47). The Lonely Planet production has therefore clearly been created as a reference work for those who merely need a fine 'Indigenous' bookshop to drop into (e.g. Hobart Bookshop for Tasmania; *LPG*, p. 327), an 'Indigenous' library collection to peruse (e.g. that of the Battye Library of Western Australia; *LPG*, p. 386), an 'Indigenous-flavoured' exhibition to study (e.g. 'The First People of Western Australia' displays at the Perth Cultural Centre; *LPG*, p. 389), a quick place to sample Indigenous fare (e.g. The Flamin' Bull Australian Indigenous Restaurants of Melbourne and Warragul in Victoria; *LPG*, p. 366), or a quick interpreted walk Black-in-time, perhaps (e.g. 'the Loontitetermairrelehoiner Aboriginal Heritage Walk' and 'the Bush Tucker Stroll' of the Swansea/Freycinet National Park region of the east coast of Tasmania; *LPG*, p. 328). But it has also been encoded or put together for those on more ardent or dedicated 'travel-missions'. It has been written for those, for instance, who are on a specific quest to precisely determine, perhaps, just who are and where are the world-renowned Warlayiriti

Artists (*LPG*, p. 428), and (possibly having been inspired by the recent *Rabbit Proof Fence* film on international release which covered the subject of 'The Stolen Generations')[2] just what and where was the Board for the Protection of Aborigines (*LPG*, p. 354), and which are/where were some of the so-called bush mission educational centres established for Aboriginal/non-Aboriginal children (*LPG*, p. 394). This text can therefore be read in terms of worldmaking effectivity at many different levels of commitment to subject or angles of interest.

At times, the *LP Aboriginal Australia Guide* is plain and forthright in its attempt to capture Indigenous voice. Consider, for instance, Exhibit 8.1 giving the views of Trudy Ridge from the Karimba skin group (south of Broome in

Exhibit 8.1 Massacre sites: the need to know – slaughter commemorated

Notes on the Grange Bay massacre of 1865, South of Broome, Western Australia, where approximately 20 Aboriginal men and women of the Karajarri people in Western Australia were massacred in response to the death of three 'white' explorers working for the pioneering Roebuck Back Pastoral company.

> This could be any story you read about any [Indigenous] massacre site in the country – but this one is our story and happened to my own family.
>
> We don't have a monument erected at the massacre site; we know where it is. There are children of the survivors of this slaughter still alive today (and now grandchildren and great-grandchildren).
>
> We don't have cemeteries or headstones in place for these areas. Not all massacre sites are known to the general public and we don't want everyone to be able to access these areas. If you do come across a burial site, please treat it with respect, just as you would behave in a considerate manner on any holy ground. Remember that, like any final resting place, someone will feel upset if the area is desecrated.
>
> For this reason we don't want to see these areas open to the general public to be trampled over, with no thought to the actual events that took place there.
>
> In all my writing, I have failed to show where massacre sites are located – this is in respect to the event, my people, my culture, and on a personal note, to my own family.
>
> In recent years, a plaque has been erected at [the Pastoral Company Monument] stating:
>
> This Plaque also commemorates all other Aboriginal who died during the invasion of their country.
>
> MAPA JARRIYA-NYALAKU. LEST WE FORGET.

Source: Trudi Ridge – whose mother had a European ancestry, and whose father emanates from Karajarri and Yawuru language groups in Western Australia (*LPG*, pp. 414–15).

Western Australia). The exhibit is taken from a 'Massacre Sites' boxed text, attributed to her within the *LPG*, that is devoted to a slaughter location near La Grange Bay in the north of Western Australia where 20 Karajarri people were killed. The father of Trudy Ridge hails from the Karajarri-Yawuru language group, and she is keen to reveal 'truths' about the European invasion of Aboriginal lands, and the good and the bad of the condition and aspirations of the 600 to 700 Aboriginal 'nations' across Australia today.

Description of the field: 'intelligent tourism' as worldmaking practice

For the purposes of this critique, the *LP Aboriginal Australia Guide* could be deemed to be a contribution to the field of 'intelligent tourism', as recently detailed in Horne's (1992) ironic and acerbic treatment of the power of tourism and special events to normalise and/or naturalise peoples, places, pasts or presents. To Horne, the vast majority of interpretation and exhibitry in tourism and travel is not only uninquiring, it is uninspiring: to him, current practices of representation and interpretation in tourism far too frequently consist only of essentialising and trivialising superficiality. Horne concedes that interpretation in tourism must always be entertaining – given the brevity of its contextual setting and the mobility of its main target 'travelling audiences' – but he argues that it can also be routinely much more decently *enlightening* in its encoding without necessarily becoming highbrow or intellectual. In this regard, Horne views tourism as a, or the main, vehicle through which the public culture[3] of a population or territory is communicated and confirmed. He therefore explores the fashions by which governments and/or interest groups take hold of narratives about capital cities, historic settlements, cultural landmarks, natural-historic drawcards and sites of sacred or secular pilgrimage in order to encode or project particular storylines of a people, a place or a past and thereby to legitimate certain versions of that region's potential public culture. To Horne, the public culture currently articulated through the storylines of tourism and travel is decidedly *unintelligent* in that it fails to develop a decent degree of 'awe' among travellers both in terms of critical awareness about the precious sites they are visiting and the sites that are precious to them in their own lives. To him, too much of the representation and the projectivity of *unintelligent tourism* (not his own words, *sic*!) is about the mere uninvolving act of *sightseeing* rather than the more engaged act of *sight-experiencing* (Horne, 1992: 132–7, 382–3). He calls for more management bodies at tourism sites, landscape settings, and interpretive centres to build a critical dimension into what they exhibit in order to make it plain that the narratives they seek to advance or reveal are not just particular acts of make-believe, but that they are acts of make-believe in accordance with vogue values concerning history, nature and/or cosmology. In this way, Horne calls for more public culture/heritage presenters in the tourism/hospitality/events industry to admit rather than to deny or cloud over the ideological character of the selectivity behind the presentations they highlight.

To Horne, all such inscribed or encoded make-believe storylines in tourism – all such public culture interpretations of a people, a place or a past – are inherently ideological: they each normalise certain visions of being, living and knowing. In this light, the everyday interpretations and the everyplace interpretations of tourism and travel have an 'always-there' *evocative material symbolism* to them, as the exhibitions and representations of the industry serve as a coding machine to version the cultural gene bank and the natural gene bank inheritances of the populations they cover or relate to (Horne, 1992: 377). Horne simply wants site interpreters (who are engaged/employed in the businesses of tourism and place exhibitry) to be much more aware of the evocative material symbolic power that they have at their disposal. He thinks that tourists and travellers-to-special-cultural-events are not routinely and inescapably dumb: he maintains that each of us who journeys to experience 'other-cultures'/different-ways-of-life can readily respond to sensitively pitched enlightenment, and through it each of us can reasonably distinguish between the claims of decently-pitched competing value-based versions of history and nature (see here, Hollinshead's (1999) critique of Horne's (1992) work on 'thoughtful tourism', 'critical tourism', 'tourism imagining', 'autonomic tourism' and 'the performativity of tourism' as distilled from *The Intelligent Tourist*).

Accordingly, in many ways the *LP Aboriginal Australia Guide* is a timely work to study as a contributory text to the art and craft of intelligent tourism, and to aid in understanding about the under-examined practices/artifices/games of cultural encoding and cultural decoding. The book clearly targets inquiring minds from the outset:

> Whether you are interested in tasting bush foods or learning to speak Nyoongar, in listening to Anangu creation *stories* [original emphasis retained] in the desert or live Indigenous pub rock in Sydney, you'll find it here. Or perhaps you're a non-Indigenous Australian curious to find more about the people whose traditional land your house is built on.
>
> (*LPG*, p. 21)

Clearly, the text seeks out to be corrective:

> Indigenous cultures are rich and varied and non-Indigenous people often have a skewed impression of Australia's First Nations. The time has come to debunk the clichés, and the only way [for you the tourist] to do this is by meeting and spending time with Indigenous people themselves.
>
> (*LPG*, p. 21)

And the work does not seek to hide its edifying mission through tourism, thereby benefiting hosts and visitors in complementary ways:

> At its best, tourism is education, enabling Indigenous people to teach outsiders about their culture in a way in which they can control the access to and

> interpretation of their information, and also make a living out of it. That's not to say that the book is full of cheery tourist stuff. There are plenty of off-the-beaten-track places and thought-provoking personal stories included here. With this guide in your backpack or glove-box, you'll find a very different Australia from the one most often presented to the world.
>
> (*LPG*, p. 21)

Such is the field of educational tourism – or, in Horne's terms, *intelligent tourism* – that the *LP Aboriginal Australia Guide* implicitly targets as it seeks to encode and inspire travellers to new levels of appreciation about Aboriginal lands, traditional spirituality and Indigenous hope. And certainly, the work has much of cultural worth and adventure value to milk, for, as it records itself, there are already approximately 17,000 registered 'Aboriginal sites' in Western Australia (*LPG*, p. 403) alone – that is, there are thousands and thousands of known and classified special or significant 'locations' in the mere western third of the dry continent.

In distilling what the 2001 Lonely Planet publication registers in terms of its contribution to 'intelligent tourism', the text will not so much be regarded as a neutral or an objective account which seeks to give indifferent commentary on Aboriginal Australia – even though the company itself claims to give independent advice (*LPG*, inside-front cover),[4] but rather as one that is offered by a production team deeply indentured to Black 'Australian' society or richly in covenant with Indigenous life-spaces. Thus the *LP Aboriginal Australia Guide* stands as a pungently encoded manuscript that is profoundly engaged with Aboriginal outlooks and committed to the re-representation of Indigenous realities. Hence it is assumed (by the authors of this chapter scrutinising worldmaking authority and agency (i.e. Hollinshead and Suleman)) to serve as a vehicle by and through which many Aboriginal groups and many communities can claim much of the form and detail of the projectivity of tourism for themselves. It is a work which attests to the in some senses *gradual* and in other senses *sudden* emergence of new subjects and new intercultural positions as the tourist sites which are now being unveiled comprise paramount sites of struggle from which many Black 'Australians' can speak to the outside/global world for the first time. Hence, on the back cover of the first edition, Dr Irene Watson – the Aboriginal lawyer, writer and activist – is quoted at length:

> There are many common stereotypes of Aboriginal peoples. One is that we are all the same and conform to the idealised image of the naked Aborigine standing with spear in hand watching the sunset. This is a picture which quickly dissolved into the reality of the 21st century. [The Aboriginal peoples of 'Australia'] are as different as the landscapes of coast, desert, rainforest and snowy mountains. The land is different and so are we, the first peoples of the land.
>
> (*LPG*, p. 99)

In this regard, the four hundred and fifty pages of the Lonely Planet publication stand as not so much a travelogue, but as a regardful and awakening account of contemporary Black 'Australia' from the-bottom-up, so to speak – duly encoded for the faithfully inquiring reader of course. Thus, the back cover of the first edition not only seeks to explain in detached fashion

> What is the significance of dots in contemporary aboriginal painting? [And] how many languages were spoken in Australia before colonisation? [And, again] what did the *Mabo*[5] and *Wik*[6] decisions mean?
>
> (Original emphasis retained)

but it claims to give the reader 'an overview of the main issues affecting Aboriginal and Torres Strait islander people today' and thereby explain the meaning and significance of all of those tours/festivals/interpretive sites 'where Indigenous people [wish to] share their culture' (*LPG*, back cover). In this regard, the tourism sites and sights of visitor itineraries to Australia potentially begin to comprise a most powerful locale from which the voice of the othered 'original Australian' can speak, although many Indigenous groups and institutions in Australia maintain that the long-standing peoples of the dry continent are neither 'Aboriginal' (largely a non-Indigenous aggregate-misinterpretation of tribal Indigenous being) nor 'Australian' (largely a forced non-Indigenous projection of *national belonging* upon Indigenous groups and communities) (see Horton, 1995; Taylor *et al.*, 2005; and various contributors in Grossman, 2006). In this sense, the exhibits and the interpretations of Aboriginal 'Australia' in everyday actuality, and again reflexively in the co-opted pages of the *LP Aboriginal Australia Guide*, constitute an important vehicle of corrective 'marginalised advocacy'. They compose a place of powerful promise for the decades of Indigenous and self-articulated exhibited culture ahead as the twenty-first century progresses.

In those fashions, the intelligent tourism (that may be deciphered within the 2001 Lonely Planet publication) acts as a worldmaking vehicle for *the articulation of counter-identity* – that is of counter-identity-through-tourism-exposition … a much under-researched subject (Buck, 1993; Hall, 1994; Hollinshead, 2002). As Hall (1997: 22) has opined, identities are always negotiated against some other perceived 'difference', that is they are routinely judged in the course of things against some understood homogenous entity. All populations – particularly all dominant or privileged populations – like the identities which they accord themselves and which they afford their others to be stable. In this regard, tourism may readily be seen (during the twentieth century) to be a hand tool of the dominant and a medium of the privileged, as it is harnessed half-wittingly and half-unwittingly to concretise the identities which particular governments wish to sanctify and/or which particular corporate interests wish to sanction (Fjellman, 1992; Lanfant, 1995; McKay, 1994). Consonantly, tourism has very much become a collaborative and universalising mechanism for explaining identity (Kirshenblatt-Gimblett, 1998) – or it has grown to become what Robertson (1997) would style as an example of *a globally authoritative paradigm for locating and explaining difference*. Hence, in terms of cognition about worldmaking authority and agency, the *LP Aboriginal Australia Guide* may be read as a vehicle of intelligent tourism which serves to resist those forms of colonised Other (i.e. the externally manufactured and projected Aboriginal) as constituted within routine regimes of representation of the urban-industrial tourism system. As such, the *LP Aboriginal Australia Guide* may be examined for what it can offer as a text of worldmaking 'cultural resistance' – even one initially conceived and ambivalently positioned in an industrial company (namely in the Lonely Planet 'corporation' with its metropolitan offices in Melbourne, Oakland (California), London and Paris)! This, in terms of Horne's intelligent tourism, is the potential usefulness of the new book. For too long, tourism has been in thrall to uninquisitive nationalist interests within governments (Hall, 1994) and to uninquisitive commodifying interests within the corporate world (Meethan, 2001) who have not at all been nuanced in their treatments of matters of sub-national identity and inter-cultural difference (Fjellman, 1992; McKay, 1994). For too long, the tourism, hospitality and events industry has blindly and blithely peddled myths about national image and cultural integration which have routinely disenfranchised and de-represented 'the Other' (Hollinshead and Kuon, 2015). Thankfully, given the initiative possibly taken (*circa* 1998) in Victoria, in some Footscray boardroom or in some east-suburban-Melbourne creative coffee-house, we have an ambiguously positioned little blue book which can richly advance the positive recontextualisation of what Aboriginal contemporaneity is and where it may be faithfully and (shock-and-horror!) *intelligently* witnessed.

The encoding: clarification of the authorial purpose

Perhaps not enough has so far been clarified about the company purpose in producing the 2001 publication out of its Melbourne offices. Allegedly launched in modest circumstances by ardent traveller Tony Wheeler, the first Lonely Planet Guide (*South East Asia on a Shoestring*, 1975) was a round-the-kitchen-table enterprise produced by Wheeler and his wife, Maureen. Wheeler – British born – continued to direct the company from his second home of Melbourne for many years, and (at time of the appearance of the *LP Aboriginal Australia Guide*) was responsible for over 650 of such travel titles. Sometimes regarded as a specialist backpacker's publisher, the Lonely Planet company then consolidated sales to such an extent that – according to the Booktrack organisation which tabulates retail sales across the UK (cited in Hodson, 2002, p. 510) – its UK sales, for instance, even outshone that other redoubtable travel publisher in Great Britain, the Automobile Association.

Claiming to gather information 'for everyone who is curious about the planet – and especially for those who explore it first-hand' (*LPG*, p. 18), the company generates an impressive list of activity guides, maps, TV guides, phrasebooks, etc. Indeed, the *LP Aboriginal Australia Guide* is explicitly (through some self-referential advice) offered as a companion guide to the company's famous *Australia* guide (*LPG*, p. 20), and implicitly supplied as a cousin book for the company's *Outback Australia* work (*LPG*, p. 130), among others. For the *LP Aboriginal Australia Guide*, the compiled list of principal authors (from Sarina Singh to Belinda Scott) is a long one with some eleven individuals profiled in some detail

(*LPG*, pp. 7–9). Thereafter, each of these principal authors provides a monster list of other contributors, advisors and aides who have helped him or her (*LPG*, pp. 10–13), an act which an unkind observer might suggest thereby guarantees the text large and immediate sales – at least within Australia, among people who like to see their own name or interest group in print!

But, of course, the list of production colonels and commanders (within this encoded and seemingly 'corrective' publication) does not end there. Indeed, we learn that the manuscript (having endured the *standard* Lonely Planet production process!) was submitted to Mick Dodson (Australia's first Aboriginal and Torres Strait Islander Social Justice Commissioner) and to Les Ahoy (Aboriginal Tourism Product Manager at the Australian Tourist Commission). In this respect, these prominent individuals kindly agreed to have their own staff check that the text was appropriate, and to additionally provide other sorts of critical and operational advice 'from an Indigenous perspective on [the involved or featured] cultural issues' (*LPG*, p. 15). Yet – just in case anyone should doubt the degree to which this co-opted text won particular and esteemed sorts of Indigenous credibility – we are also pointedly informed who wrote which of the many boxed exhibits within the publication. It is made clear to the reader that Esther Managku – the oldest living member of the Kunwinjku people – wrote 'Bush Medicine' notes (with assistance; *LPG*, p. 98). Similarly, we learn that the multivalent Mandawny Yunupingu – the first Arnhem Land Aborigine to earn a university degree, the former school principal, the band-leader of the Aboriginal group Yothu Yindi and the Australian of the Year in 1992 – generated the 'Maintaining Culture' note (*LPG*, pp. 204–5), while (for comparison) a host of other 'surf-culture'/'urban-dwelling'/'between-cultures' Aboriginal individuals pitched in with other useful boxed pieces. The emergent inner dialectic of Indigenous community-hood and individual self-hood proved to be a rather broad Lonely Planet 'church'. Such a publication – such a vehicle of cultural communication situated discursively in 'Western' industrialese and thereby within the syntax of marketplace production – can never be expected to capture the views of those Aboriginal elders and leaders who do not have ongoing dialogue with non-Aboriginals and who might be expected to be either circumspect or hostile about the flow of stranger-tourists and alien-travellers to the communal hearths and the revered tribal lands of the Aboriginal realm (see Langton, 2006; Moreton-Robinson, 2006).

Nonetheless, the strong collaborative processes which the Lonely Planet company appear to have gone through plainly have helped the large editorial team to steer clear of many of the sorts of closed, over-integrated and over-systematised accounts of places which otherwise tend to litter the tourism industry literature of the turn-of-the-century world (Kirshenblatt-Gimblett, 1998). The deliberate coalescive character of both the writing pool and the publication process adopted at Lonely Planet appears to have enabled the company to not only capture much of the throbbing present that certain Aboriginal groups and communities do want to reveal, but to situate those expressions of reality and those forms of emergent being in a pleasing variety of *semi-traditional*, *pseudo-traditional* and *transitional* contexts, something which is not all that easy to achieve (Duelke, 2005; Horton,

1995; Palmer, 2005; Toussaint, 2004: 207, note 1.2). Clearly, such a broad school of contributors could never yield any one solid or unequivocal view upon what Aboriginality is or on what 'it' seeks to attain from tourism or from any large cross-cultural encounter, today. Communal standpoints and cultural identities are always contradictory phenomena anyway, perpetually capable of being 'understood' from a sizable set of different vantage points (Morrissey, 2006).

Consequently, the broadly conceived Lonely Planet editorial and publication team have evidently been able to capture an immense range of the enormous latent spread of Indigenous voices which exist to be heard. Here and there in the text, we learn that lost identities appear to have been recently recovered across 'the continent' of Australia – read, for instance, the comments of Geoffrey Angeles (a Kungarakan-Gurindji man born and bred in Darwin) about the rejuvenation of ancient fishing traditions by and among his 'Paperbark people' folk (*LPG*, pp. 202–3). Here and there in the text, we learn that new identities are crystallising – read, for instance, the observations of Janzey McDonald (an individual of mixed Aboriginal and South Sea Islander heritage (from her mother) and Scottish heritage (from her father)) on *the new dreams* that are unfolding for young and restless 'Aboriginal' individuals today (*LPG*, p. 262). Anyone reading the *LP Aboriginal Australia Guide* will find that, taken *in toto*, the collated manuscript echoes the views of Hall (1997: 47) that identities – even 'traditional' ones – are never complete and never finished; they are always in process of formation, as Jones and Jenkins (2008) have implied for Indigenous peoples across all continents. Helpfully, and presumably intentionally, the Lonely Planet crew capture much of and about these rather contradictory spaces. There is nothing 'already produced', nothing 'totalised' and nothing 'neatly stable' about the Aboriginality (read Aboriginalities) one can find in this turn-of-the-century Melbourne text. No reader could suggest that the Black 'Australians' encountered – and the Black 'Australia' uncovered – in these pages are trapped by the tourism industry that has come to spy upon them for external digestion by other Australians and for the interest and intrigue of all sorts of other individuals overseas. It would not be fair to say that the Indigenous correspondents unearthed – or perhaps, 'earthed' and 're-earthed' – in the *LP Aboriginal Australia Guide* are reasonably contained in the local/cultural/historic settings from which they speak. Through being open-ended and dialogic, the text does not so much 'capture' these enormous Aboriginal voices, but it does enable them to escape a little from what in many instances were their previous representational straitjackets. The Black 'Other', the Indigenous 'Other' and the ambivalent/interstitial 'Other' are slowly and uncertainly breaking loose, here and there, from the industry's incarcerating pre-judgements, it seems.

Given the sorts of new understandings and the new kinds of 'intelligent tourism' freedoms which one can sense within the *LP Aboriginal Australia Guide*, one may ascertain that the relentless bombardment of Indigenous culture by the global tourism and events industry is not inherently and not inevitably a crippling thing. There is, indeed, hope for Indigenous or colonised populations where the cultural and community visions being won are being, decidedly and creatively, cultivated in open-ended empathy or in contingent sympathy, as Venn (2006) suggests is possible within all industries and across each continent under the undulations and recalibrations of 'alternative postcolonial possibility' (i.e. read *compossibility* here). Aboriginal identities today are not just about a matter of the sequestration of fixed places distinct from non-Aboriginal worlds: Aboriginal identities today are diverse and on the move – particularly where the sad realities of the colonial and the post-colonial presence have destroyed meaningful territorial anchorage. We already know that tourists tend to be rather mobile people; we now also know (via panoramic culture sketchbooks like the *LP Aboriginal Australia Guide*) that Indigenous populations are themselves rather mobile in hope and aspiration, too.

Overall worldmaking critique: the *LP Aboriginal Australia Guide* as a vehicle of 'intelligent tourism'

The critical question involved in this assessment of the value of the *LP Aboriginal Australia Guide* as a vehicle of and for intelligent tourism is whether such a publication cannot just destroy localism and the coherencies of cultural belonging, but can help specific 'Indigenous' or 'local' populations endure (Meethan, 2001). As various sorts of travellers take on new positive attitudes towards the sacred 'Other' and towards the excluded 'Other' (Featherstone, 1995: 96), it is important to understand how indeed the new representational projectivity of international tourism can help engender a new sort of 'collective effervescence' – with due apologies to Durkheim (1961) – for Indigenous peoples and essentialised populations, as small-scale/traditional/semi-traditional communities are pitchforked into the bustling commodity aesthetics of the twenty-first century. *This chapter therefore queries whether tourism only has a role to play in the disembedding of tradition, or whether it can (through due forms of intelligent tourism) play a large part in the resilience and/or the reinvention of assailed cultures.* Can tourism indeed become both 'the methodological key and the actuality of the contemporary world' – as Featherstone (1995: 154) thinks it indeed can as sacred cosmologies are incrementally entrusted to it and are increasingly dissipated through it?

In these sage and philosophical respects, is the *LP Aboriginal Australia Guide* just another modernistic intrusion upon the life of a traditional/semi-traditional population, or just another instrument of colonialist cum imperialist interference? Or will the *LPG* prove to be of large value to Indigenous populations in 'Australia', thereby helping the oppressed there to speak back – through appropriately intelligent tourism – to the industrial/metropolitan world that they have suddenly become tethered to and within? Can a widely distributed publication like those produced (anywhere) by the Lonely Planet company help the non-West speak back, through inquisitive tourists, to the commanding and encroaching cosmopolitan world, thereby helping enable local Aboriginal groups to increasingly network together transformatively as their identities, their traditions and their concepts of selfhood become manifestly reimagined through the new representative power and articulated force of tourism?

In Australia, will carefully conceived and refreshing handbooks like the *LP Aboriginal Australia Guide* help Indigenous populations out of the recent but tenacious psychological hold of external Euro-Australian understanding, and away from externally imposed definitions of 'self' towards new cultural syncretisms and towards new and dynamic dreams of people-hood? Or will the publication and the industry it services only be yet another means for drawing out painful, cultural memories? These are the key questions for any substantive assessment of the worth of so-called 'intelligent tourism' to the heartbeat of Indigenous-traditional and hybrid-transitional life.

The merits of the text as a communicator of worldmaking notions of 'home country'/'host lands'

The publication produced in Footscray, Melbourne, during the opening moments of the twenty-first century is a massive contribution to broader understanding about Indigenous 'being' and restless/halfway 'becoming'. At almost breakneck speed, an immense but very readable tome has been produced which gives *authorised* insight into Aboriginal Australia, *tested* advice on visitations to difficult-to-reach places and *quite comprehensive* information on the states/territories/islands of the Great Southland. The text is massive in comparison to Kauffman's (2000) serviceable and compact but inchoate 175-page text which Hyland House put out the previous year – also in Victoria.

Although the Lonely Planet publication is serious in tone, it is not stuffy, and it has clearly been a labour of much love for senior authors like Paul Greenway, who we learn was 'gratefully plucked [by the Lonely Planet company] from the blandness and security of the Australian public service' (*LPG*, p. 8). Indeed, an inspired production team appears to have been put together for the book – as the publishers themselves acknowledge (*LPG*, p. 16). One of the delights of the work are the little blue-box pen portraits given of the Indigenous/Indigenous press contributors, so many of whom have brought such a rich range of experiences and a wide admixture of working backgrounds to the study.

As an 'intelligent tourism' text, the collation has clearly been assembled with impressive and relevant care. The publishers claim that all traditional Indigenous country names have been checked with appropriate local Elders (*LPG*, p. 16), a fact with indicates that the final production is not just a corporate publication, but in reality is a joint private-public sector production sanctioned by Indigenous populations. In these careful and deliberate fashions, the handbook captures a reasonable polymorphic mix of views on Indigenous life and lifestyles from all corners of the country, but yet it remains an entirely user-friendly output. The casual reader, who conceivably knows a little bit about Aboriginal songlines (perhaps from the incursive writing of an outsider like Bruce Chatwin; see *LPG*, p. 399 for a brief mention of the maverick British author of *Songlines* fame), can easily dip here and there into the book because the table of contents and the index are both cleanly and clearly provided. Yet the work will also undoubtedly be of functional value to the keen activist who wishes to stiffen his/her knowledge of agency policy on Indigenous affairs (see, for instance, the useful listing of political websites: *LPG*, pp. 42–3).

Above all, an intelligent tourism text (in the call of Donald Horne) must be engaging, and in many respects this Lonely Planet publication is such. On occasions, the manuscript deploys wee pieces of irony of which the paradox-lover Horne, himself, would be delighted. For example, Joseph Kennedy – a descendent of the Trawlwoolway people of north-east Tasmania – delights the reader by revealing how at Bunjilaka (Melbourne's much-praised Indigenous centre), the interpretation of things has been so radically reworked recently that it is indeed Baldwin Spencer (the early twentieth-century anthropologist and one-time director of that very museum) who is now '[prominently] rendered in plaster and displayed under glass' (*LPG*, p. 362), rather than the exhibits of the long-time Indigenous culture he had delved into, itself! In such small ways, the text is always captivating. Many of the contributions are highly personal – such as that of Lorraine Mafi-Williams, who we learn 'was one of the last babies to be born in the traditional way [out-bush]' (*LPG*, p. 25), and who was herself 'a Stolen Generations child'. She pointedly notes that 'The last time I saw my mum she was crying' (*LPG*, p. 25). Yet this self-exposive writing is direct, is sonorous and is stirring, without ever becoming maudlin, contumelious and vituperative. We may, for instance, learn that a small group of Pintupi people may indeed (in 1984) have been the last group of Aborigines to abandon their autonomous hunter-gatherer lifestyle (when they walked into the Kintore community, 350 miles north-west of Uluru (Ayres Rock); *LPG*, p. 318), but such a potentially momentous Western Desert 'incident' is offered in plain cant: the 'last-of-the-nomads'[7] opportunity to over-romanticise things is refused.

Taken *in toto*, the Footscray 2001 publication is thus something of a brave and in some degrees balanced 'intelligent tourism' text. We are 'educated', but in simple and illuminating terms. For example, the novitiate reader learns of the English place-names (in Victoria) which have borrowed Aboriginal words, but the listing is suggestive and generative rather than being dully comprehensive (*LPG*, p. 356). Elsewhere, the novitiate reader learns how culture is usually transferred through group *moieties*, but neither the Indigenous-anthropological detail nor the social-science anthropological detail is overbearing (*LPG*, p. 204). And, later on, the novitiate reader learns that in the rock art of New South Wales, the human beings are shown in front view while animals are shown in profile: again the petroglyphology whets the appetite for more but does not drown it out. This Lonely Planet publication team have clearly produced many instructive travel handbooks that have sold!

Moreover, copious maps are provided in painstaking style with easy-to-follow legends, and yet the editors remain perpetually attentive not to render access to precious Aboriginal sites (for instance, the rock art region of Ku-ring-gai, north of Sydney; *LPG*, pp. 150–1) over-easy. And the work is not a work that sinks into over-romantic or unadulterated traditionalisms; for instance, the info-nauts of the contemporary electronic age are well served with three detailed pages of 'internet resource' insight on matters of Aboriginalia such as 'art and culture', 'the struggle', 'reconciliation', etc.

At the same time, for one of the authors of this chapter – i.e. for someone who has worked for long periods in Western Australia and in the Northern Territory (among several Australian states) – the *LP Aboriginal Australia Guide* was plenteous in the potential of its reflexive delicacies. As a former community worker in the Ngaluma country of Roebourne in the north of Western Australia, it is now reassuringly uplifted for him to be reminded how (at Karratha) one had been living and working in 'good, soft earth country' (*LPG*, p. 406). As a former administrator working out of Kalgoorlie, in Wongi Country, all sorts of memories are now rekindled for him about the Kalkula Tjukurr (Silky Pear) Dreaming which had hung over the Kalkula Tjukurr (loosely, Kalgoorlie) township. As a former 'Cultural Studies' researcher in the Kimberleys, during the 1980s, it is now fascinating for him to see how the Lombadina Aboriginal Community (at Cape Leveque; *LPG*, p. 418) and the Bardi people (at Kooljaman) have, during and since the 1990s, moved towards a gradual embrace of tourism (*LPG*, p. 418). And as a former management official at the Yulara International Tourist Township in the Northern Territory, it is now intriguing for him to read of the weight of effort which certain sections of the Pitjantjatjara and Yankunyttjatjara peoples (apparently) put into tourism at the turn of the century in order to communicate some of their precious stories about their 'Central Australian' territory and about their long-standing desert inheritances (*LPG*, pp. 249–53).

The weaknesses of the text as a communicator of worldmaking notions of 'home country'/'host lands'

Although the Lonely Planet text has many virtues as a work promoting 'intelligent tourism' it has its feeblenesses, too. Indeed, the guidebook is rather insipid in terms of its coverage of the realities of *change* and *influence* which conceivably come hand-in-glove with tourism. While the book indeed acknowledges that 'things change fast in the travel industry' (*LPG*, p. 19), it does not seriously acknowledge the fact that 'things change fast *through* the travel industry'! While the text contains sections that cover 'assimilation' (*LPG*, pp. 43–4) and 'conflict and assimilation policies' (*LPG*, p. 381), it only covers the matter in general terms and does not consider the role of tourism/hospitality/events management in the assimilative or neo-colonialist cum neo-imperialist control of people. In similar fashion, the threat of the external tourism industry appropriating things Indigenous and entities Indigenous is glossed over (notably in terms of the expanding interest in Aboriginalia among electronic citizens of the world on the World Wide Web). And, in contrast, there is little that is positive about the manner in which new declarations of being, identity and inheritance *in and through* tourism, per se, can in fact be of uplifting or enriching value. The eugenic enunciatory worth of tourism and related inscriptive industries thereby also goes unstated. One would have thought that careful clarifications thereon would tally with the book's essential encoding purpose in raising not only world-made imagination about Aboriginal people among contemporary travellers, but in also cultivating imagination within Aboriginal people about the new possibilities of life and community for them in the contemporary world through the careful and controlled development of apposite forms of representation through tourism. Or would it have been difficult to appear anything but 'patronising' in speaking expressly on such a matter?

While the Footscray 2001 text has so clearly been edited with considerable observance of detail, the work sometimes falters with regard to the depth of emphasis or the strength of advice it gives to things. Readers are reminded about the harsh travel conditions that apply in those remote areas of Australia where 'traditional'/'semi-traditional' Indigenous populations live (for instance, see *LPG*, pp. 287, 313, 425) but these warnings tend to be small and are either buried almost irresponsibly in small one- to two-inch boxes, or are lost mid-paragraph somewhere. The use of in situ Aboriginal guides by travellers/visitors is recommended (for instance on *LPG*, p. 373), but the pros and cons of how such a guide is actually obtained is not treated substantively anywhere in the book. There are also insufficient reminders in the 450 pages of the text as to how permits to travel on Aboriginal land can and ought to be obtained: this critical information is merely relegated to four small print columns on pages 126–7. Other weaknesses of emphasis concern the limited attention given to the fact that in Australia the Aboriginal Areas Protection Authority has the right to prosecute individuals who disturb sacred sites or even enter and litter specific lands – the point is secluded within a small 'legal matters' paragraph (*LPG*, p. 134) – and the dangers of introducing or using alcohol at Indigenous sites is reduced to a small number of asides (for instance on *LPG*, pp. 125 and 248). Indeed there is not much consolidated coverage in the text anywhere on the sorts of activities that would be deemed 'infelicitous', 'improper' or 'infiltrative' at Aboriginal sites or on Indigenous land. Tourists, from overseas especially, must not be expected to know these things, notably when they can reach arrival points like Alice Springs International Airport within a day or two (or even within a matter of hours) flying-time of all of the world's metropolitan centres.

And furthermore, could the *LP Aboriginal Australia Guide* not have given greater prominence to differences in gender practices – compared to Western/ Euro-Australian/non-Aboriginal cultural pursuits? A very small box (*LPG*, p. 138) does warn that 'it is not appropriate for women to play the didjeridu', for example, but the *LPG* generally skirts around differences in gender role maintenance across cultures. Perhaps the Melbourne editorial team was not too keen to stir up unrest among certain independent travellers from overseas who may be antagonised by what to them may appear – in traditional or neo-traditional 'Australia' – to be sad, artificial or debilitating classifications of life via gender. Few tourists are ever immediately ready to suspend their own judgments on how each and every society should be ordered. Few tourists may even know that their own worldmaking value judgments and preconceptions are actually hard at work as they inspect this or that in new cultural realms and landscapes overseas. But here the Lonely Planet team say far too little about the intrusions of tourist-borne gender perspectives which, in this case, have evolved in urban-industrial/cosmopolitan-city settings. As with the in-society use of the bullroarer (at male initiation ceremonies; *LPG*, p. 150), an attempt to interculturally educate (or at least 'clarify') the traveller about the sorts of gender-based thinking that persist within Indigenous traditional culture-scapes has thereby been refused.

In terms of what one could call the sort of 'quiet' but 'informed' criticality that Horne is anxious to see developed at cultural and natural tourist sites – to raise the level of intercultural awareness over and above the dull and trivial (Horne, 1992: 137; see also p. 131 for a specific comment on Australian Aborigines) – the Footscray 2001 text occasionally disappoints. For instance, some large debates concerning the different meaning of 'art' and 'the authenticity of, production' to so called 'Aboriginal Artists' is sadly omitted when lead Aboriginal painters like Clifford Possum (*LPG*, p. 302) are covered. See Myers (2005) for a mature critical reflection on the unsteady juxtapositions and the foggy interpolations that fast crop up when matters of authentic Aboriginal art rub up against received tradition and new business possibility.

Likewise, elsewhere, little is said about the ongoing conflict between certain non-Aboriginal and Aboriginal views over matters of ownership, possession and inheritance at key sites of Indigenous protest like the Old Swan Brewery in Perth (*LPG*, p. 383). These are the kind of conflicts of attachment which Ryan (1996: 153–95), Read (1996: 67–8) and Haynes (1998: 261–80) have written about in contrasting but accessible ways, and about which twenty-first century Indigenous intellectuals across Australia have much to admonish, emend and reprove (see Langton, 2006; Moreton-Robinson, 2006). And there is no mention of a key custodial site like Coronation Hill in the Northern Territory, where different Aboriginal interest groups have clamorously contested legitimacy of ownership (see Gelder and Jacobs, 1998: 68–81 on this case). And when the *LP Aboriginal Australia Guide* provides a useful listing of 'special events' which feature Indigenous groups which are promoted by Indigenous communities (*LPG*, pp. 134–7), there is no attempt to distinguish those happenings which have a deep legitimating purpose to them from those which are mere shows of knockabout fun and entertainment: 'educationally' and 'interpretively', they are all thrown in the same dilly bag![8] The reader might wonder, for instance, whether the Weipa Croc Eisteddfod (*LPG*, p. 289) has any substantive spirituality (open or closed?) to it regarding sacred/totemic reptilian life, or is just a free-and-easy intercultural playtime merely primed by the heavy thematic-cum-commercial 'capture' of the primordial toothy monster.

There are a number of other small blemishes in the intelligent tourism quotient of the *LP Aboriginal Australia Guide*. It might be churlish to condemn the book for not giving much insight into Aboriginal life and culture in a huge region like the Purnululu National Park (and the Bungle Bungle Ranges) in the Halls Creek area in the north of Western Australia (*LPG*, p. 425), for the Kija and Daru people of that region are one of many over-visited populations who may simply not want to excite much further external visitation to their removed but highly alluring hearth and homelands there. And while the immensely important 'Mabo' and 'Wik' High Court land ownership/land rights cases have been given prominent coverage in the text (*LPG*, pp. 28–9, 31), little attempt is made to relate those sorts of native-title cum cultural-inheritance decisions with what is going on elsewhere around the world (where tourists might themselves visit or hail from) where like battles are being waged over questions of traditional ownership. Indeed, the book does not offer a reading list from which the curious traveller can read up on such parallel developments of cultural inheritance and contemporary litigation around the world. The book therefore lacks a useful cross-cultural and cross-continental dimension of the 'intelligent' sort that Horne has always been seemingly eager to promote, where the encoding has to recognise and admit the styles and fashions of decoded understandings and misunderstandings that lie inevitably in wait, in their *almost natural* ethnocentricity (see Hollinshead and Suleman on 'Eurocentrism' and on 'naturalisation', Chapter 11, this volume).

In terms of structure to the text, the Lonely Planet decision to identify 'places' primarily by the Aboriginal 'country' they are located within has already been praised. Sometimes, however, this practice means that the geographic relationship of these sites with major cities/largish townships are hard to fathom for the newcomer to Australia. It might have been helpful for the editorial team to have provided a larger and louder tabulation at the back of the text cross-indexing these modern-day settlements with the traditional Indigenous 'lands' they are on or are otherwise associated with.

Other small elements in the construction of the book disappoint. The book could have done with a number of line-drawings to explain key features or elements of Indigenous life – such as what 'shell middens' are (see, for instance, the reference to the 500 midden mounds of the Weipa Peninsula; *LPG*, p. 289) and how they were formed. The same could have been provided for bora rings – i.e. for 'the circular areas of banked earth used for ceremonial purposes' (*LPG*, p. 139), for Wiltja (Mulga tree shelters) and for quandong (small 'native peach' fruit trees), etc. Then, again, the final index of the text could have been more comprehensively treated. Although matters of *authenticity* and *culture-keeping places* are both frequently addressed topics in the book, they do not appear in this index, while 'Bradshaws' (i.e. the small ethereal rock-art figures depicted in mysterious ceremonial/dance settings) are also mentioned rather frequently in the work, but are only listed in the index as being on pp. 71–2, per se. And perhaps other terms like thalu sites (tribal increase sites) could have been explained less frugally, without any degree of vital, life-sustaining or secretive knowledge being unduly given away as that insight-giving is expanded.

And to close, among the weaknesses found, certain handy 'intelligent' features of the book could have been summarised in better fashion. The text mentions a number of videos on Aboriginalia in passing, but does not offer a broad re-cap of the production and availability of these films in its end-pages. In this respect, hopefully later editions of the handbook will be much more pointed in these reflexive matters internationally as they contour the richer web resources and the eclectic digital productivity of our later (post-video) decades. And the text lists a number of agencies which have responsibility for matters Aboriginal (for example, *LPG*, pp. 42–3, 144) but only provides terse insight on how their institutional roles and functions differ. The tourist/visitor/reader is evidently expected to comprehend these critical differences *before* he/she delves into their respective listed websites, or else he/she must probe all such electronic sites. Moreover, the text occasionally lists a 'course' on Indigenous themes (such as the Indigenous Learning Centre course at the University of Technology Jumbunna Centre in Sydney; *LPG*, p. 145), but it does not make it clear whether they are full-time tertiary courses of study or are otherwise walk-in classes which the insight-craving tourist can more flexibly drop in upon. Finally, the Footscray 2001 blue book does offer a heap of recommended reading for those interested in other Lonely Planet subjects and other 'Lonely' territories (*LPG*, pp. 130, 433–5), but it does not offer a lengthy listing of texts for unschooled or schooled readers who wish to know that little bit more about Arnhem Land, Western Desert Aboriginal populations or the Uluru-Kata Tjuta cultural landscapes. Perhaps such a substantial listing might date the book unduly, but then that would reveal an absence of confidence in estimated sales and expected production updates! No … that cannot be right! The book lists a torrent of web addresses which were probably out of date a few years after the book's appearance, so that cannot be the reason. The absence of a reading list – other than a hasty 'ten' standards such as *The Encyclopaedia of Aboriginal Australia* (*LPG*, p. 130) – is a large drawback for any supposed intelligence-generating and insight-transferring vehicle.

Prospect: future encoding for and about 'Indigenous imagination' and 'decoded intelligence' on Aboriginality

It is clear from a fast inspection of this compact Footscray blue book on 'Indigenous Australia' that the Lonely Planet Group has come a very long way since the first 'classic travel adventure' (*LPG*, p. 18) across Europe to Australia from company founders Tony and Maureen Wheeler in 1972. Now the company is the largest independent travel publisher in the world – a well-articulated operation able to so speedily conceive of, produce and edit such an extensive guidebook on a pioneering subject. Who is now going to follow their impressive lead and produce the same for the 'public' 'national' cultures of the First 'Americans' of North America, the viewable inheritances of the Indigenous populations of Africa or the heritage-tourism sites of the cultures of Polynesia/Micronesia/Melanesia, for example?

Maybe, over the years, the *LP Aboriginal Australia Guide* will be condemned here and there because it just does not offer enough depth on this nor sufficient treatment of that. But it is hard to offer a comprehensive coverage of the history of a continent of people, as well as a thorough treatment of the sociology/anthropology/political science/natural history/and all, and yet still fundamentally remain a pocket *tourist* handbook for those long-standing inheritances and that viewable culture gene bank. The danger exists that this little blue book will be judged in terms of higher aims than its editors could ever reasonably have been expected to set out to achieve. It has perhaps raised the bar considerably in terms of what is available to read on Indigenous culture/Aboriginalia in Australia (or anywhere in the world!), yet (ironically) will possibly be judged for not raising that bar enough in terms of the degree to which it offers *critical* analyses of the development of Indigenous tourism in and across Australia.

By Horne's criteria though, the Footscray 2001 publication is a sudden and (hopefully) propagative arrival at the world's cultural and travel bookshops. Assessed in its entirety, it is, broadly speaking, a brilliant set of first-person accounts of Indigenous being and of Aboriginal life-spaces. It may lie too quiet on the neo-colonialisms and the over-determinations of *tourism* and of *event development, ipso facto,* but it is a most useful positive tool for those Aboriginal and non-Aboriginal interest groups who want to see Indigenous groups operating, alive and kicking, in different and dynamic ways of being and ways of being-in-business through this new century. It may be a text that is light in both its early history of Aboriginal existence – just precisely how, when and where did the very first Aborigines enter Australia via the north-west of Western Australia? (*LPG*, p. 380) – and in its longitudinal history of Aboriginal-European relations across the dry continent, but it constitutes a wonderful primer on both 'traditional' cosmology and on contemporary 'transitional' happenings. And the text may generally appear to treat Aboriginal concerns with a sense of perceived cohesion and even a sense of polished grandeur which the vicissitudes of real life in raw city-block, townscape and dry-riverbed circumstance across Australia can never actually yield up for travellers/visitors in such 'elegance'. *Pace*, the book does boldly bring home for tourists all sorts of new insights about the existence of the 'Stolen Generations', all sorts of new insights about the political doldrums which native title lease-holders and lease-claimants find themselves caught up within. Thus the Lonely Planet handbook is not merely a text that grieves for the vanished 'Other': it is indeed a compendium that helps forge new understanding (and thereby new hope) for the living 'Other' … and thereby is itself promissory for fresh sorts of world-made figurations, refigurations and configurations about Indigenous being and becoming.

It is, then, rather early to judge how good the work of Sarine Singh, David Andrew, bryan Andy *et al.*, is. In our wide and ever-changing world, there is an inherent lack of long-term equilibria in most things – there is certainly considerable instability and uncertainty in Aboriginal being at the moment, and this book not only touches on those sorts of hybridities and third-space interstitialities (after Bhabha, 1994), but it conceivably adds heat and light to that intercultural friction as it quietly demonstrates not only what Indigenous populations can freshly do via tourism, but what some Indigenous populations are already doing in tourism.

Just as there is no fixed, single, underlying set of principles for all Aboriginal societies (Morrissey, 2006), so there is no sure route to success or to sustainability through tourism. What counts at each cultural crossroad is the quality of imagination which can fit new ways of attaining things to old ways of valuing things. In this sense, the *LP Aboriginal Australia Guide* is a new-ways book, or rather a new-wave book. While its primary purpose may have been to correctively encode and thereby inform travelling culture-seekers about the riches of Indigenous edifices of nature and culture across the dry continent, the scintillating breadth, love and care by which the book has been produced will also inform the proud ancient culture-holders of 'Australia', themselves, that they have an inheritance that the world-beyond genuinely wants to know about. Hence, the book is an important first step in the provision of dinkum[9] intelligence about the appropriately knowable Indigenous heritage of Australia and the appropriately viewable sites and sights of Aboriginal being. This well-packed Lonely Planet blue book is an important beginning in terms of intercultural intelligence; let us hope that as the book expands and foliates, that future editions are tended with the same evidential degree of care and control in those places where the 2001 edition was silent or where it otherwise hiccoughed a little.

The need for non-Indigenous travellers to sites and non-Indigenous visitors to events to be given decently inculcated interpretations which host-group and locative-community populations are happy with – normally after much painstaking and demonstrable cultural-stakeholder discussion – is acute. The ultimate aim must not be just to draw the culture-thirsty journeyer to top-soil sites and scenes of Aboriginal lands, but to cultivate respect for the bottom-soil Indigenous cosmologies (as much as can be 'told'!) that underlie those viewable materialities/those surface objects. None of these strategically audienced dialectics between the hailed and encoded Indigenous inheritance and the often-overweening decoded desire to see/to experience/to indulge in Aboriginalia is easy to engage in. And all the while, these enticing cultural forms and the descriptive worldmaking narratives about them are being steadily remade and subtly de- or re-appreciated by both Indigenous and non-Indigenous populations alike, both seemingly at increasingly fast paces. These matters of cultural syntax and cosmological grammar are deep and protean: they are not simple games to play in. The demands of corrigibility are very very tall ... for all parties.

Notes

1. Readers of this chapter should be aware that any mention of the personal name of an Indigenous person who has died recently can cause considerable hurt and suffering within many Aboriginal cultures. Indeed, this very chapter may contain the names of individuals who are now no longer alive. In order not to deeply offend, readers communicating within or to Australia should use this chapter with considerable care and respect.
2. The 'Stolen Generations' are those youngsters in Aboriginal communities who have 'white'/'European' physical features and who were forcibly removed from Aboriginal settlements to be brought up in non-Aboriginal environments. The term is usually applied to government-authorised police-work to locate and then 'capture' or 'save' these mixed-blood youngsters during the early and middle decades of the twentieth century. As a named concept, it was first used in 1996 during an inquiry chaired by Sir Ronald Wilson, a human rights and equal opportunities commissioner (Ham, 2001; Moreton-Robinson, 2004: 22–9; Toussaint, 2004: 17).
3. In inspecting Horne's use of the term 'public culture' vis-à-vis 'intelligent tourism'/'intelligent events', it is helpful to compare Horne's journalistic-style engagement with the very term 'public culture' with that of the editors of the academic journal *Public Culture*. In the eponymous journal within the humanities, the rubric 'public culture' is used to cover the cultural flows which ripple and rush around the world, and which draw cities, societies and states into larger transnational relationships and global political economies (*Public Culture*, 1998: ii). The term is therefore used

within this relatively new academic journal to refer to the global transformations of culture which characterise the contestations of contemporary life, notably in the spheres of identity, mediation and consumption (Appadurai and Breckenridge, 1998). While Horne's (1992) own use of the term 'public culture' broadly reflects much of the above as is privileged in the humanities journal, he tends to deploy the term (within his own books) to address the presiding represented culture and the asserted celebrated heritage of a population or place. Thus to him – in his own works – the public culture of a people or locale is a dominant, pre-selected mix of the 'national' and 'exhibited' cultural narratives about locally revered heritage and locally revered nature (see Hollinshead (on Horne), 1999: 270). In Horne's view, all modern nations/governments/elites develop distinct and cleverly scripted versions of the championed inheritances of important places. These privileged or mainstreamed storylines and interpretations tend to make use of the legendary sites and sights of tourism to naturalise particular objects, events and settings. Hence, Horne is more concerned about the fabricative character of the held representations of places than in the flows and transformations (*ipso facto*) which course between places, or through and over them.

4. Independent advice: the encoding. Clearly, here, the Lonely Planet company might still claim to be able to meaningfully give informed (i.e. insider or community-approved) advice in terms of knowledge about particular Indigenous sites and singular interpretive events and attractions, while remaining actively and interestedly engaged in the development of visitations to Aboriginal settings and drawcards in general. Such mixed aims are not always easy to honour faithfully and 'objectively', of course.
5. The Mabo case – as resolved by the High Court (of Australia) – in 1992 was a highly important judgment in terms of questions of Aboriginal land ownership. The Mabo decision constituted an assault on the received tenet of *terra nullius*, that is the received and rather convenient outlook that Australia was effectively 'uninhabited' and therefore not owned by anyone at the time of British colonisation. The case concerned the land rights claim of Eddie Koiki Mabo and four other Mer (Murray Islanders) in northern Queensland. The Mabo legal team took ten years of difficult struggle to obtain their victory (on appeal) over the Queensland state government in this case (Toussaint, 2004: 1–2, 133–4).
6. The Wik decision: worldmaking contextuality. In 1996, the High Court (of Australia) determined (in another critical Queensland case) that – four years after Mabo (see note 5 above) – the granting of pastoral leases in Australia did not rule out native title rights. Hence, native title was deemed to be capable of running alongside pastoral leases – a decision in favour of the interests of Aboriginal land, cultural and spiritual interests which caused much upset among pastoral companies who felt that their security of operation was under threat (Toussaint, 2004: 94–5, 143–4). In the late 1990s, the conservative-minded Liberal party government of Prime Minister John Howard worked ardently to iron out what it sees as some large loose ends pertaining to the Wik ruling.
7. The term 'last of the nomads' is taken from the title of W. J. Peasey's account of the attempt in Western Australia in 1977 to rescue two 'lost' Aborigines in the aridness of the Gibson Desert. The two individuals, Warri and Yatungka, had broken traditional marriage laws and had supposedly endured several decades of exile in isolated and drought-stricken country. The tale about the 'rescue' – namely that of the supposedly last people to live a life untouched or unsullied by contact with the outside world – caught the imagination of the national and international press (Peasey, 1983).
8. Dilly bag: a small over-the-shoulder traditional bush-bag, woven out of natural grasses and frequently dyed with local bush colours. It is rumoured that a second edition of this book by Tomas Pernecky will come provided within a special purpose Routledge dilly bag!!
9. Dinkum: Australian-English colloquial term (derived from much older forms of regional English) for that which is sincere, proper and committed – i.e. for that which is 'full-on'!

References

Altman, J. C. and Finlayson, J. (1991) *Aborigines and Tourism: An Issues Paper Prepared for the Ecologically Sustainable Working Group on Tourism*. Canberra: Centre for Aboriginal Economic Policy Research, Australian National University.

Appadurai, A. and Breckenridge, C. A. (1998) 'Why public culture?', *Public Culture*, 1: 5–11.

Bhabha, H. (1994) *The Location of Culture*. London: Routledge.

Bhattacharyya, D. P. (1997) 'Mediating India: an analysis of a guidebook', *Annals of Tourism Research*, 24: 371–89.

Bodley, J. H. (1982) *Victims of Progress*. Palo Alto, CA: Mayfield.

Brown, F. (1998) *Tourism Reassessed: Blight or Blessing*. Oxford: Butterworth-Heinemann.

Buck, E. (1993) *Paradise Remade: The Politics and Culture in Hawai'i*. Philadelphia: Temple University Press.

Crick, M. (1988) 'Sun, sex, sights, savings, and security', *Criticism, Heresy and Interpretation*, 1: 37–76.

Duelke, B. (2005) 'Knowing tradition, dealing with history: on concepts, strategies and practices', in L. Taylor, G. K. Ward, G. Henderson, R. Davis and A. Wallis (eds), *The Power of Knowledge: The Resonance of Tradition*. Canberra: Aboriginal Studies Press, pp. 199–213.

Durkheim, E. (1961) *The Elementary Forms of Religious Life*. New York: Collier.

Featherstone, M. (1995) *Undoing Culture: Globalization, Postmodernism, and Identity*. London: Sage.

Fjellman, S. M. (1992) *Vinyl Leaves: Walt Disney World and America*. Boulder, CO: Westview Press.

Gelder, K. and Jacobs, J. M. (1998) *Uncanny Australia: Sacredness and Identity in a Postcolonial Nation*. Melbourne: Melbourne University Press.

Goeldner, C. R., Ritchie, J. R. B. and McIntosh, R. W. (2000) 'Tourism's economic impact', in C. R. Goeldner, J. R. B. Ritchie and R. W. McIntosh (eds), *Tourism: Principles, Practices, Philosophies*. New York: John Wiley, pp. 411–42.

Grossman, M. (ed.) (2006) *Blacklines: Contemporary Critical Writing by Indigenous Australians*. Melbourne: Melbourne University Press.

Hall, C. M. (1994) *Tourism and Politics: Policy, Powers, and Place*. Chichester: J. Wiley & Sons.

Hall, S. (1997) 'The local and the global: globalization and ethnicity', in A. D. King (ed.), *Culture, Globalization and the World-System: Contemporary Conditions for the Representation of Identity*. Minneapolis, MN: University of Minnesota Press.

Ham, P. (2001) 'Doubts on "stolen" Aboriginal children', *Sunday Times* (London), 4 March.

Haynes, R. D. (1998) *Seeking the Centre: The Australian Desert in Literature, Art and Film*. Cambridge: Cambridge University Press.

Hodson, M. (2002) 'Which guides deserve precious space in your suitcase? Mark Hodson tests the best', *Sunday Times* (London), 28 April, pp. 5.10–5.11.

Hollinshead, K. (1996) 'Marketing and metaphysical realism: the disidentification of Aboriginal life and traditions through tourism', in R. Butler and T. Hinch (eds), *Tourism and Indigenous Peoples*. London: International Thomson Business Press, pp. 308–48.

Hollinshead, K. (1999) 'Tourism as public culture: Horne's ideological commentary on the legerdemain of tourism', *International Journal of Tourism Research*, 1: 267–92.

Hollinshead, K. (2002) 'Tourism and the making of the world: the dynamics of our contemporary tribal lives', *Excellence Lecture Series: The Honors College*, 1 (2), April. Miami, FL: the Honors College, Florida International University.

Hollinshead, K. (2009a) 'Tourism and the social production of culture and place: critical conceptions on the projection of location', *Tourism Analysis*, 13, 639–60.

Hollinshead, K. (2009b) 'The "worldmaking" prodigy of tourism: the reach and power of tourism in the dynamics of change and transformation', *Tourism Analysis*, 14: 139–52.

Hollinshead, K. and Kuon, V. (2015) 'Events in the liquid modern world: the call for fluid acumen in the liquid modern world', in O. Moufakkir and T. Pernecky (eds), *Ideological, Cultural, and Social Aspects of Events*. Wallingford: Cabi, pp. 12–27.

Hollinshead, K., Ateljevic, I. and Ali, N. (eds) (2009) 'Introduction: worldmaking agency/ worldmaking authority – the sovereign constitutive role of tourism', *Tourism Geographies*, 11: 427–43.

Horne, D. (1992) *The Intelligent Tourist*. McMahon's Point, Australia: Margaret Gee Holdings.

Horton, D. R. (ed.) (1995) *Encyclopaedia of Aboriginal Australia*. Canberra: Aboriginal Studies Press.

Jones, A. and Jenkins, K. (2008) 'Rethinking collaboration: working the indigene-colonizer hyphen', in N. Denzin, Y. S. Lincoln and L. T. Smith (eds), *Handbook of Critical Indigenous Methodologies*. Los Angeles: Sage, pp. 471–86.

Kauffman, P. (2000) *Travelling Aboriginal Australia: Discovery and Reconciliation*. Flemington, Australia: Hyland House.

Kirshenblatt-Gimblett, B. (1998) *Destination Culture: Tourisms, Museums, and Heritage*. Berkeley, CA: University of California Press.

Lanfant, M.-F. (1995) 'Internationalization and the challenge to identity', in M.-F. Lanfant, J. B. Allcock and E. M. Bruner (eds), *International Tourism: Identity and Change*. London: Sage, pp. 24–43.

Langton, M. (2006) 'Introduction: culture wars', in M. Grossman (ed.), *Blacklines: Contemporary Critical Writing by Indigenous Australians*. Melbourne: Melbourne University Press, pp. 81–91.

McKay, I. (1994) *Quest for the Folk*. Montreal: McGill & Queens University Press.

Meethan, K. (2001) *Tourism in Global Society: Place, Culture, Consumption*. Basingstoke: Palgrave.

Moreton-Robinson, A. (ed.) (2004) *Whitening Race*. Canberra: Aboriginal Studies Press.

Moreton-Robinson, A. (2006) 'Introduction: resistance, recovery, and revitalisation', in M. Grossman (ed.), *Blacklines: Contemporary Critical Writing by Indigenous Australians*. Melbourne: Melbourne University Press, pp. 127–31.

Morrissey, P. (2006) 'Moving, remembering, singing our place', in M. Grossman (ed.), *Blacklines: Contemporary Critical Writing by Indigenous Australians*. Melbourne: Melbourne University Press, pp. 189–93.

Myers, F. (2005) 'Unsettled business: acrylic painting, tradition, and Indigenous being', in L. Taylor, G. K. Ward, G. Henderson, R. Davis and A. Wallis (eds), *The Power of Knowledge: The Resonance of Tradition*. Canberra: Aboriginal Studies Press, pp. 3–33.

Palmer, K. (2005) 'Dependency, technology, and government', in L. Taylor, G. K. Ward, G. Henderson, R. Davis and A. Wallis (eds), *The Power of Knowledge: The Resonance of Tradition*. Canberra: Aboriginal Studies Press, p. 101–15.

Peasey, W. J. (1983) *The Last of the Nomads*. Fremantle: Fremantle Arts Centre Press.

Public Culture (1998) 'Journal aims', 1: ii.

Read, P. (1996) *Return to Nothing: The Meaning of Lost Places*. Cambridge: Cambridge University Press.

Robertson, R. (1997) 'Social theory, cultural relativity and the problem of globality', in A. D. King (ed.), *Culture, Globalization and the World-System: Contemporary Conditions for the Representation of Identity*. Minneapolis, MN: University of Minnesota Press, pp. 69–90.

Ryan, S. (1996) *The Cartographic Eye: How Explorers Saw Australia*. Cambridge: Cambridge University Press.

Singh, S., Andrew, D., Andy, b., Choy, M., *et al.* (2001) *Aboriginal Australia and the Torres Strait Islands: Guide to Indigenous Australia*. Melbourne: Lonely Planet Publications.

Taylor, L., Ward, G. K., Henderson, G., Davis, R. and Wallis, A. (eds) (2005) *The Power of Knowledge: The Resonance of Tradition*. Canberra: Aboriginal Studies Press.

Toussaint, S. (ed.) (2004) *Crossing Boundaries: Cultural, Legal, Historical and Practice Issues in Native Title*. Melbourne: Melbourne University Press.

Venn, C. (2006) *The Postcolonial Challenge: Towards Alternative Worlds*. London: Sage.

9 Ethnography in the diaspora

Indian cultural production and transnational networks

Alison Booth

Introduction

This chapter will describe how my approach to research is framed by ethnography. I focus my research on the producers of Indian cultural events in the global and localised contexts. I am particularly interested in the processes and relationships that support their activities, with specific reference to events that are of interest to and/or produced by New Zealand's Indian communities. In this chapter, I discuss my own research as a vehicle for describing strategies for gathering research information and reporting findings set in the context of complex global production networks. Ethnography, as a research method, can prove challenging when the process of data-gathering engages cross-cultural relationships and global networks.

The term 'ethnography' has a double meaning: it refers both to a set of research methods used in fieldwork and to the report presenting that fieldwork, usually a written, richly detailed narrative account of people's everyday lives (Ybema *et al.*, 2010: 348). My research aims to explore and understand Indian cultural identity as a global phenomenon. I work in a web of transnational networks spanning space and time that underpin the heart of my research. The underlying argument to my research premise is that sustainable production networks have the potential to weave together events, diasporic communities and transcultural networks to not only create economic gains but also to empower cultural communities (Booth, 2014).

This chapter begins with a description of my approach to ethnographic research and demonstrates how developing case studies is central to my research findings. I describe how I gather information as well as my positioning in the research environment, and how these frame the core of my findings. This is followed by a consideration of the problems, challenges and limitations encountered 'in the field'. To finish, I offer a descriptive narrative of a dance performance at a local cultural festivity as a means of demonstrating how I develop case studies.

Methodology and reflections on gathering data

In my approach to ethnography, I recognise that when we describe something, even when the story we are telling is our own (in the normal course of events), the voice of our own culture – its many voices in fact – comes through in what we say. In the process of gathering data, I was challenged by the limitations of my role as an 'outsider' and a woman.

Ethnographies are said to be portraits of diversity in an increasingly globalised world, displaying the intricate ways in which individuals and groups resist the presumption of a shared order (Clifford, 1988). Ethnography as a research method rests on the dual techniques of participant observation and interviewing. The researcher commits to 'engagement with' and 'participation in' everyday situations in social life. The ethnographic way of knowing builds upon 'inter-subjectiveness' grounded in theoretical sampling, theoretical saturation and theoretical analysis in order to shape the context in which the researcher makes their own judgments (Botterill and Platenkamp, 2012: 83–4). This is supported by a commitment to writing up findings as 'thick descriptions' to assist in identifying the commonalities of the case studies that have been carried out in the course of the research.

The process of gathering data that can be presented as thick descriptions allows observations of local behaviours to be contextualised, presenting the findings in the anthropological tradition of Clifford Geertz. One can – and this in fact is how the field progresses conceptually – take a line of theoretical attack developed in connection with one exercise in ethnographic interpretation and employ it in another, pushing it forward to greater precision and broader relevance, but one cannot write a 'General Theory of Cultural Interpretation'. Or, rather, one can, but there appears to be little profit in it, because the essential task of theory building here is not to codify abstract regularities but to make thick description possible, not to generalise across cases but to generalise within them (Geertz, 1973: 26). From this theoretical perspective, an ethnographer presents 'thick' descriptions, which are composed not only of facts ('thin' description) but also of the interpretation of the context of informant comments, observations and fact building in settings in which the researcher participates.

As my ethnographic research focuses on the complex nature of culture production, I employ a mixed-methods approach by gathering primary and secondary data. This process ensures that the data are reliable (Creswell and Clark, 2007). One of the biggest challenges confronting qualitative researchers is ensuring the quality and trustworthiness of their research findings, which can be addressed by evaluating the research results against established criteria. Reliability, validity, generalisability and objectivity are fundamental concerns for quantitative researchers.

To understand the meaning of 'reliability' and 'validity', Golafshani (2003) presents various definitions and differing perspectives from qualitative researchers, taking into account that the use of these terms is commonly used in quantitative research. Golafshani demonstrates how the concepts of 'reliability' and 'validity' need to be reconsidered, as the qualitative research paradigm has moved away from the traditional positivist (scientific) paradigm. The ethnographic literature offers a vast collection of methodological examples for qualitative research inquiry (Geertz, 1972; Harnish, 2006; Johnson, 2010; Mackley-Crump, 2015; Picard and Robinson, 2006) demonstrating findings that are valid in the research context.

Validity is established through a process of triangulation, which refers to the use of more than one approach to the investigation of a research question in order to enhance confidence in the ensuing findings (Guba and Lincoln, 1989; McMurray *et al.*, 2004; Yin, 2014). When social science research relies on a single method, it may suffer the limitations inherent to that method as applied to the topic or phenomenon being studied. Triangulation offers the prospect of enhanced confidence because it may offer multiple methodological perspectives on the topic of study (Cox and Hassard, 2010).

In the case of my PhD research, triangulation was achieved through the use of ethnographic, archival and participatory methods and through the representation of data in textual case studies and graphic form. In addition, reflexive analysis was used to ensure that I, as a researcher, remained aware my own influence on the data (Krefting, 1991: 220). I kept a journal during the data collection period to record my thoughts and reflections on my experience within the framework of the research. What I found particularly important was to remember to always return to the research question and the scope of the inquiry.

I identified that I was really interested in researching the processes through which local and global network formations shape Auckland's Indian cultural performances and the consequent images of India that are received/consumed by the wider New Zealand audience. I framed my research around the following central research question: what are the processes and relationships that support the production of cultural events, with specific reference to events that are of interest to and/or produced by Aotearoa/New Zealand's Indian communities?

With this in mind, it is important to reflect on one's own place in the research context, as this will impact the discussions and findings. Reflexivity 'sets the scene' by explaining the background of the research inquiry from the researcher's perspective. The process provides a glimpse into the researcher's personal journey and how the researcher is situated in the field of inquiry. Setting the scene is a means of placing the ethnographer within the scope of the research inquiry. As the voice of the researcher is often not evident in case study research, it is important to understand the perspective of the researcher and how this informs and validates the findings.

Reflexivity: positioning myself in the research inquiry

My academic research journey began with my first conference presentation at the 2008 Annual Meeting of the Society of Ethnomusicology (Booth, 2008) and led to subsequent research opportunities and the completion of a PhD (Booth, 2014). The research central to this story was based on 25 years of professional experience in 'world music' concert production and participant observation research among performers, managers and other actors. I considered the various roles that producers play in the distinctive nature of advocacy in intra-cultural and extra-cultural concert productions, with specific reference to Indian cultural productions in Auckland, New Zealand.

To understand how I came to research this specific topic, it is important that I situate myself in the research context and clarify how my interest in this research topic began. I was born in the multicultural world of San Francisco, California and am not of South Asian heritage. I have had a lifetime interest in performing arts and specifically the arts of Asia. One of the most memorable moments of my teenage years was ushering for a concert by sarod master Ali Akbar Khan with Mahapurush Mishra accompanying on tabla, an experience which opened in me a deep appreciation of the classical music tradition of North India. Over the years, I have had the opportunity to live, work and study in this tradition, in the USA, India and New Zealand.

Professionally, I have worked as an event producer across various industry sectors, although I have a strong preference for the creative industries. The community of Indian musicians I have been connected to, for most of my adult life, has provided me with transnational networks. My husband has had a long history as a writer, concert reviewer, performer and assistant in many Indian performances in Auckland as well as internationally. These circumstances, under which my family arrived in New Zealand in 1993, opened up opportunities to work with touring musicians, university students and local Indian musicians. This background and past experiences inform my teaching, research and writing (Booth, 2014: 17–19).

Taking the stage: research beginnings

The following is a portion of the introduction to my first international conference presentation (Booth, 2008) that allowed my research voice to be heard for the first time. This story continues to be woven through my research even today, as it assists me in remembering who I am and where I am situated in my research.

When I moved to Auckland, New Zealand, in 1993, the music of India was not visible. I did meet people, of South Asian heritage, who had attended one or both of two concerts by Pandit Ravi Shankar and Ustad Alla Rakha that had taken place in 1973 and 1981. Many of these migrants arrived in New Zealand in the late 1960s and 1970s to work as doctors and accountants and in other white-collar professions. From my experience working within this community, I came to discover the importance of these concerts as they remained imbedded in their collective cultural memory.

The first Auckland Ravi Shankar concert that I have record of took place in 1973. It was attended by a recently arrived Pakistani immigrant who had learned sitar from his father in Lahore. He recalls the sell-out crowd at the Auckland Town Hall, then Auckland's premier classical venue. Although my friend and his wife were both employed in relatively prestigious white-collar professions, tickets were nevertheless very expensive for recently arrived migrant families. My friends sat in the cheapest seats available. Nevertheless, the concert experience made my sitar player friend feel at home in his new country and remains a pleasurable memory 35 years later (Booth, 2008).

In the process of writing these words and researching the tale, the cultural production of India in a transnational context never strayed far from my creative thoughts. My PhD thesis is dedicated to this sitar player friend who passed away during the final stages of my writing. He gave me ephemera (past posters and correspondence) from the many events we were either involved with producing or attended together over the years. His voice gives me confidence and adds authority to my research and validity to my findings.

Navigating the research puzzle

The process of gathering information began in the form of conversations and reviewing ephemera with friends and colleagues who shared in Auckland's Indian cultural production experiences. This process helped me frame the scope of my research. My office is full of boxes filled with memories that have nurtured my life as a producer, performer and participant in a myriad of cultural contexts. At the early stages of my PhD journey, I had to focus on how I could contain and prioritise the mass of information that I had collected.

I began by poring through the boxes, which had not been opened in years, and in some cases decades. As the Indian diaspora is based on transnational networks that are mobile, growing and expanding, I was able to draw on my past Indian cultural production experiences in India, Europe, North America and Australia. Putting the whole story together was challenging, as the research process became an ever-expanding, gigantic jigsaw puzzle.

One of many useful documents that surfaced in my archival search was a copy of *Festival of Asia: What's On* (Asia 2000, 1997), a document prepared for festival sponsors by Asia 2000, now referred to as the Asia New Zealand Foundation. This document had sat untouched in a filing cabinet for 15 years. As a researcher, I always struggle to decide what to keep and what to throw out, especially if you move from your hometown and live in other cities, countries and continents. In this case, I had kept a vital document that I was able to use in the design of my initial research questions. This document contained a wealth of historical information including confirmation of the identity of the sponsors, a record of the production relationships at play, and the history of performances by both local and international artists representing the Asian continent in New Zealand. This document proved useful as a means of confirming stories in subsequent interviews and media reports, which contributed reliability to my data.

I assisted in the production of the 1997 Festival of Asia as part of my involvement with the University of Auckland and the Indian community, and having participated in the delivery of the festival brought depth to my understanding of this historical occasion and the role that Asia 2000 has played over the years in supporting pan-Asian cultural events. This participant experience gave me the ability to pick up the phone and discuss my research questions and the intention of the document with the person who had created it, as she still works for the organisation. This mixed-method approach to data collection – historical documents, participant observation and informants – contributes to authenticating findings. This is just one example of how I compiled hundreds of minute stories that became the pieces required to complete the research puzzle that serves as the foundation of my ethnographic research.

New Zealand's expanding Indian diaspora

To understand the scope of the field in which my research sits, it is essential to understand the people central to the research focus. Through academic resources and government reports, empirical data can be identified. New Zealand's Indian population increased by 48 per cent between 2006 and 2013 to over 155,000, in a total New Zealand population of just over 4.4 million (Friesen, 2008; StatisticsNZ, 2013). Many of the more recent Indian migrants have arrived as international students, while others are skilled workers from major Indian cities as well as Africa, Europe and North America. The majority of students attend private tertiary institutes, polytechnics and universities located in Auckland. These new student arrivals, alongside the young new professional workforce, have brought with them new performance perspectives that challenge the more traditional concept of 'Indianness' practised by the longer-term residents.

There are many Indian cultural organisations in New Zealand representing a variety of linguistic and cultural identities. These identities can be roughly apprehended by examining Figure 9.1, which shows the number of speakers by Indian language over three consecutive census periods (StatisticsNZ, 2013).

The community organisations create festivities that serve the traditional function of networking and providing opportunities for preserving the traditional culture of

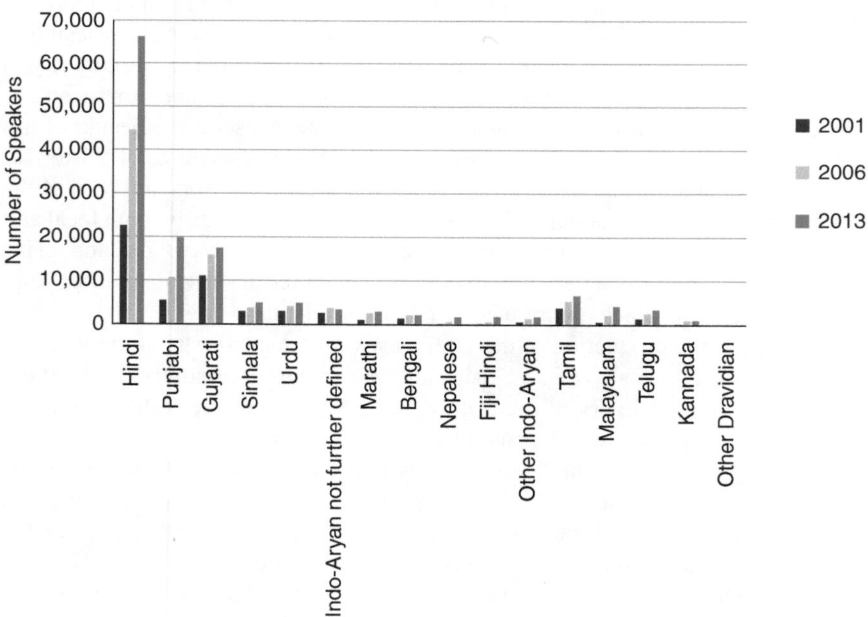

Figure 9.1 Comparison of the growth and diversity of Indian languages spoken in New Zealand between the years 2001, 2006 and 2013

their original homelands in the cultural site of their new homes (DeSouza, 2011; Mankekar, 2015; Turino and Lea, 2004; Vertovec, 1997). This is in contrast to the influx of new migrants that includes a population of young, educated professionals and tertiary students wanting alternative cultural experiences such as night clubs and dance raves, readily available in other cities around the world with large Indian populations. As the size and diversity of Auckland's (and New Zealand's) Indian population has grown significantly in numbers and cultural diversity over the period of my research, in many ways my research has involved focusing on a 'moving target'.

This is also the case with the smaller and less visible South Indian communities. The population with Tamil Nadu roots was over twice the size of those from Andhra Pradesh (Telugu speakers) and Kerala (Malayalam speakers) in 2006. By 2013, the proportions of community representation had changed (see Figure 9.2), although the Tamil population continues to be in the majority.

The 2013 New Zealand Census reveals the growth in the small South Indian population (StatisticsNZ, 2013) and is illustrated in Figure 9.2. This information demonstrates that during the period of my research, demographic profiles have not remained stable. With the growth and diversity in the population have come advances in technology and global understandings of what Indian culture is perceived to be in New Zealand. Understanding the Tamil population and their consumption of culture provides significant data to the case study that features later in this chapter. As an ethnographer, the accuracy of my research is dependent on understanding my research focus in the broad sense as well in the minutiae.

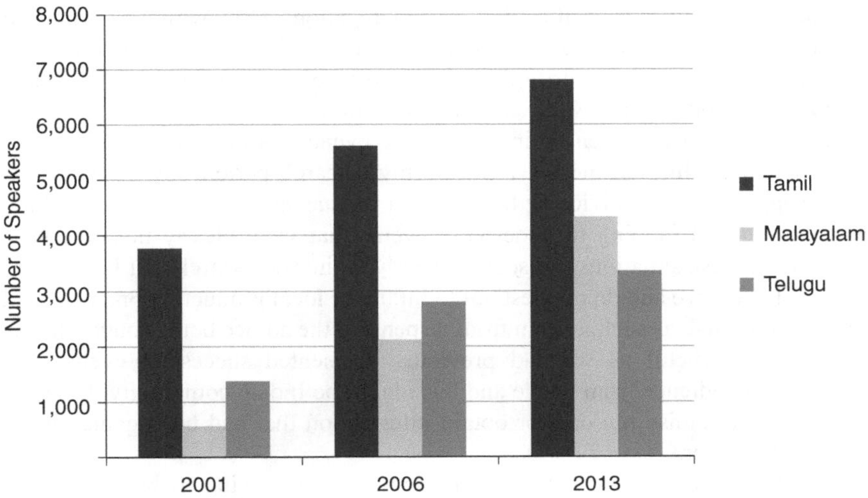

Figure 9.2 Census comparison showing the population growth of the three major South Indian linguistic affiliations in New Zealand between the years 2001, 2006 and 2013

Research limitations and cultural challenges

Reflecting on the limitations of any research methodology and the research context is important in order to understand how the role of researcher affects the outcome of the findings. In my case, I have identified several important factors: language, gender, culture, professional factors and ethical considerations.

I first should note that, in some cases, my husband was able to assist with his Hindi language skills when required and in situations requiring social interplay in this male-dominated field. Often, the older Indian migrant women come from rural areas and do not learn to speak English until after their arrival in New Zealand, rendering conversations stilted and gaining a common understanding difficult. This is not true of many of the younger migrants, who are often better educated and have lived in large cities in India and around the world. Those with local experience and children, including myself, find common ground with new migrants in our ability to give education-related advice, for instance engaging in long debates on the prestige of the different schools to which they might send their children. It can be quite difficult for me to have meaningful conversations and build friendships with those who do not have a good command of English and who are not well educated. My role as an academic and educator can be threatening. This raises an ethical dilemma: how much about yourself do you reveal when collecting data?

The scope of the data that I can gather is limited by my inability to attend every concert, performance and festival produced and/or interview every producer. I have purposely limited the scope of my research by not focusing on private events, although I do attend them – and often those involved in this side of the business become valuable informants. I also have opted not to consider events produced primarily for specific religious congregations. Even with the events that do not fall under these categories and theoretically fit into my focus, it is not possible – nor even necessarily desirable – to take into consideration each and every event produced by every cultural association.

One of the other challenges in researching events has been my own personal involvement within the industry. During my research period, my husband and I were approached for advice by Indian event producers. Often they were seeking sponsorship and funding to underwrite events that were clearly not otherwise feasible. In these situations, I discovered early on in my research that I needed to step back, observe and do my best not to influence local production practices and relationships and, as such, refrain from dispensing the advice being sought. It was often quite difficult as we had previously presented successful events that attracted an audience from inside and outside of the Indian community. I did not want to compromise my data or obtain information that had been gained in an unethical manner.

Those approaching me were mainly new migrants trying to break into the industry and seeking advice, while many of the established producers were aware of my research as I did not keep secrets. Often, it was assumed I was interested in interviewing musicians, in particular Bollywood stars and others perceived as rich and famous. I had to make it clear I was interested in the producer perspective from an event production angle. At some points it was very difficult watching promoters lose large amounts of money on events. I found, during the course of this study, that it was easier for me personally and more beneficial for my academic career to focus on my research and limit my arts management role in the community. I did make the decision to accept complimentary tickets from friends to events as my research budget was not sufficient to cover concert tickets, which could range from $20 to $600 in price.

Our University Ethics Committee brought another layer of cultural complexity to my role as an ethnographic researcher. In terms of the preservation of informants' anonymity, the Committee does not like researchers replacing informants' names with 'A' and 'B' as identifiers, instead encouraging the use of pseudonyms. In a culture where names easily connect a person to cultural community, religion, region, class and caste, a pseudonym can obscure the cultural context that the informant's real name provides. For this reason, I use either the real name or a generic indicator with no cultural strings attached (such as 'A' or 'B') beside an in-depth description of the person within the case study.

Overcoming challenges

Gender was an especially important factor in my research because the production of Indian events globally is dominated by male producers. This meant that there were some circumstances in which my gender acted as a barrier to the accessing of information. Women are rarely concert producers, and if they are involved in this side of the production practice, they are normally assisting their husbands or producing dance performances for their students.

Women do play other vital roles in the delivery of live events, as cultural teachers and publicists, and in stage design and support networks, including hospitality. Many women offer a wide range of experience in and knowledge of event delivery through their own participation and I am grateful for their friendship and sharing of knowledge.

In some situations I was accepted as part of the community and in other instances I remained a cultural 'outsider'. There are certain situations where I am unable to participate actively, due to language, cultural and religious barriers. To overcome participation barriers, I have found that by engaging in careful observation, it is possible to pick up visual details that would be missed if engaged in the conversation. This situation happens most frequently when I am assisting my husband in his research in the field. In other situations, I am viewed as being on an equal footing and can engage in a more active manner, as in the example of the many established classical musicians and well-educated friends in Mumbai who are women and treat me as a friend and colleague.

Recently, at a festival in Ahmedabad in the Indian state of Gujarat, a gentleman sitting next to my friend asked her how I could listen to Indian classical music for hours and not get bored. This gentleman was working on the assumption that a person of European heritage, and particularly a woman, could not possibly understand the complexity of the melody (*Raga*) and rhythm cycles (*Taal*). My friend, who is from Ahmedabad, replied, 'She understands more than you do,' thus shutting him down. This is not an uncommon experience for me in India or New Zealand and forms part of my research experience. My husband, who has the advantage of fluent Hindi and being male, rarely experiences such issues.

Cultural representation and cultural transmission are themes that interweave through my findings. Also important are cultural identity and issues of power, which can arise not just for participants in the study but also for the researcher. With this in mind, the following case study illustrates some of the vast variations on the concept of 'Indianness', interpretations of classical performance and new migrants' experiences, which can be challenging for me to capture and interpret from my research data. In this ethnographic context, my gender, cultural expertise and lack of language skills are embedded in the 'voice' of the thick description process central to the development of the case study.

Case study: the sound of ankle bells

Introduction

This case study focuses on Tamil cultural production practices: the vital role played by dance performance in Tamil cultural transmission, and the role cultural events serve in building local and transnational community. The performance that inspired the following thick description serves as an illustration of the issues I have encountered in the process of gathering ethnographic data, as discussed above: culture barriers, language barriers and access. In the process of developing this into a full case study, I had time to reflect on various notions of classical and popular culture meanings and the transnational interactions of culture in the context of a globalised world. The small size of Auckland's Tamil community makes research easy on one hand – everybody knows each other and it is easy to track changing trends – but difficult on the other, as members of the community are often competing for the same resources, including sponsorship, students and audience.

I take as my starting point a public performance of Indian dance that illustrates the flow of mediated cultural content as a form of cultural representation that moves across multiple pre-media and mediated classical, hybrid and commercial traditions, highlighting the interplay of locality. In this case, I do not speak Tamil and my contacts within this specific local community organisation are limited. Initially, I had not planned to attend as a researcher but rather to accompany my husband, who had been asked to introduce a well-known performer, the father of a member of the association. The performer had travelled from India and was performing in the second half of the programme.

In the first half, there was one performance that stood out from the rest, sparking my curiosity: a dance with classical and modern elements, skilfully executed by two young women. Although I could not understand the language being spoken around me, I could feel the excitement of the audience and the power of the dance. This led me to interview the choreographer, consider the aspects of the dance that made it so compelling and situate the performance within its larger cultural context. By unpacking the cultural elements behind the dance, I considered how one dance performance forms part of a larger, global cultural and economic phenomenon, denoting the movement of people, media and cultural content.

Shiva Dance

The venue was a spacious school hall in Mt Roskill, an area of Auckland with a large Indian population. The Auckland Tamil Language and Cultural Society, a community group known in Tamil as Muthtamil Sangam, celebrated their tenth anniversary in 2011. Muthtamil Sangam is a secular and non-profit organisation promoting social contact between Tamil speakers, and providing a support base for new arrivals to Auckland. The organisation aims to foster and promote Tamil language, literature, values, traditions, culture and art. The 'Shiva Dance' was the final item in a longer section of a still-longer programme that featured young local dancers representing Auckland's various South Indian dance teachers and community dance schools. The programme content of this section varied from re-enactments of commercial Tamil film scenes, in which young boys with pasted-on moustaches gyrated to Tamil film music, to South India's official dance genre, Bharatanatyam.

The 'Shiva Dance' performance displayed excellent dance technique, including classical Bharatanatyam repertoire. There was also a modern/Bollywood twist to the choreography. I understood the performance paid homage to Shiva, the Lord of Dance, through an exciting, devotional and unconventional performance. Observing the audience's enthusiastic reaction to the 'Shiva Dance', as well as noting my own positive response, I became curious as to what I had witnessed. I had no idea who the choreographer was or the context in which the dance had been created.

Later, I established contact with the two dancers. Dancer B lived on the same street as a close South Indian musician friend and he gave me her contact information. When I called Dancer B, I learned that she had arrived in Auckland from the land of her birth, Botswana, as a young Tamil girl, in 2007. She referred me to Dancer A. She, in turn, is part of a growing number of young people coming from India for postgraduate study in Auckland. With her arrival she has brought new perspectives on classical dance traditions. She was very open and generous with her information and supplied me with her personal story as a dancer, as well as the name of the song and the popular Tamil film in which the dance was performed. This led me to begin exploring the academic literature on the role Bharatanatyam plays in the expanding South Indian diaspora and to track down a copy of the film in Auckland.

Bharatanatyam in the diaspora

O'Shea (2003, 2008) has written on the role of Bharatanatyam and the relationship of the dance with India's national identity. The Bharatanatyam dance repertoire expresses Hindu religious themes, recounting episodes from pan-Indian mythologies. This dance tradition played an important role in the reinvention of India's classical performance identity in the 1920s and 1930s, as reformers sought to shift dance and music from their hereditary sites of transmission and performance, Hindu temple complexes, to new institutional sites in performing arts academies, supported by middle- and upper-class South Indians.

Since the 1920s, dance academies have followed the movements of the Indian diaspora, and have become increasingly popular since the 1960s (Peterson and Soneji, 2008). Students from the diaspora travel to Chennai to study Bharatanatyam, while teachers from Chennai travel the world teaching, and their students, having studied in Chennai or outside India, set up dance schools in their new localities. With this process has come innovation and new choreographic work (O'Shea, 2003; Ram, 2011).

Bharatanatyam is currently widely practised in South Indian communities throughout the world, with specific examples recorded by David (2008) in the United Kingdom and Ram (2000) in Australia. Dance academies and individual teachers thrive by preparing girls for their *arangetrams*, or 'debuts' into the world of dance; these have been reconceptualised in diasporic understandings as 'graduations' from the academy. *Arangetrams* represent years of training in the Bharatanatyam dance tradition and are widely staged in Chennai as well as in South Indian communities worldwide. Chennai's dance teachers often travel abroad, teaching young members of the often wealthy South Indian diaspora. They also market online training videos; indeed, in Auckland, many Bharatanatyam dance teachers rely on YouTube for instruction and on training videos downloaded from the dance academies in Chennai for lesson plans. Besides their training in Auckland, many daughters of the Tamil elite visit Chennai to train for their *arangetrams* in the prestigious academies. *Arangetrams* have come to provide a way for diasporic parents to define, through their daughters' dance performances, what it means to be Tamil.

There is a great deal of competition among the women who teach Bharatanatyam in Auckland. Over the years, I have not become close to many of them. As the 'outsider' conducting research, it can be quite difficult negotiating community politics. I learned that Dancer B began studying with an established local Bharatanatyam teacher for her *arangetram*. Recognising Dancer A's prestigious training and experience, Dancer B's parents asked Dancer A to tutor their daughter in a series of 'authentic' lessons to boost the quality of her upcoming *arangetram*. At the time of her 'Shiva Dance' performance, Dancer B was studying solely with Dancer A. She has since completed a successful *arangetram*.

Dancer A clearly understood that what she had taught Dancer B was not classical in the understandings of Chennai's conservative dance standards, but chose the film scene as it is popular and one of her favourites. The content of *arangetrams* in Auckland is rarely restricted to pure classical Bharatanatyam and almost inevitably includes items based on film choreography. Shresthova (2008) has argued that performances of dances copied from Indian films by the members of diasporic Indian communities at cultural events have become 'performances of cultural identity', forcing an acknowledgment of the public performance as a form of cultural representation that flows from mediated hybrid traditions into live performances. In this way, a cultural performance like the 'Shiva Dance' performed in Auckland is part of a much larger emerging, expressive and inherently hybrid vernacular movement of tradition representing Tamil culture that goes beyond a form of diasporic cultural nostalgia.

Dancer A, the 'Shiva Dance' choreographer, creates innovations in Bharatanatyam. Before arriving in Auckland in 2008 to complete a PhD in science, she studied and taught at one of Chennai's oldest and most prestigious dance academies, established in 1939. Along with her studies, she was trying to secure a niche teaching dance in the highly competitive local scene. She also has dance academy friends in the USA and Europe who teach dance classes in their new localities. The choreographer, as a new teacher, was seen by some as an asset, but by others as a threat to the established local dance community.

Some dance academies focus on teaching classical repertoire while others include modern repertoires offering Bollywood dance styles as well as hip hop, tap and other popular global dance forms. Dancer A is the first in her family to study dance and is considered by them as a bit of a rebel. Although formally trained in the classical dance tradition, she is young and loves other forms of dance, including folk, modern, hip hop and belly dancing, and she includes these in her teaching and choreography.

'Nada Vinodangal': sound of ankle bells

'Nada Vinodangal' is a well-known song from the famous and much loved Telugu film, *Sagara Sangamam*. This was the first time the song had been choreographed and presented live in an Auckland public performance. The audience would have been aware of the song and the dance scene featured in *Sagara Sangamam*. Other amateur dance renditions of 'Nada Vinodangal' produced in other parts of the diaspora, including the United States, Dubai and India, can be found on YouTube. As is common in the South Indian global film market, this popular film was prepared for release into three South Indian language markets. Following its initial 1983 Telugu release, *Sagara Sangamam* was dubbed into Tamil and Malayalam, with these versions released as *Salangai Oli* (1983) and *Sagarasangamam* (1984), respectively.

Because the performance I witnessed was to the Tamil version of the song, I refer to the song by its Tamil title, 'Nada Vinodangal', which translates as 'the sound of ankle bells'. Although only the Tamil version of the film was available for purchase in Auckland, all three versions of the song scene – and, indeed, of the entire film – are available online as full versions and YouTube clips. I was able to purchase *Salangai Oli*, complete with English subtitles, at the Tamil-language video shop in Mt Roskill, the heart of Auckland's Indian 'ethnoburbs' (Li, 2008).

The 'Shiva Dance' provided me with a story to unravel revealing a complex a cultural web of traditional vs. the innovative. Without spending the time researching the background information through interviews and secondary sources, I could not have created an academic conference presentation on this performance, which I gave in Australia (Booth, 2012), or written 'Case Study One: Classical Content in a Tamil Diasporic Dance Performance', a section of my PhD thesis in which this thick description is further developed (Booth, 2014: 73–94).

Conclusion

In this chapter I have tried to demonstrate how the ethnographic research method allows for a deep and contextual analysis. Thick descriptions push the boundaries of observation, as they challenge the writer not only to describe an observation they have made but also to place that observation into context by exploring and questioning the narratives that emerge from the initial observation. This process can be slow and frustrating and requires patience in order to capture the portrait in an ever-expanding globalised world.

Writing case studies taking a mixed-methods approach, combining primary data from interviews and participant observation with secondary data from government and media reports, contributes to the contextual trustworthiness of my research findings. Both quantitative and qualitative data play a crucial role in creating context within an ethnographic research method. The fact that communities transform in terms of demographics and social networks inevitably means that the research picture captures only a glimpse into a specific time and place. Revisited, the story will be told differently as the contexts of stories are forever changing as will my own placement in the story, as I, too, am part of the picture: the participant observer must be recognised as playing a role in the ethnographic framework.

Crossing paths over the decades with academics, producers and performers has opened further research opportunities for my larger research projects which are currently unfolding. I am in the slow and methodical data collection stage of a project that requires expanding my networks beyond the boundaries of New Zealand and comparing the history and production networks of similar phenomena of transnational production of Indian culture taking place in other countries. Ethnography depends on respect, honesty and love for people and their cultural expressions. It all comes down to the trust that you have in people and that people have in you.

References

Asia 2000 (1997) *Festival of Asia: What's On*. Wellington: Asia 2000.

Booth, A. (2008) *Representing Culture: Performance Production as Advocacy from Ravi to Anoushka*. Presentation given at the Annual Meeting of the Society of Ethnomusicology, Wesleyan University, Middletown, CT, October.

Booth, A. (2012) *The Sound of Ankle Bells: The Flow of People, Culture and Media in the Indian Diaspora*. Presentation given at the Annual Meeting of the International Association for the Study of Popular Music (Australia/New Zealand Branch), University of Tasmania, Hobart, Australia, December.

Booth, A. (2014) *Performance Networks: Indian Cultural Production in Aotearoa/New Zealand*. Doctoral thesis, University of Otago, Dunedin, New Zealand. Retrieved from: https://ourarchive.otago.ac.nz/handle/10523/4826.

Botterill, D. and Platenkamp, V. (2012) *Key Concepts in Tourism Research*. London: Sage.

Clifford, J. (1988) *The Predicament of Culture: Twentieth-century Ethnography, Literature, and Art*. Cambridge, MA: Harvard University Press.

Cox, J. W. and Hassard, J. (2010) 'Triangulation', in A. J. Mills, G. Eurepos and E. Wiebe (eds), *Encyclopedia of Case Study Research*. Thousand Oaks, CA: Sage, pp. 945–9.

Creswell, J. W. and Clark, V. L. P. (2007) *Mixed Methods Research*. Thousand Oaks, CA: Sage.

David, A. R. (2008) 'Local diasporas/global trajectories: new aspects of religious "performance" in British Tamil Hindu practice', *Performance Research*, 13 (3): 89–99.

DeSouza, R. (2011) '"All of me meets here, an alchemy of parts": negotiating my identities in New Zealand', in P. Voci and J. Leckie (eds), *Localizing Asia in Aotearoa*. Wellington: Dunmore Publishing, pp. 231–45.

Friesen, W. (2008) *Diverse Auckland: The Face of New Zealand in the 21st Century*. Wellington: Asia New Zealand Foundation.

Geertz, C. (1972) 'Deep play: notes on the Balinese cockfight', *Daedalus*, 101 (1): 1–37. Retrieved from: http://www.jstor.org/stable/20024056.

Geertz, C. (1973) 'Thick description: toward an interpretive theory of culture', in *The Interpretation of Cultures: Selected Essays*. New York: Basic Books, pp. 3–30.

Golafshani, N. (2003) 'Understanding reliability and validity in qualitative research', *Qualitative Report*, 8: 597–607.

Guba, E. G. and Lincoln, Y. S. (1989) *Fourth Generation Evaluation*. London: Sage.

Harnish, D. D. (2006) *Bridges to the Ancestors: Music, Myth, and Cultural Politics at an Indonesian Festival*. Honolulu, HI: University of Hawai'i.

Johnson, H. (2010) 'Lighting up Aotearoa: presenting Diwali to a multicultural nation', in S. Bandyopadhyay (ed.), *India in New Zealand*. Dunedin: Otago University Press, pp. 149–63.

Krefting, L. (1991) 'Rigor in qualitative research: the assessment of trustworthiness', *American Journal of Occupational Therapy*, 45: 214–22.

Li, W. (2008) *Ethnoburb: The New Ethnic Community in Urban America*. Honolulu, HI: University of Hawai'i Press.

Mackley-Crump, J. (2015) *The Pacific Festivals of Aotearoa New Zealand: Negotiating Place and Identity in a New Homeland*. Honolulu, HI: University of Hawai'i Press.

Mankekar, P. (2015) *Unsettling India: Affect, Temporality, Transnationality*. Durham, NC: Duke University Press.

McMurray, A., Wayne, R. and Scott, D. (2004) *Research: A Commonsense Approach*. Southbank, Australia: Thomson Learning.

O'Shea, J. (2003) 'At home in the world? The Bharatanatyam dancer as transnational interpreter', *Dance Review*, 47 (1): 176–86. Retrieved from: http://www.jstor.org/stable/1147037.

O'Shea, J. (2008) 'Serving two masters: Bharatanatyam and Tamil cultural production', in I. V. Peterson and D. Soneji (eds), *Performing Pasts*. New Delhi: Oxford University Press, pp. 165–93.

Peterson, V. and Soneji, D. (eds) (2008) *Performing Pasts*. New Delhi: Oxford University Press.

Picard, D. and Robinson, M. (2006) 'Remaking worlds: festivals, tourism and change', in D. Picard and M. Robinson (eds), *Festivals, Tourism and Social Change: Remaking Worlds*. Clevedon: Channel View.

Ram, K. (2000) 'Dancing the past into life: the Rasa, Nrtta and Rāga of immigrant existence', *Australian Journal of Anthropology*, 11: 261–73.

Ram, K. (2011) 'Being "rasikas": the affective pleasures of music and dance spectatorship and nationhood in Indian middle-class modernity', *Journal of the Royal Anthropological Institute* (serial online), 17: S159–S175.

Shresthova, S. (2008) 'Dancing to an India beat: "Dola" goes my diaspora', in S. Gopal and S. Moorti (eds), *Global Bollywood*. Minneapolis, MN: University of Minneapolis Press, pp. 243–63.

StatisticsNZ (2013) *People and Communities: Asian People*. Wellington: StatisticsNZ. Retrieved from: http://www.stats.govt.nz/browse_for_stats/people_and_communities/asian-peoples.aspx.

Turino, T. and Lea, J. (2004) *Identity and the Arts in Diaspora Communities*, Vol. 40. Warren, MI: Harmonie Park Press.

Vertovec, S. (1997) 'Three meanings of "diaspora", exemplified among South Asian religions', *Diaspora*, 6: 277–99.

Ybema, S., Yanow, D., Wels, H. and Kamsteeg, F. (2010) 'Ethnography', in *Encyclopedia of Case Study Research*. Thousand Oaks, CA: Sage, pp. 348–52.

Yin, R. K. (2014) *Case Study Research: Design and Method*, 5th edn. Los Angeles: Sage.

10 Collapsing social distance with cake and tea

The influence of Indigenous methodologies

Jared Mackley-Crump

Introduction

A central concern for researchers using qualitative and ethnographic methods in event studies is the negotiation of relationships that arise from the field. These relationships not only govern the fieldwork but also determine its outcomes. The success (or not) of the way in which we establish relationships with those who we interview and from whom we are gifted knowledge, in large part determines the quality and depth (or not) of the data that emerges, and therefore the success of the resulting ethnography (e.g. Geertz, 1988; Hammersley and Atkinson, 2007). The 'crisis of representation' in the social sciences, which (re)emerged from the mid-1980s, questioned the interpretive nature of ethnographic accounts and challenged the authority of disciplinary frameworks that had long guided empirical research (Geertz, 1988; Marcus and Fischer, 1986). As a consequence, attention has been forced onto the role of researcher and their positionality within the field, of considering how factors such as age, gender, ethnicity and cultural difference impact the research process and therefore the research findings. Parallel to this has been a focus on the relationships between researcher and researched, how they are formed, negotiated and maintained, and how differing power relationships impact the research process (e.g. Taylor, 2011). Much of this has emerged from various sociological and anthropological perspectives, such as feminist critique, queer theory and Indigenous studies. Thus, a significant body of work offers insight into the process of researching within particular social contexts, interrogating the nature of these relationships. While this has been discussed widely at a theoretical level, a gap remains for discursive narratives of fieldwork experiences, demonstrating how relationships were formed and how the distance between researcher and participants was negotiated.

This chapter offers insight into this area by exploring the (unorthodox) interview method practised during my doctoral research, and it contributes to the body of knowledge concerned with methodological practices, especially for the burgeoning area of event studies. In short, I baked and took cakes, slices and/or muffins with me when meeting participants for interviews (Mackley-Crump, 2012). Drawing on key moments from my fieldwork experience, I highlight how this instinctive interview method was effective in collapsing the social distance between myself as a (relatively) young, male, *Pākehā* (European) New Zealander, and the approximately fifty people I interviewed. In doing so, several concepts become important, such as the symbolic meaning of domesticity, of home, and of carrying out research in these domestic environments. Ideas about reciprocity, of gestures and acts that give thanks to participants, and the importance of rapport, of establishing relationships of respect and trust in order to achieve successful research exchanges, are also foregrounded. Together these ideas can be contextualised within the area of Indigenous studies, where they represent fundamental tenets of the research method.

In a slightly unorthodox structure, though, I begin the chapter in the field, recounting the key moments that construct a narrative of both auto-ethnographic reflection and also of encounter. This narrative explores the context of my pre-fieldwork hypothesis, and shows how it was borne out once I entered the field and began interviewing. I begin this way to demonstrate how my approach was driven by instinct rather than by any overriding theoretical considerations. It is after this that I move into the discussion of theoretical context, addressing how domesticity and domestic situations provide a possibility of creating fruitful research encounters, the importance of rapport and reciprocity and, finally, how notions of Indigenous methodologies were influential. Within this, broadly, comes the notion of *vā,* of space, and the belief that space is not something that separates people, but rather it is space that holds people and relationships together (see, for example, Ka'ili, 2005; Wendt, 1996). The appropriation of this idea calls for a (re)consideration of space in the research process, of the importance of nurturing space as a conscious practice. The use of baking (and of cups of tea) provides a demonstration of how *vā* was nurtured throughout my research; how, rather than separating, space was used to establish and build relationships and facilitate successful interviews.

The issue, the method and the context explained

In preparing to go into the field, I knew that I would generally be interviewing relative strangers but, paradoxically, hoping to collect rich, qualitative data, as if I held long-established relationships with these participants. My research was about the development of Pacific festivals in New Zealand and, for this, I was going to interview key organisers and performers involved with the two largest festivals, in order to understand the importance and meanings of these festival spaces. Participants, therefore, were primarily drawn from various Pacific communities, communities that first began to migrate to New Zealand in large numbers from the 1960s, and communities that have cultural and ancestral ties to other island states located throughout the South Pacific Ocean. Broadly, these communities share various historical and cultural connections, as well as shared experiences of migration and socio-cultural adaptation in the new New Zealand homeland (e.g. Macpherson, 2006). As a group, my participants shared these broad cultural similarities but also represented the communities' otherwise divergent characteristics: some were long-term migrants, some arrived more recently, many were born in New Zealand; for some English was a second language, for others their first; some were community elders, some had only just completed secondary education. The majority I met for the first time at the interview moment, or briefly met/spoke to beforehand to facilitate the interview.

Reflecting on these circumstances, I made the simple decision to use baking as a way of creating rapport, offering reciprocity and otherwise trying to overcome the research paradox. I also knew, though, that this decision had broader, contextually relevant social and cultural meaning. Having grown up in and around various Pacific communities, including many who were immediate and extended family members, I knew that food carries deep cultural significance; it acts as a social glue, a way in which social relationships are nurtured, the idea of abundance being historically and culturally tied to ideas and memories of bountiful harvests and of collective celebration (e.g. Kahn and Sexton, 1988; Manderson, 1987). As one of my interviewees would later reflect:

> Food is comfort, friendship, family … [it] plays a big role in who we are. We're always offering food to someone coming to visit. We always have a cup of tea, and whatever is in the pantry, we eat.
>
> (J. Monolagi, interview, 21 June 2010)

Moreover, though, food as a social glue, a medium through which ideas of culture, community and companionship are communicated, is something that transcends geography and is global in orientation (see, for example, Counihan and Van Esterik's 2013 edited collection; Mintz and Du Bois, 2002). Furthermore, baking for participants simply seemed like an appropriate thing to do, a way of attempting to quickly establish an environment conducive to relaxed but informative discussion. This instinctive approach felt like an obvious course of action: a small but symbolic display of thanks to those who were so generously to give me their time, their stories and their knowledge, material that would ultimately help me to gain a doctoral degree. I didn't think twice about it. I did not think this approach unorthodox; in fact I assumed it was – in a general sense – the kind of approach widely practised.

Additionally, I had begun to read broadly about ethics in research and notions of reciprocity, and this reinforced my intuition. Much of the reading, though, centred around researchers working in developing communities and countries, where clear economic and power imbalances existed. In these scenarios, reciprocation often took the form of assisting with community development, supporting education and travel, and providing needed resources (technology, books, food, energy and so on). In my setting, this form of reciprocation was neither needed nor appropriate. However, still wishing to incorporate this general ethos, I concluded simply that I would undertake little actions wherever possible, which would – hopefully – go some way towards offering reciprocation for the generosity shown by those I interviewed. Once in the field, numerous opportunities to support collaborators arose, such as attending concerts and other events, buying books and calendars, and supporting funding applications. These actions, in addition to baking, represented my attempt at reciprocity.

Stories from the field

The first person I interviewed for my research was Tala Cleverley, the person responsible for bringing about one of the earliest Pacific festivals in the early 1980s. She was also the first Pacific Islander elected to a local body council in New Zealand and, as a community leader, had been interviewed extensively since the 1970s. The interview took place at her home. From my fieldnotes:

> Tala greeted me and led me down the hallway and into the kitchen, where the interview was to take place. As I sat at the table, in a home full of family and memories, she made us a cup of tea. 'Here, I've brought something for your afternoon tea,' I offered (an apple and cinnamon loaf). Turning around, she seemed genuinely surprised, and was greatly appreciative. 'You know what,' she told me, 'so many people have interviewed me over the years, and all they do is take my knowledge and go away. They never bring me anything. So, your gesture … means more than all of them.' It was not the only time my gift was mentioned during our time together.

The impact of this exchange was immediate, and it remains one of the most profound memories of the fieldwork experience. It reinforced my thinking about food and social values and that my intuition was correct. It validated my belief that bringing home-baking would help to facilitate successful research encounters, and indeed we enjoyed several hours in each other's company, exchanging stories and general discussion. More fundamentally, though, it shocked me to think that, in almost four decades of being interviewed as a public figure, not one researcher had considered that making the same (small) gesture was appropriate. It was this experience that set in motion the reconsideration that my approach was not as universal as I had assumed.

Reactions continued along similar lines as interviews progressed. Participants who were older, and generally migrants, were impressed but also intrigued by the fact that I was – to them at least – a young person baking, but also that I was male, the perception being that baking was a female pursuit. I was able to counter – honestly – that I was trying to teach myself to bake and was glad to have the opportunity; as a single person living away from family I had otherwise little reason to bake. It created instant warmth by creating an instant conversation starter, something to help ease the process of building rapport; we were chatting before we realised we were chatting, and from there it was easy to transition into interview mode. It also provided a way for me to demonstrate a degree of 'cultural awareness', and the conversation would often move easily to discussing different types of Pacific cuisine, which dishes I liked or wanted to know more about, and what was going to be available at the festival. In the case of the interviewee quoted above, Fijian Joana Monolagi, our conversation canvassed the cultural and symbolic importance of food in Fijian culture, Indigenous Fijian cuisine and the influence of Chinese and especially Indian migration on food culture in Fiji, and how this had been adapted to the New Zealand environment.

The discussion went on for so long that she finally exclaimed, ‘Well, I guess we’d better get on with the interview.’

On each occasion where baking was involved, an entire batch was made and offered in a container that could be left with participants. This offered a complement to the invitation that always opened interviews in home settings: the invitation to share tea, which often turned into multiple cups. At the time that these interviews were taking place, I also had casual employment taking notes from focus groups for a commercial research company. Coincidently, the focus groups’ topic was tea drinking; the client, a historic New Zealand company looking to refresh its brand. Thus, at the same time as I was listening to groups of strangers discuss the cultural importance of tea – its symbolic role as a form of communal socialisation, woven throughout the fabric of their lives and fused with memory and nostalgia – I was becoming a tea drinker myself and experiencing these emotions play out over and over in interview situations. Tea, then, deserves to be considered alongside baking, as it also helped to establish the relationships that created successful research environments. As Lee Joliffe (2007: 249) notes, ‘tea is closely related to hospitality in many cultures and societies: it is offered as a sign of hospitality; and it forms an important part of hospitality’ (see also Pettigrew and Richardson, 2013). That it was consistently tea, and not coffee for example, offered by my hosts, reinforces this link. Like food, tea carries special socio-cultural significance as a social glue, and this is particularly so in Pacific communities, where tea consumption is widespread (Haden, 2009: 72–3).

The process of taking baking to interviews with younger people, either around my own age or younger, made me nervous. I wondered whether this attempt at collapsing social distance might result in the inverse: awkward reactions from those without perhaps the same cultural or social influences of elder community members. Nonetheless I persevered, and the response, while different, still achieved the desired results. One early example was an emerging rock band, TribalState. My (concerned) assumption – that a group of heavy metal enthusiasts were possibly going to look at a plate of mini muffins and be confused by the intention – was disproven. Rather, as struggling musicians (and students some of them) they gratefully and greedily inhaled the food, thankful that I had provided sustenance for the long night of practising ahead. The time spent eating before the interview started properly provided an opportunity to ‘break the ice’, my explanation once again offering an easy conversation starter that naturally progressed to music (‘I bake and I also play music’) and then to the festival.

On another occasion I went to interview Te Awanui Reeder, the lead singer of iconic New Zealand band Nesian Mystik. Again, I was apprehensive about my method; again based on his age being similar to mine, but also based on his standing within the music industry and myself as something of a fan. I need not have worried: without hesitation he invited me into his house where I met his father and fiancé, and the conversation unfurled with familial ease in a comfortable social setting. In this instance I had made a chocolate and raspberry brownie and the response was somewhat cultural: my attempt at reciprocity was reciprocated. I was invited to stay for lunch, where his fiancé made sandwiches to eat alongside the brownie once the interview was over (although, unsurprisingly, with the brownie sitting before us the entire time, not all of the brownie survived until lunch!). I was also given an advance copy of the band's latest CD which was just being released to retail outlets. They were so impressed – via repeated praising – that I felt it necessary to state that the brownie was in fact a simple recipe, and easily replicated; I told Awanui I would email it to him. A short while after this, he emailed specifically to thank me again. He had made the brownie for a *whanau* ('family') gathering and it was hugely successful; he received widespread praise for having made it. And, in the couple of times we have crossed paths in the intervening years, it is something he makes a point of recollecting. The brownie is fondly remembered. This demonstrates well not only the social impact that this initial exchange had, and the success of this approach in achieving the desired outcome, but it also acts as a demonstration of the ongoing connection created in that moment, one that has been remembered and reflected upon in the now five years that have passed (the second meeting occurred in early 2015). In the same sense, in the several times I have encountered Joana Monolagi since 2010, we inevitably end up talking about food, of Fijian curries and my latest baking attempts. And, likewise, the same thing occurred with a number of other participants I have had the chance to reconnect with, including staff members from the two festivals where case studies were completed. Baking and the memory of this unconventional introduction continues to be a way we are connected and reconnect; it allows our conversations to continue.

Some of these connections are based on interviews that took place at workplaces, such as the festival offices, community radio stations and social agencies. A number, in fact, unfolded in this manner as interviews often took place during standard office hours to best fit with participants' timetables and commitments. In these situations, my approach remained the same but the intention became twofold. I still wanted food to act as a social ice-breaker, something to create conversation, but I also wanted it to act as something that symbolically if not physically removed us from the office environment, something that signalled a break in the working day. In short, I wanted to bring the comforts of domesticity into office environments. This intention played out well, as we generally moved into a kitchen or meeting room to conduct the interviews; the baking, in this sense, seamlessly fitted into the physical movement away from strictly work spaces. The curiosity of myself as a young(er) male having baked again played a central role in establishing an easy dialogue, especially when interviewing community leaders and elders. In only one situation was this approach unsuccessful: when the interview took place in a building lobby, and the exchange was constrained by the period of a timetabled lunch break. The provision of baking did not fit the environment. It was loud, busy and the interview somewhat hurried; we did not have the luxury of time to create familiarity. In retrospect, that it was refused and I subsequently left with baking in hand was not surprising. Although the interview was still successful – the particular perspective being sought was gained – it lacked the warmth and personal nature of other exchanges and the casual pace which with other interviews proceeded. And, although impossible to prove, it led me to reflect on how much more successful that exchange may have been had the creation of social space unfolded in a different way.

One final key learning from the fieldwork experience is worth reflecting on, and this is where my approach was not able to be carried out at all: where interviews took place in neither home nor office, but in public places, generally cafes or other food establishments. In these situations, the locations were chosen by interview participants, but I emphasised it should be somewhere local to them, where they would be comfortable and where we could 'grab something to eat and drink'. Although I adopted the same general intention, in that I 'provided' by paying for food and drink – often after having to repeatedly encourage participants ('it's the least I can do') – some of these exchanges were less successful. As above, the environments were often loud and busy and so, from the outset, it was harder to create the environment required for a fruitful discussion to take place. Additionally, there was a lack of the obvious ice-breaker that baking provided, and I had to try and tease out another topic to take this discursive focal point. As an example, my interview with Mina Leolahi, an elderly Niuean migrant and community leader, took place in a loud and bustling local eatery. In contrast to my experiences with other community leaders, such as described above, the first part of the interview plays back as stilted and slightly awkward; it took a noticeable period of time for the conversation to begin to become more fluid, and the social distance between myself as an outside researcher and her as a community member is obvious. Again, it is impossible to know whether our conversation would have been any different had it taken place in more personal settings. Again, though, upon reflection it reinforced my belief that my instinctive approach had created the most successful research exchanges, or most successfully created environments in which interviews resulted in rich stories and observations. Thus I ended my fieldwork experience with a determination that, for future research, I would make a more concerted effort to replicate the method and environments that had worked so well. It reinforced to me the importance of considering research interviews to be a sum of much more than a simple exchange of thoughts and discussion between parties. The space in which these encounters take place is vital, and the way in which that space is deliberately created and used to establish relationships is extremely important.

Discussion: domesticity and Indigenous method in event studies research

The approach I adopted to collapse the social distance between researcher and researched is one that is essentially rooted in domesticity. It stems from the belief that, as cook and writer Nigella Lawson often describes, the kitchen represents the heart of the home, and that bringing this warmth, this familiarity, into the research environment establishes relationships conducive to successful exchange. As Alison Blunt (2005) more broadly notes, 'the home is a material and an affective space, shaped by everyday practices, lived experiences, social relations, memories and emotion' (p. 506). This notion of domesticity as a research environment, whether food-related or generally, is not a significant theme within existing literature. However, it is visible in fragments of disparate accounts of fieldwork experiences and research projects. Anne Larsen (2010), for example, provides an account of time spent researching in a close-knit hamlet, recounting the benefits but also the pitfalls of living with a family and detailing how relationships were formed by spending time with participants in their homes. With more specificity, Lynette Sikic-Micanovic (2010) notes the chosen location of her interviews: 'This was most frequently the kitchen/family room, where the most important domestic or "inside" functions of the household take place – where women cook, members of the household gather, eat, sleep, etc.' (p. 49). In both accounts, the home (and kitchen, even) is reinforced as central in creating environments in which trust was established and the relationships formed, from which successful research resulted (and see also Al-Hindi, 1997, who notes the levelling experience of researching domesticity; of reducing the research hierarchy by entering participants' homes as a guest). And, from a different perspective, teachers of research methods have been challenged to encourage students to value experiences, like the sharing of food, that fall outside the traditional boundaries of 'research' but which nonetheless impact the resulting fieldwork (Hammersley *et al.*, 2014).

Others are more explicit in illuminating the role of food in these processes. Linda Henderson (2013: 101), for example, in discussing the apprehension she felt approaching a group interview that blurred professional/personal/researcher lines, describes food and drink as something 'definitely needed' to help facilitate the process. Likewise, in interviewing female artists in their homes, Bette Kauffman (1992) notes how food and drink helped to enable an easy progression into interview mode. Here, participants were offered tea or coffee, and food was served as a discrete event; however, she recounts, 'the events were not entirely discrete … at some point lunch talk moved toward interview talk' (p. 203). Ann Oberhauser (1997) experienced the same, where initial bonding between researchers and participants occurred through a process of preparing food that was then shared, which allowed for a natural progression from one state to the other. In this case, the experiences 'became more than just an interview' but represented a chance 'to engage with [participants] on their own terms, in their own space' (pp. 170–1). And in a similar finding, Allison Hayes-Conroy (2010) describes how being invited to share time and food within people's homes allowed the ethnographic data to reveal itself, rather than coming from interview processes. As she reminds researchers who have become caught up in formal processes of the academy, 'food and people go together in a kind of obvious but often forgotten way' (p. 741). Finally, in a project about the experiences of migrant women in New Zealand, the kitchen and the informal sharing of food helped to establish the relationships needed for successful research to be conducted. As the researchers note, 'we found that visiting women at home tended to create a positive rapport', as it was built in an environment that allowed them to eat their own food, listen to their own music, and shake off their performances of 'Kiwi' cultural conventions (Longhurst *et al.*, 2009: 336). Noting the visible comfort created by being within their own domestic spaces, they thus conclude that 'visiting migrant women in their home to share food and stories was an intense and visceral way of finding out more about their lives' (p. 342).

In the above discussions, domestic spaces and food are all shown to be influential in creating social spaces that facilitate successful research encounters. This focus on space, and on using tactics of domesticity to dissolve the social distance between collaborators, stems from broader methodological concerns in which notions of rapport are a key theme. Many different suggestions have been made for creating rapport, ranging from emulating community patterns and lifestyles in order to fit in (e.g. Rapport, 2010), sharing personal experiences (e.g. Cuomo and Massaro, 2014; Oakley, 1981), adopting openness (e.g. Roberts and Sanders, 2005), incorporating therapeutic modes like empathy and problem-solving (e.g. Undheim, 2003), 'walking methods' (e.g. Jones *et al.*, 2008), to a wholesale rejection of alterity, advocating instead for recognising and embracing the inevitable personal investment and emotional attachment that researchers have to those they are researching (e.g. Taylor, 2011). Being aware of techniques for creating rapport, and incorporating these into a researcher's own practice, is important because, as has been noted, 'it is the interviewer's responsibility to create a friendly, relaxed atmosphere and put the respondent at ease' (Jorgenson, 1992: 151). The quality of rapport directly impacts the quality of the data collected. Thus rapport should not be considered as a strategy to manage interviews and participants, but as a fundamental element in conducting successful ethnography (Reeves, 2010).

It is within this body of work that I situate my own account of methodological suggestions; food was used as a deliberate tactic to create rapport and collapse social distance. It was also used – among other actions, in some cases – as an attempt to foreground notions of reciprocity into the development of my practice. In doing so, it was a recognition that reciprocity is an important consideration in planning fieldwork-based projects, an important need to 're-centre' research around notions of reciprocity, to 'relate on a human level rather than always reconciling a research agenda' (Wesner *et al.*, 2014: 6–7). In theory, reciprocity revolves around seemingly straightforward questions: how do I give back? How do I repay participants for sharing their time, knowledge and experiences (Kelly, 2014: 2)? Although answering these questions can lead to complex negotiations and considerations of power and ethical conduct (Sawyer, 2014), it is increasingly argued that reciprocity can be simply found in small acts, in the everyday interactions that take place in the field. This can be providing material assistance, but it can also be as modest but meaningful as 'helping in a garden, giving rides, babysitting, or sharing food and medicine' (Gupta and Kelly, 2014: 5). It can simply be 'looking at another human being and giving with no agenda other than to say, thank you' (Finney, 2014: 4). In this sense, then, the actions taken to reciprocate time and knowledge gifted to me can be understood as 'gestures', as meaningful symbols of gratitude where material difference to participants' lives does not occur and is not necessarily appropriate (Gupta, 2014).

Up to this point, I have pulled together accounts from a variety of sources in order to construct my narrative. There is, in fact, a disciplinary area where the importance of rapport and reciprocity in research design and method, and of collapsing the distance between researcher and researched, are a central concern. The area of Indigenous studies and methodologies are founded on these notions, and many of the sources cited above are drawn from this area. In Indigenous studies, ideas of desirable relationships between research parties, the responsibility that each has for the other and reciprocity are all interwoven and represent the fundamental tenets of the research process (e.g. Cram *et al.*, 2013; Smith, 1999). Furthermore, research is viewed as 'ceremony': 'Indigenous research is a ceremony and must be respected as such. A ceremony … is not just the period at the end of the sentence. It is the required process and preparation that happens long before the event' (Wilson, 2008: 60). This focus draws attention to that which occurs before the fieldwork and the interviews. It calls on researchers to engage in 'setting the stage correctly' (p. 69), a determined focus to ensure that the relationships required to successfully exchange ideas are in place, that issues of power are addressed (e.g. de Leeuw *et al.*, 2012; Paine *et al.*, 2013). Here the possibility of a multiplicity of cultures, worldviews and cultural practices are considered and importance placed on incorporating these into research methods as appropriate (Tipa *et al.*, 2009). Fundamentally, Indigenous methodologies represent a challenge to academic thought and unchallenged processes that place the academy at the centre of research and research processes; it challenges us to think beyond our own (research) agendas, to relinquish power and to become part of a reciprocal process. Within this paradigm, the (cultural) significance of sharing food in order to create social spaces conducive to successful exchange becomes not radical but instinctive, encouraged, an ethos of *manaakitanga*, of hospitality (Smith, 2013). As has been noted:

> An interview is a social situation and in a social situation giving and accepting food is a traditional way of welcoming someone … the serving of a plate of food when a person comes to a home for a visit or to a gathering is common.
>
> (Christopher *et al.*, 2005: 134; see also Dickson and Green, 2001; Walker *et al.*, 2014).

I should be clear that I am not asserting that I conducted my research from a holistic Indigenous studies framework; I have neither the authority nor feel that I have a comprehensive understanding of what this exactly means. However, I am making a connection, that, from an Indigenous studies perspective, the particular method I adopted is appropriate, as an action rooted in the desire to create relationships that 'de-centre' the research process, that are based on respect and exchange. And this, finally, brings me back to space, and the Sāmoan proverb, *la teu le vā*, care for the *vā*, the relationships. Writer and literary academic Albert Wendt (1996, 'Vā') famously explained that '*vā* is the space between … not empty space, not space that separates but space that relates, that holds separate entities and things together … the space that is context, giving meaning to things.' Here, space is considered in relational terms, as something that connects you and me, writer and reader, researcher and researched, not as something that separates us. To care for the *vā* therefore means to nurture relationships in order to strengthen connections across space so that it metaphorically reduces the distance. Tevita Ka'ili (2005) extends this by proposing the Tongan concept of *tauhi vā*, the practice of reinforcing connections across space through reciprocal exchange, strengthening and reaffirming ties and relationships in the process (and these relationships can be both spatially and temporally (dis)located). There is – unfortunately – no room here for a detailed exploration of these concepts, and again I do not seek to assert that I conducted research using them as guiding principles. I hope that my appropriation does not superficially dissolve the complexity and cultural significance of these ideas into single paragraph sound bites. My intention, rather, is again to draw a link between my instinct and theoretical models that reinforce this approach. I hope also, by employing them, to extend these ideas and my approach into new disciplinary areas. The *vā* and caring for it means that we look at space not as something that separates us, but as something that connects us. To nurture the *vā* means to foster this space, to take actions to strengthen and maintain connections across space. In this context, my methodological approach of baking can be viewed as a way of trying to nurture space as a relational construct, to dissolve the distance between myself as a researcher and those who collaborated with me and transform it into something that connected us, and connects us still. Food, as a culturally significant, universal social glue, became the means to nurture the *vā* in the fieldwork process.

Conclusion

In this chapter, I have outlined the approach I adopted during my doctoral research to collapse the social distance between myself as a researcher and those who participated in my project by being interviewed. This approach – the provision of home-baking – was instinctual, driven by a belief in the role of food as a social glue, a medium through which people communicate and maintain relationships. In recounting my fieldwork experience, I have not only shown how this approach was successful, but underscored how it relates to the importance of building rapport and of reciprocity in research processes, as well as how it relates to space as a construct that needs to be purposefully considered in order to create the research exchanges we desire. The rich quality of the stories and reflections I received from my participants is, I believe, a direct result of the time taken to 'set the stage' correctly. If I had not done so, the information may not have otherwise been so freely given. The implication here is that using unorthodox methods in order to establish rapport between collaborators may positively impact the research exchange and, as mentioned at the outset, it is the quality of these exchanges that ultimately determines the outcomes of our research projects. While the space between researchers and their collaborators can be seen as barriers, I argue that it instead should be seen as something that connects us and therefore needs to be nurtured; it is this nurturing – through sharing food and drink, through respect and reciprocity – that created the relationships that underpinned the success of my project. I challenge researchers to adjust their thinking; we owe it not only to ourselves and our research, but to those with whom we collaborate.

References

Al-Hindi, K. (1997) 'Feminist critical realism: a method for gender and work studies in geography', in J. Jones III, H. Nast and S. Roberts (eds), *Thresholds in Feminist Geography: Difference, Methodology, Representation*. Lanham, MD: Rowman & Littlefield, pp. 145–64.

Blunt, A. (2005) 'Cultural geography: cultural geographies of home', *Progress in Human Geography*, 29: 505–15.

Christopher, S., Burhansstipanov, A. and Knows His Gun-McCormick, A. (2005) 'Using a CBPR approach to develop an interviewer training manual with members of the Apsáalooke Nation', in B. Israel, E. Eng, A. Schulz and E. Parker (eds), *Methods in Community-based Participatory Research for Health*. San Francisco: John Wiley & Sons, pp. 128–45.

Counihan, C. and Van Esterik, P. (2013) *Food and Culture: A Reader*, 3rd edn. New York: Routledge.

Cram, F., Chilisa, B. and Mertens, D. (2013) 'Introduction', in D. Mertens, F. Cram and B. Chilisa (eds), *Indigenous Pathways into Social Research*. Walnut Creek, CA: Left Coast Press, pp. 1–40.

Cuomo, D. and Massaro, V. (2014) 'Boundary-making in feminist research: new methodologies for "intimate insiders"', *Gender, Place and Culture: A Journal of Feminist Geography*, pp. 1–13.

de Leeuw, S., Cameron, E. and Greenwood, M. (2012) 'Participatory and community-based research, Indigenous geographies, and the spaces of friendship: a critical engagement', *Canadian Geographer/Le Géographe Canadien*, 56: 180–94.

Dickson, G. and Green, K. (2001) 'Participatory action research: lessons learned with Aboriginal grandmothers', *Health Care for Women International*, 22: 471–82.

Finney, C. (2014) 'Doing it old school: reflections on giving back', *Journal of Research Practice*, 10 (2): art. N3. Retrieved from: http://jrp.icaap.org/index.php/jrp/article/view/412/357.

Geertz, C. (1988) *Works and Lives: The Anthropologist as Author*. Stanford, CA: Stanford University Press.

Gupta, C. (2014) 'Reflections on giving back and giving thanks', *Journal of Research Practice*, 10 (2): art. N7. Retrieved from: http://jrp.icaap.org/index.php/jrp/article/view/400/361.

Gupta, C. and Kelly, A. (2014) 'The social relations of fieldwork: giving back in a research setting', *Journal of Research Practice*, 10 (2): art. E2. Retrieved from: http://jrp.icaap.org/index.php/jrp/article/view/423/35.

Haden, R. (2009) *Food Culture in the Pacific Islands*. Santa Barbara, CA: Greenwood.

Hammersley, L., Bilous, R., James, S., Trau, A. and Suchet-Pearson, S. (2014) 'Challenging ideals of reciprocity in undergraduate teaching: the unexpected benefits of unpredictable cross-cultural fieldwork', *Journal of Geography in Higher Education*, 38: 208–18.

Hammersley, M. and Atkinson, P. (2007) *Ethnography: Principles in Practice*, 3rd edn. London: Routledge.

Hayes-Conroy, A. (2010) Feeling slow food: visceral fieldwork and empathetic research relations in the alternative food movement', *Geoforum*, 41: 734–42.

Henderson, L. (2013) 'Reconceptualising the interview: an assemblage of affect', in M. Vicars and T. McKenna (eds), *Discourse, Power, and Resistance Down Under*, Vol. 2. Rotterdam: Sense Publishing, pp. 99–110.

Joliffe, L (ed.) (2007) *Tea and Tourism: Tourists, Traditions and Transformations*. Clevedon: Channel View Publications.

Jones, P., Bunce, G., Evans, J., Gibbs, H. and Hein, J. R. (2008) 'Research design: exploring space and place with walking interviews', *Journal of Research Practice*, 4 (2): 1–9.

Jorgenson, J. (1992) 'Communication, rapport, and the interview: a social perspective', *Communication Theory*, 2: 148–56.

Ka'ili, T. (2005) 'Tauhi vā: nurturing Tongan sociospatial ties in Maui and beyond', *Contemporary Pacific*, 17 (1): 83–114.

Kahn, M. and Sexton, L. (1988) 'The fresh and the canned: food choices in the Pacific', *Food and Foodways: Explorations in the History and Culture of Human Nourishment*, 3: 1–18.

Kauffman, B. (1992) 'Feminist facts: interview strategies and political strategies in ethnography', *Communication Theory*, 2: 187–206.

Kelly, A. (2014) 'Drawing lines in the mud: giving back (or trying to) in northern Cameroon', *Journal of Research Practice*, 10 (2): art. N2. Retrieved from: http://jrp.icaap.org/index.php/jrp/article/view/394/356.

Larsen, A. (2010) 'Some reflections on the "enchantments" of village life, or whose story is this?', in P. Collins and A. Galliant (eds), *The Ethnographic Self as Resource: Writing Memory and Experience into Ethnography*. Oxford: Berghahn Books, pp. 63–77.

Longhurst, R., Johnston, L. and Ho, E. (2009) 'A visceral approach: cooking "at home" with migrant women in Hamilton, New Zealand', *Transactions of the Institute of British Geographers*, 34: 333–45.

Mackley-Crump, J. (2012) *The Festivalisation of Pacific Cultures in New Zealand: Diasporic Flow and Identity Within 'a Sea of Islands'*. Doctoral dissertation, University of Otago, New Zealand.

Macpherson, C. (2006) 'Pacific peoples in Aotearoa/New Zealand: from sojourn to settlement', in K. Ferro and M. Wallner (eds), *Migration Happens: Reasons, Effects and Opportunities of Migration in the South Pacific*. Vienna: Lit Verlag GmbH & Co. (Austrian South Pacific Society), pp. 97–126.

Manderson, L. (ed.) (1987) *Shared Wealth and Symbol: Food, Culture and Society in Oceania and Southeast Asia*. Cambridge: Cambridge University Press.

Marcus, C. and Fischer, M. (1986) *Anthropology as Cultural Critique*. Chicago: University of Chicago Press.

Mintz, S. and Du Bois, C. (2002) 'The anthropology of food and eating', *Annual Review of Anthropology*, 31: 99–119.

Oakley, A. (1981) 'Interviewing women: a contradiction in terms', in H. Roberts (ed.), *Doing Feminist Research*. London: Routledge, pp. 30–61.

Oberhauser, A. (1997) 'The home as "field": households and homework in rural Appalachia', in J. Jones III, H. Nast and S. Roberts (eds), *Thresholds in Feminist Geography: Difference, Methodology, Representation*. Oxford: Rowman & Littlefield, pp. 165–82.

Paine, S., Priston, M., Signal, T., Sweeney, B. and Muller, D. (2013) 'Developing new approaches for the recruitment and retention of indigenous participants in longitudinal research: lessons from E. Moe, Māmā: maternal sleep and health in Aotearoa/New Zealand', *Mai: A New Zealand Journal of Indigenous Scholarship*, 2: 121–32.

Pettigrew, J. and Richardson, B. (2013) *A Social History of Tea: Tea's Influence on Commerce, Culture and Community*. Danville, KY: Benjamin Press.

Rapport, N. (2010) 'The ethics of participant observation: personal reflections on fieldwork in England', in P. Collins and A. Galliant (eds), *The Ethnographic Self as*

Resource: Writing Memory and Experience into Ethnography. Oxford: Berghahn Books, pp. 78–96.

Reeves, C. (2010) 'A difficult negotiation: fieldwork relations with gatekeepers', *Qualitative Research*, 10: 315–31.

Roberts, J. and Sanders, T. (2005) 'Before, during and after: realism, reflexivity and ethnography', *Sociological Review*, 53: 294–313.

Sawyer, S. (2014) 'Failing to give enough: when researcher ideas about giving back fall short', *Journal of Research Practice*, 10 (2): art. N12. Retrieved from: http://jrp.icaap.org/index.php/jrp/article/view/413/366.

Sikic-Micanovic, L. (2010) 'Foregrounding the self in fieldwork among rural women in Croatia', in P. Collins and A. Galliant (eds), *The Ethnographic Self as Resource: Writing Memory and Experience into Ethnography*. Oxford: Berghahn Books, pp. 45–62.

Smith, C. (2013) 'Becoming a Kaupapa Māori researcher', in D. Mertens, F. Cram and B. Chilisa (eds), *Indigenous Pathways into Social Research*. Walnut Creek, CA: Left Coast Press, pp. 89–100.

Smith, L. T. (1999) *Decolonizing Methodologies: Research and Indigenous Peoples*. London: Zed Books.

Taylor, J. (2011) 'The intimate insider: negotiating the ethics of friendship when doing insider research', *Qualitative Research*, 11 (1): 3–22.

Tipa, G., Panelli, R. and the Moeraki Stream Team (2009) 'Beyond "someone else's agenda": an example of indigenous/academic research collaboration', *New Zealand Geographer*, 65: 95–106.

Undheim, T. (2003) 'Getting connected: how sociologists can access the high tech elite', *Qualitative Report*, 8 (1). Retrieved from: http://tqr.nova.edu/.

Walker, M., Fredericks, B., Mills, K. and Anderson, D. (2014) '"Yarning" as a method for community-based health research with Indigenous women: the Indigenous women's wellness research program', *Health Care for Women International*, 35: 1216–26.

Wendt, A. (1996) 'Tatauing the post-colonial body', *Span*, pp. 42–3. Retrieved 14 January 2015 from: http://www.nzepc.auckland.ac.nz/authors/wendt/tatauing.asp.

Wesner, A., Pyatt, J. and Corbin, C. (2014) 'The practical realities of giving back', *Journal of Research Practice*, 10 (2): art. M6. Retrieved from: http://jrp.icaap.org/index.php/jrp/article/view/426/346.

Wilson, S. (2008) *Research Is Ceremony: Indigenous Research Methods*. Winnipeg, Canada: Fernwood Publishing.

Part IV

Conclusion

11 Events and the framing of peoples and places

Acts of declaration/acts of devilry

Keith Hollinshead and Rukeya Suleman

Introduction: Quinn and disengaged Event Studies research

In order to examine what ought to be researched in the domain of Event Management/Event Studies today, it is useful to begin this chapter on the contextuality of special events and drawcard festivals by taking time to distil what one of the lead analysts of event development says about the state-of-the-art of event operation and event promotion. Thus this chapter opens with Quinn's (2009) compact but insight-loaded inspection of the quality and coherency of inquiry into the administration and articulation of events in our time. In her review work, Quinn has traced what could be described as the soundness and the wholeness of received research into the staging of special events, particularly with respect to Tourism Studies.

In her broad-brush reflection on how events are currently viewed and evaluated, she finds 'Event Management' to be one of the vogue areas of coverage in Tourism Studies, but one that is somewhat uneven in its attention. In Quinn's judgment, the assembled literature on events is almost exclusively characterised by inquiry into concerns of production and supply: to her, it is decidedly but overly 'applied' in focus. In her view, investigations into the presentation and promotion of events is conventionally seen to be an ordinary *management* or *operational* matter and there is a noted lack of critical assessments of the juxtaposition which events have with the broader spectrum of cultural, social, psychic and political value. Consequently, in the subfield of Event Studies, there is a distinct tendency of both practitioners and researchers to separate events from their wider public and temporal trajectories, and the special events of our time are almost repeatedly analysed with regard to merely their germinative capacity to boost tourism, instead of also being scrutinised with respect to their relevance to and within the wider societal importances of the contemporary moment.

In these respects, Quinn furthers the point that special events are only infrequently investigated in terms of their conceivable role as naturalising or essentialising acts of community celebration or *en groupe* ritual, though she does admit that a number of recent scholars have probed the identity-making/identity-confirming function of events especially with regard to concerns over sense of place and/or space. To Quinn, the found shortfall of attention may be registered by the fact that intelligence about special events which has been generated from social science and humanities domains has substantively been secondary to the knowledge that has been forthcoming from operational management/event marketing approaches. In her judgment, the role of events as serviceable vehicles for the inculcation of the governing ideologies (that come embedded within the spread and flow of the globalising development of place and/or space) has been notably impoverished.

Quinn's significant contribution to the Jamal and Robinson (2009) state-of-the-art inspection of Tourism Management/Tourism Sciences (*The Sage Handbook of Tourism Studies*) amounts to a reflective and penetrative commentary of the lead imperatives and the suppressed orientations which crop up in Event Management/Event Studies. In calling for much richer criticality in the unfolding literature on 'events', Quinn (2009: 490) points out that there is continued preoccupation with given events as 'singular and contained phenomenon', and she calls for the winning of rather more connected interpretations of events as entities that come freighted with or in their own specific panoply of cultural, social, political and spatio-environmental trajectories.

In this light, Quinn praises the advances made by investigators such as Shepherd (2002) who refrain from regarding aspects of authenticity as the distinct property of an object or idea (highlighted at a particular event of significance) but who look for the interest group esteem or the collateral worth which it possesses as an outcome of historic or contemporary 'social processes'. In like fashion, Quinn acknowledges the insights of Boyle (1997) who mapped the political contours and the ideological figurations which are embedded within the social construction of particular events, and she applauds the painstaking efforts of researchers such as De Bres and Davis (2001) who have traced the generative profiles of events as instantiations of governing playmakers in terms of what is exhibited and what is neglected or ignored. Decidedly, Quinn (2009: 490) pays homage to the labours of Larson and Wickstrom (2001; and also of Larson, 2002) to energise inquiry into host/playmaker 'stakeholder connectivities' through the use of 'political market square' techniques in Event Studies research, and she considers such oxygenated styles of the scrutiny of 'public power' at work to be a distinct leap forward in this research domain. Undoubtedly, if Quinn is to be accepted in her review work for the Jamal and Robinson handbook, there is a good deal that is actually fresh and healthy in the Event Management/Event Studies literature today with respect to inquiry into the 'mediated' political articulation of special events, but it only crops up within a limited number of the research teams, i.e. among the more open-minded and conjugative investigative teams.

Overall, Quinn bemoans the general shortfall of interdisciplinary cum multidisciplinary investment into the political profile of events, and thinks that lack has stymied conceptual awareness in the demesne of event development. She salutes Crespi-Valbona and Richards (2007) who had already registered the view that only a limited proportion of field investigators had ever worked in tandem to scrutinise *which found network of sanctioning players* indeed share orientations and outlooks in the power-plays which always inevitably accompany the selection and promotion of grand or large special events (Quinn 2009: 495). She commends Boyle's (1997) judgment that there has been all too little effort placed upon inquiry into how special events are indeed *consumed* in the marketplaces of tourism and leisure by various publics and different sub-populations (Quinn 2009: 496). Moreover, in giving comment upon Yardinici's (2007) examination of the community and market 'shadow' special events in Turkey (mainly in Istanbul itself), she consequently declares that special event occasions and drawcard festivals are almost axiomatically aligned in their de facto development with regard to external/global interests (in lieu of with respect to local constituencies) and they tend to be scaffolded vis-à-vis Western and lukewarm-in-piety interpretations of human/socio-economic/technical/cosmological advance. To Yardinici, the understandings that drive vogue 'externally networked' event management and development practices across the world (through the business of tourism and within the travel industry 'system', *ipso facto*) are pointedly 'Euro-Western' in profile, and are thereby somewhat minimalist in their exhibited religiosity and in their felt local communal reflexivity.

As a consequence of these uncovered plus and minus points in the strength and reach of the 'Special Event' literature, Quinn (2009) thus insists upon the generation of much more resolution in the work to assess the political range and interest group support base of large events and drawcard festivals. In recent years, Hollinshead *et al.* (2015) have taken heed of Quinn's critical reflections. In this respect – and in terms of distinct Quinnian forms of action – Hollinshead *et al.* (2015: 18) suggest that on the ground, she is mainly asking for:

- more sustained inquiry into matters of community identity (as distinct from 'image identity');
- more discerning inspection of the juxtaposition of global homogeneities with local heterogeneities (after Fox Gotham, 2005); and
- more nuanced scrutiny of the degree to which meanings broadcast within and via events can be expressly read/fittingly recorded by outsider interest groups and populations (see Quinn, 2009: 486, 491, 493).

In these respects, please refer to Hollinshead *et al.* (2015) for a fuller critique – as inspired by this call of Quinn in *The Sage Handbook of Tourism Studies* – of the strategic reach of events as both 'secular pilgrimages' and as sites of corporate 'commodified aesthetics'.

Background: acts of declaration in the staging of special events

Inspired by the assessment of Quinn (2009) in *The Sage Handbook of Tourism Studies*, Hollinshead *et al.* (2015) indeed produced a useful response paper on the politics and poetics of the iconography or rather on the *iconology*! (see page 182 for definition) of peoples/places/pasts/presents which are highlighted or celebrated in and through the staging of special events. They have drawn up a primary glossary of target research terms and concepts which advanced research teams in Event Management/Event Studies can utilise to cultivate further creative approaches or inventive Quinnian angles to explore the mobilisation of competing worldviews through the ceremonialisation of things at special events and drawcard festivals. This primer from Hollinshead *et al.* (2015) – conceived to improve the state of the art of research into the connectivities of special events – constitutes a list of as yet underserviced terms which could fruitfully be deployed to probe what is declared/announced/heralded (and what is not so hailed) at special events as some inscriptions of being and becoming inevitably triumph over other potential inheritances through the monumentalisation of favoured 'social things' there/then. Thus the following short list of concepts is taken from Hollinshead *et al.* to serve as a catalyst list on matters of the normalisation/naturalisation of peoples and places for concerned researchers (in the wake of Quinn, 2009) with and across Event Studies. The dozen catalyst terms drawn up are as follows:

- *Coding machine* – the function of an event to inscribe a people/place/past/present in terms of a particular (contested) worldview.
- *Effectivity* – the degree to which an event moves the perception of others (or target interest groups) towards supporting a particular version of things, or otherwise take up an advocated identity or inheritances.
- *Emplotment* – the telling of an event in terms of the interpretations used to narrate it and the decorative exhilaration harnessed to make it captivating.
- *Evocation* – the interpretive effort to dress up an event so that it speaks to the specific and important doxa (or cultural warrants/held beliefs) of a particular homeland or target population.
- *Iconology* – the political science study of how power is mobilised in the staging of a local/regional/national event vis-à-vis the operational deployment of resonant images, symbols and cultural significations it uses – i.e. perhaps of the iconography (or the iconology) of these images, symbols and cultural significances within a particular geographical, spatial or temporal setting as obtained via ethnographic or representational mapping.
- *Inscription* – the manner in which an event is textually (or discursively) explained/justified/narrated to suit a particular assumed normalised or naturalised view of the world.
- *Invented culture* – the process by and through which an event is used to help a population manufacture or remanufacture a presumed or claimed tradition for itself or to otherwise freshly/correctively help that population imagine/perform/develop 'new' yet supposedly bona fide cultural pursuits/traits/inheritances.
- *Material symbolism* – the inherent power of signification that is embedded within the objects and the 'physical' icons used to project or propel an event, and the representational force of particular buildings or manufactured/produced/fabricated 'things' to speak to a given normalised worldview.
- *Performative activity* – the selected mix of interactive pursuits and engaged activities which are selected for an event – or which otherwise unfold at an

event – which help (in an emergent sense) to freshly/correctively/creatively 'produce' in dynamic fashion new or revised forms of lived culture for or among that population.

- *Priviligentia* – the 'ruling group' (or otherwise the recipient group) which benefits economically/psychically/politically from the presentation of a particular event, the narratives of which are loaded consciously or unconsciously in terms of their interests or their cherished inheritances.
- *Sacralisation* – the emic processes by and through which an event 'sacralises' an important idea or inheritance, whereby that belief/place/object or even that 'person' or 'being' is declared to be extremely rare/precious/sanctified by (or for) a specific people.
- *Subjugation* – the manner in which a mainstream population or a hegemonic institution consciously or unconsciously uses its dominant resources or its communicative position at an event to suppress or silence the held truths, the believed rights or the standing practices of a 'different', or 'rival', or an 'othered' community/group/organisation.

Focus: the generation of a working glossary on declarative activity

While the above brief list of catalyst terms from Hollinshead *et al.* (2015) is a handy start-up set of terms and concepts which can hopefully help get the conceptual juices of Event Studies researchers flowing, clearly a much more expansive glossary is needed given the dimensions, scope and magnitude of Quinn's (2009) dissatisfaction with the field. The purpose of this chapter is therefore to extend the preliminary thinking of Hollinshead *et al.* by providing a more substantial glossary which can prompt deeper and richer thinking on matters of research design within Event Studies. In this chapter, an attempt is therefore made to fertilise the ways in which the field talks about and appreciates what special events are and represent. In this regard – and in further recognition of Quinn's earlier call for more understanding of the wider connectives and broader positionalities of special events – a larger pool of illustrative terms and concepts will be revealed which can help stimulate deeper and fuller thought in the field about what special events can and do signify and for whom. This pool of ideas and constructions will describe (in particular ways) how event management and event development are always, and unavoidably, significant political practices which ought to be understood in terms of what is projected and performed through them, and coterminously what alternative, competing articulations of peoplehood and placedom are denied or debarred. Thus the working glossary that will be drawn up in this chapter is not one conceived around ways of speaking about a given special event as a singular 'event' or a 'fixed object of study' in and of itself, but rather as an institutionally positioned or interest-group demarcated 'commemoration' or 'happening' which addresses some lineages from the past and some traditions (or transitions?) as are exercised in the present, but *not* others. Hence, the working glossary that will be revealed in this chapter is part and parcel of the effort to satisfy what could be described as an *institutionally located Event Studies*.

In this light, it should be clarified that the articulation which undergirds the gestation of this glossary of exemplar terms and constructions about the broader meanings and the wider values behind events is not a field-contained one. Quinn's (2009) demand was for those who work in Event Management/Event Studies collectively to end their under-recognised theoretical confinement and escape from their scarcely admitted conceptual and methodological self-quarantine. It does not seek to advance specialist 'expert' knowledge of and about Event Management per se, but is rather an orientation which draws upon a wider panorama of disciplinary understandings, be they trans disciplinary and even post disciplinary ones. It is thus a glossarial 'outlook' rather than a glossarial 'inlook'. Positioning special events as important phenomena which carry all sorts of signs, representations and meanings in the ways in which they are conceived, scaffolded and promoted, the glossary is designed to draw attention to certain fashions by and through which special events are constituted by particular institutions and/or virtual structures. Such is the trans disciplinary cum post disciplinary orientation of the glossary towards those matters of power and those acts of cultural politics which may be discernible in and about them.

All told, the extended but still illustrative glossary offered in this chapter has been put together to help those who work in Event Management/Event Studies think a little more deeply about the exteriority of the special events they administrate or conduct ontological or epistemological research into. Clearly, no such glossary in a short one-off book chapter can ever be comprehensive and – to repeat the point – the glossarial definitions offered in what follows are merely meant to be illuminative or explanatory of different/richer ways of seeing and knowing what given events stand for. Thus the 30 sample terms and concepts that will be provided hereunder compose no more than a melange or bricolage of trans disciplinary avenues cum post disciplinary approaches through which the mien and the externalness of them can be more fruitfully gauged. Hence, the thirty exemplar terms and concepts each in some way speak to what the given event conscripts in political terms, connects with psychically and helps connote symbolically for its various stakeholders. Consonantly, the 30 sample constructions constitute a quick and ready attempt to attest to the declarative agency/the declarative reach/the declarative authority of special events in their myriad of potential consciously connived and unconsciously unctioned (or lubricated) ways. The 30 terms themselves will be culled from a much more extensive (three hundred word/four hundred word?) glossary on matters of iconography and iconology which the authors (Hollinshead and Suleman, forthcoming) are currently working on for publication elsewhere.

The developing glossary: events and the framing of peoples and places

In selecting the 30 illustrative terms/concepts, the initial aim has been to respect Quinn's clear view that research into event management and event development remains a somewhat stilted and logocentric activity. Thereafter, the objective behind the collation of this illuminatory glossary has been to satisfy ten platforms/areas of research inquiry which were put forward by Hollinshead *et al.* (2015) as an already published response to Quinn's (2009) call for oxygenated inquiry. The following statement explains how Hollinshead *et al.* drew up their start-up list of target platform areas:

> [The platform subjects were] selected with regard to their potential to generate what Jaramillo and McLaren (2008: 198) style as *fluid acumen* – or the capacity to generate multiple yet-each-supportable interpretations about what is politically and poetically important at the said event. Thus, the researcher who operates with 'fluid acumen' is he or she (or the interdisciplinary/transdisciplinary research team) which can learn how to interpret the meanings and the privileges carried by or generate through the said event vis-à-vis a plurality of outlooks upon it. The researcher who works with studied or developed fluid acumen is thereby one that has learnt how to creatively yet critically weigh up the sorts of authority and the kinds of reach which are embedded within the given event from a diverse (but salient!) mix of both social and psychic outlooks and cultural/political institutional arrangements 'there' and sincerely and substantively work with an informed and demonstrably supportable *multilogical imagination* (Hollinshead and Ivanova 2013). To these ends, the researcher skilled at operating with fluid acumen is one who has developed capacity at identifying the historical contingency of things, and the critical reflexivity that a range of communities/interest groups/organisations have with it or likely to have in the foreseeable future. It is thereby incumbent upon the researcher who inspects and interprets with fluid acumen to accordingly work with open-to-the-future understandings, and many will thus want to explore working to *postdisciplinary* principles (rather than just interdisciplinary or transdisciplinary ones) to that end (Coles, Hall, and Duval 2006) — notably where matters of cross-cultural interpretation are tall and questions of intertextuality and interpolation are acute.
>
> (Hollinshead and Ivanova, 2013: 22–3)

The ten platform arenas offered by Hollinshead *et al.* (2015) are:

- the social correlations of events;
- the cultural correlations of events;
- the psychic correlations of events;
- the political correlations of events;
- the historical correlations of events;
- events and salient matters of being;
- events and salient matters of becoming;
- events and salient matters of voice;
- events and salient matters of reflexivity; and
- events and salient matters of audiencing.

For each of these ten listed platform themes or beach-head subjects promoting deeper or enhanced inquiry into the politics and poetics (or, said another way, the signified politics and the signified psychics) of special events and drawcard festivals, a set of three exemplar terms will be given. Each of the three concepts addresses what are as yet under-utilised or emergent lines of inspection (with regard to the plural knowability of things) in the declaration of people/places/pasts/presents. The set of glossarial terms are housed in a respective set of boxes: Box 11.1 = The Social Correlation of Events; Box 11.2 = The Cultural Correlation of Events; Box 11.3 = The Psychic Correlation of Events; and so on.

Again, to restate the point, because of available word-ceilings, each of the ten boxes cannot offer anything like a complete or thorough inspection of the platform area in question. The 30 terms provided are merely pre-typified ones which can foreshadow the selection of future research agendas by other Event Management/Event Studies scholars or practitioners across the continents. Those offered here are taken from the chapter authors' current own respective research work on the declarative power of tourism to normalise the public culture and public heritage of places (mainly Hollinshead) and to the declarative agency of travel to validate or transmute inherited – notably spiritual and homeland – identifications (mainly Suleman). Thus the chapter authors make no apology for the fact that, among the 10 platform boxes, the 30 exemplar terms privilege the thinking of French litero-philosophers (such as Foucault on *le regard* [the institutional gaze]), of the assessments of the Hungarian political-historian Nyíri on the statist declarative of place and space in China, of the British sociologist (yet wannabe-geographer) Urry on our burgeoning contemporary global mobilities, and of the Indian-born literary critic Bhabha on the anguished restlessness of so many of the world's peoples under our postcolonial/neo-colonial moment. Such biases and unbalanced emphases are difficult to avoid in an illustrative glossary which is necessarily limited in room. But Hollinshead and Suleman (forthcoming) are working decidedly to ensure that their larger in-process glossary (from which these 30 immediate terms are summarily taken) will be substantively more eclectic across the zones of connectivity underscored by Quinn (2009) and on and around the platform subjects of declarative reach suggested thereafter by Hollinshead *et al.* (2015) in that Quinnian vein.

Box 11.1 The *social* correlation of events: some under-examined subjects in declarative event projection

Research topic 1 = regime-of-truth

The term *regime-of-truth* is taken from the French litero-philosopher Foucault and attempts to account for what governing organisations/instrumentalities do in the fields they control or work within. Foucault was not concerned with the absolute 'truth' of a statement (where it remains universally 'so', once uncovered, whatever the period or context), per se.

He was more interested in working out the effectiveness of particular apparatuses of authority whose control of *power/knowledge* made a particular understanding/interpretation/truth 'true' in the real world with real effects at a given point in time. Thus, to him, organisations/institutions/populations are inclined to work with (or rather *within*) regimes-of-truth (which may or may not be absolutely 'true') but which have significant consequences if everyone under the influence of that organisation/institution/population indeed believes 'it' to be so or situationally accepts it as so. A distinct regime-of-truth does not, therefore, lie outside of power: indeed, it acts as a 'thing' in the world, working *in capillary fashion* through the biopower agency of those individuals who work partly consciously and partly unconsciously through the normalised modes of discourse (what is said) and praxis (what is done) which that institutional apparatus doles out. Accordingly ... in event management in North America, regimes-of-truth of one era may celebrate the seemingly natural Manifest Destiny conquest of the American West by 'White'/'European' settlers, whereas events in a later era (or 'episteme' in Foucauldian terms) might coterminously celebrate 'First American'/'Indian' narratives about the sanctity of their precious homelands alongside those which still pay homage to the so-called 'Anglo' conquest of the so-called 'Wild West'.

Research topic 2 = tourist gaze, the

Borrowing from the strong French concept *le regard* (the institutional gaze) – and particularly from Foucault's construction of the clinical gaze in medicine – Urry presents *the tourist gaze* as those systematic ways of seeing that tourists engage in and which various corporations, organisations and interest groups of the tourism industry help concretise and universalise over time. In Urry's view, there are three principal dichotomies in or through which the de-differentiating power of the tourist gaze has been (or is being) influential, namely those of (1) the romantic/collective; (2) the authentic/inauthentic; and (3) the historical/modern. Clearly, Urry's intelligences on the tourist gaze have been prodigiously helpful in helping scholars in Tourism Studies understand the when, where and why of the collaborative industrial scripting and the almost habitual projection of things through the symbolic/institutional coding of tourism. While his eponymous book *The Tourist Gaze* has perhaps become a lead work on the social, cultural and political parameters of tourism, some analysts have expressed disappointment that Urry did not venture very far in giving critique of the Foucauldian dimension of the key term (the gaze) or of the considerable weight which that very construction has in French litero-philosophy. Readers should note that, in France, *le regard* is a paramount construct in ocularcentric discourse to account for the objectifying vision of strangers and for the political institutionalisation of self and in-community understanding. Other observers have also been puzzled as to why Urry drew distinct attention to a limited number of gazes (such as the romantic and collective gaze) when conceivably within his own work there is demonstrable evidence of many other substantive sorts of gaze. Hence … in event development, in any local subject-arena in history or in nature, then, what are the vogue and unquestioned ways in which particular narratives are repeatedly told through today, if any, and which versions of those pasts/these interpretations of nature are regularly (even axiomatically) suppressed?

Research topic 3 = imagined communities

In the modern world, or rather, in the so-called postmodern world, the pace of social change is accelerating and is continually testing the capacity of prior mechanisms of social practice to cope. During the late twentieth century, in Europe, clusters of social, economic and political systems which were brought into being in the eighteenth century are now seen to be 'in dissolution'. For example, the received form of the supposedly eternal *nation state* is lately the subject of radical change during the contemporary moment, as the conventional ideology of nationalism (i.e. where it is envisioned as a sovereign device able to fix boundaries and the representations of 'countries' in terms of a certain priviligentia and certain traditions, and able to make decent 'national' citizens of those that live within that claimed state) is beginning to dissipate. Nowadays, new forms of political collectives are emerging as *imagined communities* – Anderson's (1983) much adopted term – in which an unfolding or virtual population chooses to commemorate itself in a non-locative fashion, or otherwise coalesces around an affective identity of some kind, while the supposedly long-standing territorial and national/sovereign communities are now in decline. Such apparently 'natural' but distinctively hierarchical organisations of 'great antiquity' are slowly being replaced by new models of pseudo-nationalist belonging, by new hybrid multicultural 'communities', and by new cultural/religious/ethnic/special interest diasporas which do not necessarily have any strongly coherent locational or admino-military isomorphism. The new wave of inchoate attachments and creatively imagined communities tends to produce its own particular-cum-idiosyncratic solidarities, their own inventive dreams and their own obscure futures. Thus … in event development in the particular region or city, how many of the lead events are primarily territorial in appeal, how many of them are imagino-virtual and not primarily based on geographical residency?

Box 11.2 The *cultural* correlation of events: some under-examined subjects in declarative event projection

Research topic 1 = scenic spots

In inspecting the drawcards of historic and natural eminence in China, Nyíri deploys the term *scenic spots* to classify the most famous sites and ancient relics of places/provinces/states. He suggests that these noted inherited settings – along with the lead museums, zoos and theme parks – constitute the *mingsheng*, or the canonised 'imagined multicultural community' of the historically continuous nation of China. For Nyíri, these indexed scenic spots (i.e. these *jingdian*) are vital tools of both patriotic education and modernisation, and almost all of them are prominently celebrated in literary circles, too. Hence … with regard to the leading events of our time in other countries, how many of them are deeply correlative culturally and salute long-standing culturo-national significances, and are thereby necessarily located *in situ* at historic or natural sites which are redolent with 'patriotic virtue' of this kind or which are otherwise deliberatively re-enforcive of a region's/a nation's esteemed literature?

Research topic 2 = signification

Signification is the decided act of bestowing symbolic worth upon a site, scene or storyline in terms of the manner in which it reflects the dominant visions of a place or population. 'Significance' (or *significant difference*) is always a relational matter, for no 'meaning' or 'difference' ever exists neutrally, understood in the same regard by everyone. All meaning – after Bakhtin – has to be established through dialogue with others, and is therefore inherently 'dialogic'. Thereby … in terms of the leading cultural events of a region or city, which authorising institutions/bodies/agencies (if any) have been instrumental is giving due 'significance' to them? Or, otherwise, could the events be said to be so notable and self-agentic that they have now come with their own rare and highly esteemed singularity?

Research topic 3 = culture manufacture

During the 1980s and 1990s, culture came to be less commonly regarded by anthropologists and sociologists as a distinct concrete or prime-moving force acting in and through society, and more frequently as a process rather than as a firm or stabilised entity – i.e. being increasingly seen to be a performance which can be constantly *created* or *recreated* in dynamic fashion. Moreover, given the ease of mobility and communication in late twentieth-century life, cultural phenomena were increasingly seen to less commonly 'belong' to definitive social contexts, and the cultural practices of a given population were increasingly found to involve the creative invention/manufacture of all sorts of new protean things in all kinds of new protean situations, or otherwise of the creative recombination of existing cultural forms. When anthropologists/sociologists, therefore, study the manufacture of culture today, they are particularly keen to consequentially understand who is inventing which new cultural symbols, and who is appropriating or decontextualising old ones for which particular purpose. Ergo … could a leading event (or mix of paramount events?) staged in a particular city or region effectively be said to have performatively created a significant new cultural form – or a noted novel cultural activity – which has been very well adopted 'there'?

Box 11.3 The *psychic* correlation of events: some under-examined subjects in declarative event projection

Research topic 1 = consumption

In everyday use, *consumption* is the utilisation of a good or a service until it has no remaining value. In the social sciences, however, it is part and parcel of that more complex process of production and consumption whereby particular commodities are transformed or given added value for a distinct buying or experiencing public. In contemporary capitalist societies, consumption is depicted as being the driving force of the economy, and given commodity relations are assumed to penetrate all spheres of social life and psychic aspiration. Thus … for a particular special event, in which contrasting ways (if any) do particular groups/markets differentially 'consume' it? How different are the attendant psychic resonances signalled by it in terms of the use-value/function-value/meaning-value of the event among different buying or experiencing populations?

Research topic 2 = ethnic-group-maintenance

Each distinct population (or ethnic group) lives within a symbolic universe which consists of a matrix of all socially objectivated (i.e. socially functional) and subjectively real meanings (after Berger and Luckman). This symbolic universe not only orders the past, the present and the future, it puts 'everything in its rightful place', even legitimating the 'correctness' of an individual's subjective identity within that population/ethnic group. Since all social realities are constructed in the face of danger/uncertainty/chaos, they are precarious, and when such difficulties enlarge to become 'a significant problem', specific procedures of universe maintenance become necessary by which that population confirms its own important felt identity and legitimates itself, positively projecting and normalising some things/some behaviours/some preferences and delegitimating (or denying the reality of) other things/other behaviours/other preferences. Monopolistic-style *en groupe* legitimations or normalisations of things tend to occur within those groups/populations where there is a high degree of social-structural 'psychic' stability. Where traditional definitions of reality thereby remain strong, the possibility of large social change tends to be restricted. So … with regard to the principal events staged in a city or region, which psychic affordances (or affiliatory benefits) do they each come freighted with? How do the events appear to provide psychic comfort or *en groupe* stability, and for which groups or populations/sub-populations in particular?

Research topic 3 = flâneurs

To Urry – following Benjamin and Wolf – the *flâneur* (or 'stroller') is the modern hero of our time. He/she is that person who is freely able to travel, to arrive, to gaze, to move on, to be anonymous and to exist in psychic ease as he/she is ever mobile, remaining 'comfortable' in all sorts of foreign or liminal zones away from his/her normal place of residence. Hence, *flânerie* is the continuing act of strolling, gazing and (importantly) being gazed upon 'here', 'there' and 'there'. So … does the special event being put on provide succour only to the diehard specialists active in that domain of interest – having a high threshold of knowledge/skill/engagement to be of interest – or can it also be fast or readily appreciated by the ever-mobile traveller and the scene-chasing wayfarer?

Box 11.4 The *political* correlation of events: some under-examined subjects in declarative event projection

Research topic 1 = discursive statements

Under Foucauldian thought (after Foucault, the analyst of institutional thought and practice), a 'discourse' is generally the type of 'domain language' engaged in and furthered by a group/discipline/population, and it embraces the ideas and privileged meanings which that body upholds. Thus *discursive statements* are those verbal/visual/textual articulations which carry and express the embedded values of that group, and they are regularly or routinely engaged in part-conscious/part-unconscious fashion. Under Foucauldian thought, it is the everyday talk (via discursive statements) and the everyday deeds (via matching praxis or *practical and material acts*) which enable the world to be seen/experienced/known in particular tacitly approved or naturalised ways rather than via other truths (i.e. via competing understandings). Hence … for a city or region's portfolio of annual events, which normalised outlooks on the world are supported in ongoing fashion by the statements issued and the activities associated with them … on a case-by-case basis? Does the talk and the deeds of each and all of these events reflect and further the very same normalised worldviews?

Research topic 2 = indoctritainment

In his *Scenic Spots* study of the classification of the leading heritage sites and the precious nature settings of China, Nyíri maintains that tourism in China is quite distinct from that in other nations. For instance, drawcard sites in 'The West'/'Europe' tend to constitute bourgeois forms of tourism which are founded upon the celebration of and visitation to places and spaces imbued in *authenticity*, and, in Russia, 'Soviet' forms of heritage and nature tourism tend to be built substantively upon opportunities for *rugged and selfless experience*. In contrast, to Nyíri, tourism development and management in China is regulated heavily by the state, and the scenic spots (*jingdian*) and theme parks of the People's Republic of China are harnessed in order to explain the heroic past of the nation and to further patriotic education and modernisation across it. Under such representations of *indoctritainment* in China, tourism sites and settings are pointedly bounded, approved, indexed and promoted for proper 'consumption', as preferred by the all-seeing interpreting/governing hegemonic 'state'. In this way – after Sun – Nyíri suggests that in China these classified sites are not free for interpretive contestation by viewers/visitors, but are semiotically 'overdetermined'. But is it only China that deals in indoctritainment? Accordingly … do intense ideological values come quietly or loudly articulated within the entertainment fare of other cities or regions (your own state or nation)?

Research topic 3 = ortholalia

Nyíri's *Scenic Spots* study is seemingly a study of the Chinese state 'in action'. In exploring the state's discursive practices (see *discursive statements*, above) of indoctritainment (see also, above), Nyíri maintains that the scenic spots and the theme parks of China are totalised (interpretively) to such a degree that opposing interpretations flounder and *in situ* reflection by tourists is simply not cultivated by them. Under these acts of *ortholalia* (or heavily regulated discursive control over what can be 'said' or 'enacted' there), the resultant articulation about history/culture/heritage may be seen to constitute a form of socialist repression, but not one which is just 'political' in its origin, but also 'national' and 'cultural' in its temper. Acts of ortholalia are deemed by Nyíri to be embedded 'somewhere' within the difficult-to-read 'triangle' of the state/the economy/the culture of China at this time. And, interestingly, Nyíri suggests that such efforts at totalised cultural control have conceivably increased in China over recent decades and have not diminished under the intensified information flows of early twenty-first-century 'capitalism'.

A bedfellow term for ortholalia is *orthopraxy*. Where a government or regulating authority is dominant or hegemonic with regard to what ought to be celebrated/normalised/naturalised – and where the control over the discourse and praxis of representational activity is secure/total/absolute – that government or authority could be said to indulge in *orthopraxy*. It not only privileges particular 'political' visions and versions of the world, but restrictively delimits the ways in which those truths/images/symbolisations can be articulated in everyday practice in the field or projected through industrial endeavour.

So ... do other countries exhibit strong (hegemonic?/absolutist?/imperialist?) statist control of what ought to be cherished and celebrated (and thereby understood) through the special events they promulgate? If Nyíri was justified in his assessment of ortholalia and orthopraxy in China in the last two decades of the twentieth century – and many would claim his interpretation overstates the degree of centralist control over what may be seen and experienced – does 'Beijing' operate in that same magistral or peremptory way as the third decade of the twenty-first century is reached?

Box 11.5 The *historical* correlation of events: some under-examined subjects in declarative event projection

Research topic 1 = discontinuous historical realities

The Cultural Studies/Literary Studies commentator, Homi Bhabha, has devoted much thought to populations who have suffered under the colonial yoke and under the later neo-colonial suppressions, and who have particularly suffered because they have been cut off from their revered 'history'. He has keenly traced the sensorium of such decentred peoples, although knowing that such monitoring of the changeable/emergent networks of international identifications today is something beyond our current and commonplace 'perceptual, mappable experience'. In this light, and with respect to those hybrid situations which many of the world's broken or partly broken populations are forced to endure, what intrigues Bhabha are the new spaces of *discontinuous historical reality* which now appear, flicker or inscribe themselves for such peoples here and there across the globe. What Bhabha seeks to capture are the sorts of disjunctive episodes by which received concepts of selfhood and long-standing worldviews are fragmented as old historical subjects disintegrate or otherwise become displaced by new schizophrenic and ambivalent subjectivities. Thus, as ancient and long-run historical realities discontinue, new expressive identities now appear at new 'in-between locations' and at emergent enunciative sites where there is a remaking of boundaries and an opening out of fresh potentialities for invigorated identity and rejuvenating selfhood. To Bhabha, in some neo-colonial and postcolonial settings, the future once again becomes *an open question* for such populations, instead of being one thoroughly specified by a received and closely defined past. So … in event development within a nation, is there evidence that events are being dreamed up on stage which enable or encourage particular peoples to become their old selves again, yet be a population with a new and different roseate future?

Research topic 2 = Eurocentrism

Eurocentrism is that mix of acute ethnocentric understandings by and through which 'European'/'Western' values are assumed to be the right and proper (or the only 'rational') ones to uphold about a given subject or in a given place, wherever it is in the world. Under Eurocentrism, 'non-European'/'non-Western' outlooks upon the world tend to be ignored or dismissed and 'non-European'/'non-Western' people are incrementally 'othered' as their history, their inheritances and their customary cultural practices are chastised or subjugated. While Eurocentrism is a panoply of thought that is predominantly indulged in consciously and (even more dangerously!) unconsciously by institutions/interest groups/corporations hailing from Europe and the West, it has not been infrequent (during the history of recent centuries) to find that certain non-European individuals or non-Western organisations work to Eurocentric outlooks on the world, whether (again) those views have been adopted consciously or unconsciously. Thus … in the given formerly colonised/neo-colonised nation, has a programme of events been staged which seeks to restore old and fragile non-European/non-Western worldviews, or otherwise display them in bi- or multi-interpretive fashion alongside those articulations of seeing and being which are Eurocentrist in force?

Research topic 3 = naturalisation

Naturalisation is a cousin term of *normalisation*, where the latter covers those acts which standardise understandings and render them uniform across a population. While the term normalisation tends to be used to describe how a thing or cognition is ordered and organised within and across an institution or society, the term naturalisation tends to be used when that object or idea is assumed to be implicit or innate or authentic to a particular setting or context. When a thing is thereby naturalised, the aim of the naturaliser is to fix it 'forever' via that dominant understanding or that ruling interpretation of and about it, as if that phenomenon is plainly and instinctively 'so'. To naturalise a behaviour or custom is to deny flexibility of meaning about that thing and to secure discursive or ideological closure about it. Thus a way of life is seen to be 'natural' (and therefore right, and proper for a people or territory to *naturally* uphold) and thus beyond permanence, beyond history – and being inviolate, that revered inherited thing is not therefore 'cultural' in the sense of having an ordinary or human-created growth, it is a raw and historic natural entity. Consonantly … is the given event based on a premise that the activity or subject being venerated is one which naturally and historically belongs 'there'?

Box 11.6 Events and salient matters of *being*: some under-examined subjects in declarative event projection

Research topic 1 = identification

Matters of *identification* are notably germane to representations of and about colonised or suppressed peoples, whose preferred ways of being are in peril. When individuals from a mainstream population seek to understand and then signify the reasoning of a 'different'/'other'/'subjugated' population, they generally have available to them – according to the French Neo-Marxist Pêcheux – three principal structural configurations of discourse. Under the first such form of explanatory reasoning (i.e. under *identification*), all things are axiomatically and unthinkingly assumed to exist completely within the realm of dominant/mainstream thoughtlines. Under the second such modality (i.e. under *counteridentification*), the voice adopted (or the voice appeased) is that of the uncertain and sceptical 'troublemaker' in that suppressed population, that is, capturing the outlooks of he/she who revolts against this over-determinant mainstream discourse in projecting how the world and its objects should be seen, and who seeks to reverse that imposed orthodoxy, but yet who stays predominantly captive to its carried structured ideas and its implicit biases. Under the final style of reasoning (i.e. under *disidentification*), a more resolute attempt is made to fully recognise and reject those imposed/dominant conceptualisations and replace them entirely with representations which are accounted for via either the old/subjugated cosmologies of that disempowered population or via fresh and emergent 'oppositional discourse' which in and of itself can rejuvenate that lately subjectified people. Hence, the effort to re-identify an imposed or unwanted 'identification' about a particular people/place/past/present is (under *counteridentification*) a subtle and agile endeavour to replace crippling, irrelevant and normalising 'talk' with more vibrant and locally empowering styles of ideological communication about things, but under *disidentification* that corrected effort to empower that population 'to be again' can become decidedly more committed, pugnacious and (if necessary) revolutionary/violent. Hence … is there any evidence in the events planned for a city/region/country that there are elements in the event programme which (1) counteridentify, or (2) disidentify towards the interests or the felt being of a disenfranchised population?

Research topic 2 = imaginal realm

An *imaginal realm* is that panoply of interpretations/projections/inscriptions through which a place or nation is predominantly understood and declared 'as being'. Typically, representations of or about a particular imaginal realm pay distinct reference to the unusual/special/esteemed qualities of that place or people and attempt to account for its mythical/iconic inheritances. Clearly, since tourism is fundamentally a, if not the, leading industry of 'difference project', tourism is a vital vehicle for articulation about the cherished/inherited/hailed ways of being which distinct peoples support culturally, spiritually, cosmologically. Thus it is important to monitor (in Tourism Management/Tourism Studies) the everyday role that offered tourism promotions indeed play in decently/appropriately communicating such preferred notions and inheritances of being, and in examining the degree to which the projections of a given imaginal realm in tourism conceivably tally with the ways it is inscribed through other projective/performative industries. Thereby … is the way an event on the tourism/travel calendar of a city or a region describes the imaginal realm of a people or place closely coterminous with ways in which 'it' is communicated in arts events, in film and/or in other representational industries? Do those who project this and that about the lived realities of that people or place appear *to collaborate* strategically with those who work in those other projective/performative industries when they draw up their representations of that imaginal realm?

Research topic 3 = post-tourists

While MacCannell has famously claimed that tourism is fundamentally structured around the tourist's continued search for authenticity, Feifer recognised that – these days – a significant (even substantive) proportion of travellers are actually *post-tourists* who in fact delight in the very inauthenticity of the everyday/everyplace tourist experience. Indeed, both Feifer and the sociologist Urry recognise that 'post tourists' do, in fact, find pleasure in the teeming multiplicity of tourist encounters/games in which they participate, knowing there is indeed no such singular authentic tourist experience but a veritable litany of projected 'texts' framed for them from which they can happily choose as they variously search for beauty, for information, for enlightenment, for escape, for their own solitude, or for whatever. Feifer (and Urry) thereby argue that in matters of experiencing and being while travelling, not all tourists 'be' the same, or 'desire' the same. Ergo … at the specific event being promoted, to what degree are tourists there motivated by the quest for authentic being, and to what degree are local people motivated by that like quest for authentic being?

Box 11.7 Events and salient matters of *becoming*: some under-examined subjects in declarative event projection

Research topic 1 = ambiguity

In the current context of matters of identification and representation through the declarative power of tourism and/or the projective agency of special events, the term *ambiguity* refers to those locations of existence and hope and to those significations of identity and inheritance which appear to give off vague, uncertain, obscure or 'double' meanings about people and/or things. Sometimes these articulations of being (and, importantly, those interpretations of *becoming*) are deliberately rendered ambiguous in order that a wider range across the population will be able to identify with it, or will be able to aspire towards that broadcast sentiment. Accordingly … for the particular special event, does what is celebrated/signified/symbolised there narrowly and definitively target a singular and specific interest-group/sub-population, or does it equivocally and ambiguously strategically target a broader/more loosely defined/potentially more encompassing mix of groups and peoples?

Research topic 2 = emergent peoples

An *emergent people* is that population which has learnt or which has acquired the capacity to define and project itself in new ways which are either freshly representative of a long-standing but lately subjugated/downtrodden identity, or otherwise which are representative of new forms of unfolding or refreshing 'difference' which has not before been traditional or in vogue 'there'. Such *emergent* populations tend *not* to be an absolute/totalised/thoroughly authentic reflection of any previous or pre-given cultural tradition, ethnic trait or fixed set of practices, but they do tend to draw upon some particular inherited interpretations of past being as they seek to forge a new future for themselves via a newly won counteridentification or otherwise via a strong campaign of *disidentification* (see *identification*, above, in Box 11.5). Hence … does the special event in question signify the hailed culture/the revivified spirituality/the rejuvenated cosmology of a newly 'emergent' or a freshly 'confident' population?

Research topic 3 = transgredients

Writing in the late-middle period of the twentieth-century, Bakhtin considered that when one removes the social from cognitive understanding, it is difficult to really appreciate how individuals think, reason, solve problems or recall things: to him, all those characteristics that psychologists/social psychologists had previously insisted could be understood only by focusing on events taking place *inside the individual* fail to lead us to any real or stable understanding of 'mindedness'. Thus Bakhtin and his followers believe that 'our social others' – our often difficult-to-spot conversational partners – must always be identified in given social settings, if we are readily to know how 'we' came to see, value and label things, including ourselves. To Bakhtin and his followers, it is important to know not so much the *ingredients* of a social situation (i.e. what may be found *within* that conversing person), but the *transgredients* of that contextual/intersubjective setting (i.e. what is located there *between* rather than within those individuals). Ultimately to Bakhtin, then, one's 'personality' and one's 'self' are mutually determined or transgredient phenomena – a matter of collective shaping and interpersonal/intersubjective becoming – rather than being restrictively naturally occurring ingredient entities. Thus … how *social* is the projection of the special event? Does it address highly individualistic notions of being and motivation … or does it deliberately target highly communal/highly bonded/high *en groupe* notions of collective becoming?

Box 11.8 Events and salient matters of *voice*: some under-examined subjects in declarative event projection

Research topic 1 = declarative authority

In the current context of matters of representation through tourism and/or signification through event management, *declarative authority* comprises the agency, power and reach of an institution, interest group or state to explain something, to announce something or to correctively project that entity and, in so doing, thereby celebrate a particular custom, cultural warrant or inheritance as being decent/worthy/the right thing to do or uphold. The declarative authority of an organisation/institution/interest group constitutes its worldmaking capacity and legitimated right (whether that voice is given or acquired) to designate/normalise/naturalise ideas and things through the performative/projective/inscriptive industrial activity of tourism (in concert with that of other related 'collaborative encoding industries', or through the strategic staging of mediated events. So … for the particular special event … which was the body/bodies or organisation(s) which gave legitimacy (and/or authenticity?) to it?

Research topic 2 = decoding

Decoding is the process by which an individual, group or population receives and interprets a communication, a broadcast/narrowcast or an act of signification voiced to it. Usually, the 'receiving' or 'listening' party will 'hear' the communication axiomatically in terms of its own emic history and its own doxa (i.e. its dominant ways of talking and acting). It is thereby the function of decoding specialists within (or available to) that individual/body/community to make comprehensible those involved or difficult-to-fathom external communications which have been sent to them (see *encoding*, below, in Box 11.10) and which might otherwise be unfamiliar to that party 'there'. Thus … for the given event … was it actually decoded by the target population in the manner in which it was initially voiced to them (encoded) by the body managing and projecting it?

Research topic 3 = non-statist authorisations

Non-statist authorisations or non-statist representations of culture/heritage/nature/whatever are projections/significations/narratives which emanate from sources other than the regulating 'state government' there in that province/territory/country. Non-statist authorisations of a storyline or for a place/space are notably significant where situations of hegemonic or totalised control (over what may be voiced or experienced about anything) generally apply there. Non-statist authorisations tend to be explanations/interpretations/legitimations which stem from 'external' organisations (such as those voiced from outside capitalist/corporative sources in a communist nation or command economy) or which arise from osmotic and difficult-to-regulate transnational behaviours which individual travellers have knowingly/unknowingly carried into that province/territory/country with them. (See *indoctritainment*, *ortholalia* (and *orthopraxy*) in Box 11.4, above.) Accordingly … in the particular state or nation, is the power and authority of the state being challenged at a given special event by an articulated narrative or a voiced interpretation of and about the world which has come in exogamously from 'abroad' in some fashion?

Box 11.9 Events and salient matters of *reflexivity*: some under-examined subjects in declarative event projection

Research topic 1 = interpretivism

Interpretivists hold that meaning changes over time everywhere (eventually!) and can never be finally fixed but must always inevitably require a reflexive act of interpretation. To interpretivists, meanings always have be 'read', 'informed' or 'interpreted', and so there will always be a resultant imprecision about the use of language, symbols and signs in each and every place. Interpretivists maintain that 'readers', 'viewers', 'listeners' can never precisely secure the exact meaning originally intended by a 'writer', 'image-maker' or 'speaker', and that *interpretivism* is therefore a field of thought that admits the *corrigibility* of interpretation (where knowledge is always partial and always open to different 'improved explanations' or to 'more richly informed explications' from the same or from alternative reflexive perspectives). Hence … where a long-run event is still being staged in a region/city/country … do different kinds of attendees visit it in order to commemorate or celebrate entirely different things in or about it from each other? At such a long-standing event, have the principal meaning(s) by which the event is staged/legitimated/funded/supported changed significantly, over time?

Research topic 2 = pseudo-events

Urry – the British author of *The Tourist Gaze* – acknowledges a debt to the US social commentator Boorstin, who had argued that contemporary Americans cannot experience 'reality' directly but necessarily thrive on *pseudo-events* (or rather *inauthentically contrived attractions*) while they ignore the real world outside. By Boorstin's estimation, American tourists are subject to increasingly more extravagant displays of things as they travel the world, contained within the controlled environmental bubble and controlled representational realm provided for them by the tourism and hospitality industries, and they consequently become ever more removed from the local people who inhabit the very places they visit and gaze over. Under the seeming sway of the globalisation (or Americanisation?) of all things – including reflexive experience – travellers from the rest of the world have also learnt how to survive/enjoy/take on board the pseudo-events or the hyper-realities metered out to us all, today. So … for the large event being inspected … for which visitors (if any) does it reflexively stand as 'a real/authentic event' and for which does it stand as a pseudo-event of some kind? And … for which host/local/event-staging groups does the event stand as 'a real/authentic event' and for which does it likewise stand as a recognised pseudo-event?

Research topic 3 = reflexive mobility of vision, the

In his writings during the couple of decades (or more) which have followed the initial appearance of *The Tourist Gaze* in 1990, the sociologist-cum-geographer Urry has attempted to make sterner observations on the mobility of vision in tourism and its cousin, leisure and economic practices. In this effort to more penetratingly distil how 'the tourist gaze' has been globalised and has globalised, the later Urry has worked on research agendas to distinguish between *virtual travel* (through the Internet), *imaginative travel* (through phone, radio and TV) and *corporeal travel* where individuals physically move to/through different places and bodily experience them. What now, therefore, interests the Urry of the second decade of the twenty-first century is *the tourism reflexivity* of destinations/spaces/storylines/services … i.e. of the set of disciplines, procedures and criteria which facilitate each (and every?) destination/region/country to monitor, to evaluate and to develop its accumulative 'tourism potential' under the emerging patterns of global travel. He is thereby interested in, under *the liquid modernity* (after Bauman) of our contemporary moments, how particular places are indeed reflexive with these impulses of virtual, imaginative and corporeal travel, how they are interconnected, how they are encountered multi-sensuously, and which particular forces work to aggregate those experiences and assemblies to thereby give durability and stability to those mobile visions/mobile experiences. Consonantly, to Urry, the apparatus of tourism (and the apparatuses of the global flows of intercultural experience and aspiration) yields various levels or forms of materiality to 'the gaze', 'the glance' or 'the visions' it programmes, projects and performs, and which we differentially/reflexively welcome or disdain. Thus … in terms of this reflexive appreciation of things … does large-scale special event ABC on the local/regional/national calendar cater only for *corporeal travellers*, or does it have substantial appeal for *virtual travellers* and/or for *imaginative travellers*? Does special event ABC have the same sort of appeal for local travellers/local experiencers of it as it does for those who have journeyed to it/encountered it from a considerable distance?

Box 11.10 Events and salient matters of *audiencing*: some under-examined subjects in declarative event projection

Research topic 1 = articulative reach

Laclau and Mouffe maintain that all discursive representations are 'temporary' rather than 'inevitable' significations of and about the world: they are merely projections and identifications which are *articulated* and thereby *bound together* by custom and convention in a particular place at a particular time. In this light, that which is *articulated* is not only discursively 'expressed', it conjoins other compatible representations which collectively/collaboratively help constitute and stabilise the overall institution/community/nation. The *articulative reach* of an organisation or agency thus is said to comprise those channels of communication and those territories of influence which it has sway over, whether that found effectivity be long-standing and tenacious or otherwise be emergent and 'fresh' (or 'corrective') for those 'audiences'. Cultural meaning may therefore be said to be *articulated* with the political economy and/or the industrial economy and is consequently identifiable in resultant moments or lines of 'production'. Hence … how is special event DEF *explicitly* articulated with or deliberately dovetailed with other long-standing identifications of being and becoming which are 'owned by'/known to be well associated with the hosting/presenting population? How is the private sector company or the public sector body which runs special event GHI *implicitly* articulating or dovetailing that happening with the felt customs/the hailed conventions/the cherished narratives of a particular target audience or particular mix of audiences?

Research topic 2 = encoding

Encoding is that audiencing process by which an organisation or body puts up a topic or issue for broadcasting (or for narrowcasting) to others, commonly (and often merely) reflecting the in-house or endogamous terms of reference privileged by that presenting/projecting agency, but sometimes deliberately and/or cleverly framing it within the specific 'emic syntax' or through the 'cultural grammar' used by the target population instead. It is the function of experienced encoding specialists to selectively and creatively direct the target reader/target listener towards the gain of preferred communicated meanings via an economy of well-audienced effort, coterminously foregrounding certain favoured interpretations but suppressing disapproved ones. The audiencing effort may be one that seeks to persuade the target audience towards some new experience/idea/consumptive activity, or it may just be one that wallows in the worldviews or milks the cultural warrants of that intended audience. Thus … which significant steps did the event management company for festival JKL take to soundly encode it for population MNO? And where special event PQR was poorly attended, how (perhaps) did external company/distant operators/overseas corporation STU fail to decently/effectively/propitiously encode its communication about special event UVW in terms of the doxa/the held cultural preferences/the ordinary proclivities of target population XYZ? (See *decoding* in Box 11.8, above.)

Research topic 3 = soft power

The concept of *soft power* covers those activities indulged in by institutions, populations or nations to attract or persuade other/external audienced populations (or even domestic/internal audience groups and communities) about an actual but as yet under-appreciated or a future-desired order of things. While 'hard power' mechanisms tend to comprise the ability to coerce via military or economic might, 'soft power' acts or projections comprise the nuanced capacity to present and project aspects of culture, custom or civilisation arrestively in a generalised sense to other peoples, or otherwise in a strategic/reflexive sense to a specific population or target mix of people(s). Fundamentally, the exercise in and of soft power is an act of strategic communication where the operating institution or the encoding nation seeks to be liked or have particular things savoured by others on a general level or on a specific audience-by-audience/market-by-market/country-by-country basis. Soft power communication is typically a discriminating 'game to play' or leverage, and it is often hard to initially establish, easy to lose and costly to re-establish. Thus … in terms of the soft power 'campaign' being proposed, how will its success be measured and who will carry out that evaluation? In terms of the given country's failed soft power campaign, why were the gains/outcomes from it so apparently under-appreciated or ephemeral as registered with regard to each other nation targeted by that strategic communication effort?

Summary: time for Quinnian action – onwards with the scrutiny of connective reach and declarative agency

This chapter opened with a reminder of how Quinn (2009) has pointedly called for more sustained investigation into matters of connectivity, which special events indeed have in terms of communal meaning and stakeholder/interest group support. It then inspected the related view of Hollinshead *et al.* (2015) that Quinn's assessment of the contemporary state-of-the-art research into event development/event projection vitally obligates researchers in the domains of Event Management and Event Studies to take bold and more informed steps to probe the declarative power/declarative reach/declarative authority of special events and drawcard festivals. Ten platform arenas of under-serviced Quinnian study (as registered by Hollinshead *et al.*) were adopted and a total of 30 exemplar terms pertinent to what events might indeed normalise/naturalise were defined as a fillip for future research agendas on the political and psychic constituencies of large commemorative events.

But the time for the background rationale-making is over. Commentators Quinn, Hollinshead, Kuon, Alajmi and Suleman have each variously spoken. It is time for the dinkum (bona fide/earnest) work into the political and psychic correlations of events and festivals to be undertaken with added fervour and sterner trans-disciplinary cum post-disciplinary intent. Please refer to the second edition of this Pernecky book to see how you all went on, and what edition two of *Approaches and Methods in Event Studies* can fruitfully report from across the continents, hereafter. Hopefully, the field of enlightened researchers on regimes of truth, ethnic group maintenance, discontinuous reality and soft power matters etc. can *event-ually* satisfy Bernadette Quinn over in the land of Erin.

References

Anderson, B. (1983) *Imagined Communities: Reflections on the Origin and Spread of Nationalism*. London: Verso.

Boyle, M. (1997) 'Civic boosterism in the politics of local economic development: "institutional positions" and "strategic orientations" in the consumption of hallmark events', *Environment and Planning A*, 29: 1975–97.

Coles, T., Hall, C. M. and Duval, D. T. (2006) 'Tourism and post-disciplinary enquiry', *Current Issues in Tourism*, 8: 293–319.

Crespi-Valbona, M. and Richards, G. (2007) 'The meaning of cultural festivals: stakeholder perspectives in Catalunya', *Journal of Cultural Policy*, 13: 103–22.

De Bres, K. and Davis, J. (2001) 'Celebrating group identity and place identity: a case study of a new regional festival', *Tourism Geographies*, 2: 326–37.

Fox Gotham, K. (2005) 'Theorizing urban spectacles: festivals, tourism, and the transformation of urban space', *City: Analysis of Urban Trends, Culture, Theory, Policy, Action*, 9: 225–45.

Hollinshead, K. and Ivanova, M. B. (2013) 'The multilogical imagination: tourism studies and the imperative for post disciplinary knowing', in M. Smith and G. Richards (eds), *The Routledge Handbook of Cultural Tourism*. London: Routledge, pp. 53–62.

Hollinshead, K. and Suleman, R. (forthcoming) *The Making, Demaking, and Remaking of Worlds: A Glossary on the Geopolitics of Peoples and Places*. Manuscript in preparation.

Hollinshead, K., Kuon, V. and Alajmi, M. (2015) 'Events in the liquid modern world: the call for fluid acumen in the presentation of peoples, places, pasts, and presents', in O. Moufakkir and T. Pernecky (eds), *Ideological, Social, and Cultural Aspects of Events*. Wallingford: CABI, pp. 12–27.

Jamal, T. and Robinson, M. (eds) (2009) *The Sage Handbook of Tourism Studies*. Los Angeles: Sage.

Jaramillo, N. and McLaren, P. (2008) 'Rethinking critical pedagogy: Socialismo Nepantla and the specter of Che', in K. N. Denzin and S. Y. Lincoln (eds), *Handbook of Critical Indigenous Methodologies*. Los Angeles: Sage, pp. 191–210.

Larson, J. and Wikstrom, E. (2001) 'Organizing events: managing conflict and consensus in a political market square. *Event Management*, 7: 51–65.

Larson, M. (2002) 'A political approach to relationship marketing: case study of the Starjoyran Festival', *International Journal of Tourism Research*, 4 (2): 119–43.

Quinn, B. (2009) 'Festivities, events, and tourism', in T. Jamal and M. Robinson (eds), *The Sage Handbook of Tourism Studies*. Los Angeles: Sage, pp. 483–503.

Shepherd, R. (2002) 'Commodification, culture, and tourism', *Tourist Studies*, 2: 183–201.

Yardinici, S. (2007) *Festivalising Difference: Privatisation of Culture and Symbolic Exclusion in Istanbul*, EU Working Papers, Mediterranean Programme Series, RSCAS, 2007/35, pp. 1–26.

Index